Building an
Outstanding
Legal Team

**Battle-Tested Strategies
from a General Counsel**

Bjarne P Tellmann

For Ranjay, with deep gratitude
for everything you have taught
me during AMP 194. Thank you!

For Alessandra, Mia and Liv

Managing director
Sian O'Neill

***Building an Outstanding Legal
Team: Battle-Tested Strategies
from a General Counsel*** is published by

Globe Law and Business Ltd
3 Mylor Close
Horsell
Woking, Surrey GU21 4DD
Tel: +44 20 3745 4770
www.globelawandbusiness.com

Printed and bound by Gomer Press

*Building an Outstanding Legal
Team: Battle-Tested Strategies
from a General Counsel*

ISBN 9781911078203
© 2017 Globe Law and Business Ltd (except
where otherwise stated)

DISCLAIMER
This publication is intended as a
general guide only. The information
and opinions which it contains are not
intended to be a comprehensive study, nor
to provide legal advice, and should not be
treated as a substitute for legal advice
concerning particular situations. Legal advice
should always be sought before taking any
action based on the information provided.
The publishers bear no responsibility for any
errors or omissions contained herein.

Endorsements for *Building an Outstanding Legal Team*

Bjarne Tellmann has written a deeply practical book about the challenges facing the modern general counsel. Based on his own extensive experience, the book is filled with insights that both experienced and novice GCs can immediately use to build a world-class legal department.

David B Wilkins, Lester Kissel Professor of Law, Vice Dean for Global Initiatives on the Legal Profession, Faculty Director of the Center on The Legal Profession, Harvard Law School

Bjarne Tellmann's novel approach centres on identifying and managing core legal risk, while building an innovative, connected and future-oriented team. This book is required reading for any CEO who wants to understand what the legal department should be doing.

Glen Moreno, Chairman of Virgin Money Holdings (UK) plc, former Chairman of Pearson plc, UK Financial Investments Limited and former Chief Executive Officer of Fidelity International Ltd

Bjarne Tellmann's innovative approach will help lawyers in any organization to lead, inspire and build their teams. His cross-disciplinary analysis will inform everyone involved in legal leadership.

Thomas J Miles, Dean and Clifton R. Musser Professor of Law and Economics, The University of Chicago Law School

This book is a must-read for both current and aspiring general counsel and the law firms that represent them. It highlights real-world topics that can make or break a GC and provides practical, thoughtful and innovative advice on how to successfully handle them. Bjarne Tellmann has made a significant contribution to the profession as he discusses, with great insight, the multifaceted role of today's general counsel.

Louise M Parent, Former General Counsel and Executive Vice President of American Express and Of Counsel, Cleary Gottlieb

Building an Outstanding Legal Team offers a fresh perspective from the front lines of the in-house counsel revolution. Arising out of Bjarne Tellmann's deep experience and passion for building effective legal teams, this book is an invaluable resource for anyone involved in the critical mission of preparing the next generation of corporate counsel leaders.

That mission is critical and this book is crucial because in an increasingly complex global economy, we need a new framework for corporate counsel leadership and legal teams to empower in-house lawyers to help their businesses to create long-term value through both creativity AND integrity, finding common ground at the intersection of strong corporate values and cutting edge strategy.

Scott Westfahl, Professor of Practice and Faculty Director of Executive Education, Harvard Law School

Every in-house lawyer must have this essential playbook on his or her desk which combines decades of experience into an incredibly useful and practical read on the role of the modern General Counsel in today's world. This book is my bible.

Rachel Barnett, General Counsel, Travelzoo

The curriculum of top law schools does well to prepare our graduates for high-level work at private firms, in the government, or in public interest law. Only recently have we begun to focus on the particular organisational, economic and leadership issues faced by general counsel at major institutions. Bjarne Tellmann's new book is a comprehensive treatment of those issues that in-house lawyer/leaders deal with each week, and as such will be welcome reading for law students, and lawyers of any age or seniority level.

Theodore W Ruger, Dean and Bernard G Segal Professor of Law, University of Pennsylvania Law School

As a General Counsel who has led legal department transformations in three public companies, I can assure you that Bjarne Tellmann's practical yet sophisticated battle plan has been designed to help General Counsels achieve superior performance in almost any situation. The book is articulate, easy to follow and highly instructive and a road map for new and established General Counsels to create world class premier performing legal departments.

Bobby Katz, Executive Vice President, General Counsel and Corporate Secretary, Jabil Circuit, Inc

How is the innovation revolution changing the legal profession? What do successful General Counsel and T-shaped individuals have in common? Why will change management play a critical role in your team's success? A trailblazer and a recognised change agent in the corporate legal industry, Bjarne Tellmann brings decades of in-house and law firm experience to dissect these and other questions central to building and running outstanding legal teams. His new book is a must-read for any forward-thinking legal industry professional.

Robert S Insolia, Managing Partner, Goodwin Procter LLP

A powerful and practical analysis that illustrates the complex challenges that today's general counsel face. Bjarne Tellmann's innovative book provides cutting-edge tools for in-house leaders, while giving law firm and business partners alike a deeper understanding of what excellence looks like for a modern legal department.

Jan Gustavsson, General Counsel, Company Secretary and Director of Strategic Development, Coca-Cola HBC AG

Tellmann's book will help outside counsel understand the multifaceted roles the GC serves and the types of support needed from their outside counsel. It underscores the critical need for law firms to serve as strategic partners, providing a deep and concentrated level of specialised legal expertise that is tailored to and aligned with business needs.

Jami Wintz-McKeon, Chair of the Firm, Morgan, Lewis & Bockius LLP

Bjarne Tellmann's powerful book offers invaluable insights on leadership and strategy that resonate beyond the legal department. Building an Outstanding Legal Team vividly illustrates how the General Counsel contributes to the strategic decision-making of modern corporations. Tellmann's wealth of global experience, combined with his compelling writing style, makes this book a riveting and insightful read for anyone interested in how to be a successful strategic leader.

Thomas C Lawton, Professor of Strategy and International Management, the Open University Business School, Visiting Professor of Business Administration, the Tuck School of Business at Dartmouth, and author of *Breakout Strategy* and *Aligning for Advantage*.

The insights and enduring principles contained in this book are applicable to law firm and general counsel leadership. It is a guide to navigating both types of organisation and maximising the outputs from the firm or the company.

Mark Rigotti, Joint CEO, Herbert Smith Freehills LLP

Building an Outstanding Legal Team is both accessible and actionable. Bjarne Tellmann has written a book that will be immensely useful for general counsel and business leaders alike. Tellmann lays out a path-breaking model that will help general counsel accelerate the performance of their teams at a time of disruption and change.

Kevin Michaels, Managing Director, AeroDynamic Advisory

Table of contents

Part C: The software

Part D: Critical threads

Part E: Conclusion

Foreword

During times of uncertainty, people are inclined to find comfort in guides and maps. While the primary audience for *Building an Outstanding Legal Team* may be those in the legal profession, the book is a great read for anyone seeking direction on building teams or managing their careers during periods of change.

As the former Associate General Counsel for the Bottling Investments Group at The Coca-Cola Company, Bjarne provided guidance to more than 80 legal associates in the Group and my leadership team. We have been friends and colleagues for more than 15 years and I have always known him to be a pragmatic leader with a keen understanding of the application of law.

His reputation as a leader preceded him prior to joining the Coca-Cola system. Having served in leadership roles with Coca-Cola Hellenic Bottling Company, Kimberly-Clark, Sullivan & Cromwell LLP and White & Case LLP, he has lived and worked in Asia, Europe and the United States, establishing himself as a global citizen.

Building an Outstanding Legal Team offers practical and holistic guidance on building teams, selecting partners or advising team members on dealing with change. His review and discussions of the different approaches to leadership around the world, specifically when collaborating with counterparties, business partners, and teams outside of cultural norms is exemplary. His thoughts are from real examples; tested around the globe. His observations are built on practice, not theory.

The insights in this book offer sound advice on quickly building a legal structure that allows operations teams to work collaboratively, with a minimum amount of risk while maintaining focus and generating efficiencies.

This book demonstrates Bjarne's experience in changing the perception of legal teams to enabling functions instead of cost centres. It is this type of solution-oriented thinking that benefited our system during his tenure. He played a pivotal role in educating our operational teams on the benefits of collaboration and early engagement with the legal function.

It was enlightening to find Bjarne's application of ideas to be relevant in such a variety of different contexts. This book would make an exceptional addition to the armoury of anyone entering a management role.

Irial Finan
President, Bottling Investments Group,
Executive Vice President, The Coca-Cola Company
Atlanta, February 2017

Acknowledgements

Michael Frankel, a long-time friend and classmate of mine from The University of Chicago Law School, first planted the thought of writing a book in my mind. Without his steady encouragement and inspiration over many coffees, this book would never have happened.

A book is a collective endeavour. Particular thanks are owed to: George Costello, Kirsty Devine, Silvia Hodges Silverstein, Victoria Lockie, Kyle McNeil, Denise Nurse, Stephen Rauf, Annie Scott, Julie Shapiro, Tom Steiner and Bill Stone. Each of them patiently and generously gave me their time and insights.

Special thanks go to Bobby Katz, Matt Kettel, James Neath and Joy Saphla for their professional expertise and for engaging deeply on several parts of the book, making those chapters so much better than they would otherwise have been.

There are too many other people who have contributed in various ways to mention them all by name, but I am deeply grateful for their support, energy and advice.

Thanks also to Tiffani Alexander of the ACC Docket, and Aaron Kotok of CEB for providing me with materials, and to Rachel Barnett and Louise Firestone of Columbia University Law School, Colin Carrol of Lawyers Business Development Club, Justin Connor of the Association of Corporate Counsel, Lynn Glasser of Sandpiper Partners, John Jeffcock of Winmark Global, and Dr Thomas Lawton of Dartmouth Tuck School of Business for giving me conference and teaching platforms to test the concepts I was developing. I am also grateful to Dr Kevin Michaels for always being the perfect intellectual sparring partner.

I owe a particular debt of gratitude to John Fallon and the entire executive team at Pearson plc, as well as my colleagues and friends in Pearson's legal department for supporting me in this effort and for giving me the opportunity and encouragement I needed to complete my manuscript in parallel with performing my day job.

The contents of this book are the product of experiences gained over decades, working in numerous legal organisations around the world. The people I have managed and those who have led me have all been my teachers, and I have learned so much from each of them. I would like to thank in particular Phil Hoffman, Irial Finan, Paul Mulligan, Bernhard Goepelt, Geoffrey J Kelly, Ben Garren, Leslie Turner, Jan Gustavsson, Leonard Quaranto, George H White, Petri Haussila and Göran Åseborn for showing me through their leadership what it means to build outstanding teams. Each of you has given me so much more than I can ever repay.

Many thanks to Jim Smith and Sian O'Neill at Globe Law and Business for their professionalism and for believing in this project, providing me with their wise insight and guiding this project into harbour. I owe particular thanks to managing editor Lauren Simpson and editor Derek Atkins for their incredible dedication, energy and creativity, as well as their astute editing. I would also like to thank Richard Proctor, who as typesetter made it all look and feel so perfect.

I have been fortunate to stand on the shoulders of giants while completing this manuscript. I am particularly grateful for the input and encouragement I received from Ben W Heineman, Jr, Dean Thomas J Miles, Mark Roellig and Professors Scott A Westfahl and David B Wilkins.

My deepest gratitude goes to Susan Sneider and Larry Marks of New Vistas Consulting for their tireless, selfless and exceptional support and encouragement over so many months. Susan provided brilliant editing, tenaciously and courageously killing off what needed to go. She carefully considered every page, through successive drafts. I have learned so much from her and am eternally grateful. Larry shared his deep wisdom and expertise in many key areas of the manuscript, making this a far better book than it would otherwise have been. I cannot imagine this book without their input. I have no idea what possessed them to volunteer to take such a project on, but I have been greatly blessed for it.

Writing can take a toll on families. Many thanks to my wife Alessandra and our daughters Mia and Liv for putting up with my late nights, missed weekends and perennial lack of sleep. Alessandra was a true partner in this project, helping with the design of the cover and providing me with excellent input throughout the process.

Finally, I am grateful to my Australian cattle dog, Blue Belle, who kept my feet warm as I wrote and reminded me to take walks. Nothing beats the smile on a dog.

Bjarne Philip Tellmann
New York, December 2016

About the author

Bjarne Philip Tellmann is General Counsel and Chief Legal Officer of Pearson plc and a member of its Executive Committee. A FTSE 100 company with over 30,000 employees in more than 70 countries, Pearson provides a range of education products and services to institutions, governments and individual learners. At Pearson, Bjarne leads a legal team of 170 people across six continents. He previously worked across Europe, Asia and the United States in various capacities with Coca-Cola, most recently as associate general counsel of The Coca-Cola Company. He has also held various legal positions at Kimberly-Clark and the law firms of Sullivan & Cromwell LLP and White & Case LLP.

Bjarne has received multiple awards for legal excellence. In the United States, he was recognised in 2016 as a 'Legend in Law' recipient of The Burton Awards, held in association with the Library of Congress and co-sponsored by the American Bar Association. In the United Kingdom, he was included in The Legal 500's GC Powerlist for 2016, and in 2015 *The Lawyer* magazine named him as one of its Hot 100 lawyers.

Originally from Norway, Bjarne holds a JD with honours from the University of Chicago and an MSc (Econ) from The London School of Economics. He has also completed Harvard Law School's Leadership in Corporate Counsel programme. Bjarne is a frequent speaker, panellist and lecturer in the United States and Europe, and he publishes regularly, including as the author of the "Career Path" column in ACC Docket, the award-winning journal of the Association of Corporate Counsel.

Prior to studying law, Bjarne was a professional actor, having appeared in several Norwegian and Swedish films and TV shows.

Part A: Setting the scene

Introduction

Years ago, I recruited a talented young corporate lawyer with a sterling law firm background into a senior in-house leadership position. At a meeting a few weeks into her new job, she recounted her struggle to build a team, manage difficult clients, handle multiple and simultaneous crises and cut costs. She paused for a moment, before asking me quietly, "Bjarne, is there a manual that will tell me how to do this job?" This elicited a good-natured chuckle. Yet her question planted a seed in my mind: could it be possible to articulate a framework that would, in fact, help in-house legal leaders to accelerate their performance?

The need for such a model has grown in the years since that question was raised. The demands on general counsel (GCs) from the board, senior executives and other stakeholders have increased significantly.[1] In response to these additional demands, thought leaders have raised the bar, painting bold visions of the new role for general counsel. Ben W Heineman Jr, former GE general counsel and senior fellow at Harvard Law School, captured the *zeitgeist* in his recent book, *The Inside Counsel Revolution*, in which he calls on GCs to be both partner–guardians and statesmen.[2]

Heineman's vision is appropriate given the volatile and complex environment in which companies and their legal advisers find themselves. Globalisation, regulatory expansion and risk convergence have raised the stakes and made the job much more complex. At the same time, corporate cost demands have increased and are placing downward pressure on legal department resources at a time when the internal demand for legal support is increasing exponentially. There is unquestionably a need for GCs to be well-connected strategic partner–guardians, able to advise and guide on projects that underwrite risk, while ensuring that legal resources are aligned globally and organised effectively. To avoid going the way of the dodo, GCs must adapt to these new expectations.

But how, exactly, does one adapt?

That brings us back to my colleague's question: "Is there a manual that will tell me how to do this job?" This book is an attempt to answer to that question in the affirmative, by providing a model to help GCs build outstanding legal teams and accelerate the GC's development.

The macro-political and economic forces driving the changes that GCs are facing come at a time when the legal profession itself is being convulsed by twin revolutions. The first is what is known as the innovation revolution. Driven by globalisation and technological disruption, it is unbundling the work of both individual lawyers and the traditional law firm model, presenting the GC with both opportunities and challenges.

The second revolution, occurring simultaneously, is what can be termed a 'professional convergence revolution', caused by the rapid pace of change. Good ideas are generated when people with radically different skills interact with each other in an ever more connected manner. As author Steven Johnson notes, innovation requires us "to build information networks that allow hunches to persist and disperse and recombine."[3] That in turn has increased the demand for 'T-shaped' executives, who combine deep cognitive, analytical, or technical skills with broad multidisciplinary and social ones.[4] Given their deep legal expertise and role as connectors, GCs are natural-born T-shaped professionals. These professionals are taking on a host of difficult new tasks, in addition to that of legal adviser. Role overload is an ever-present danger because the many new responsibilities that the job entails are too demanding for any one individual to successfully carry out.[5]

To succeed in this new climate, today's general counsel must effectively become her own chief executive – able to communicate, inspire and build outstanding legal teams, identify and anticipate risks, formulate and execute strategy, implement procurement and technology pipelines, control costs, ensure efficacy and nurture culture and talent. The GC must be an outstanding leader and team builder because, without a world-class legal team to support her, even the most distinguished partner–guardian will eventually fail to deliver effective support for clients. Building an outstanding legal team is the GC's acid test as a leader.[6]

While the vision of the GC as partner–guardian and statesman is both compelling and necessary, the current reality for most GCs is quite different. Crushed as they are under a daily avalanche of role overload, cost pressures, recurring litigation, major deals and periodic crises, and facing the many challenges the aforementioned macroeconomic developments and twin revolutions have wrought, most have little time to figure out how to build outstanding legal teams or move toward an ideal state. The partner–guardian vision is definitely the goal but it is not always clear how to get there. This book attempts to give you a model to help you do so.

'Model' is used here in the dictionary sense of being "a structural design".[7] It will point you in the right direction, but *you* must tailor things to your specific circumstances. An all-encompassing universal manual would have so many decision trees that it would be both endless and useless. Instead, a model such as the one presented here provides a starting point for discussion, a framework for building a team, and tools to implement a structure.

One caveat. This book is not about how to be a top-notch general counsel in the substantive sense. It does not tell you how to forge excellent relations with your CEO, provide sage advice, lead during times of crisis, and be a steady and reassuring hand for your board. It does not tell you how to tackle compliance and legal hazards, ethics, crisis management, citizenship, public policy or governance. Clearly, these substantive skills are essential to your success; but this book assumes that you already have most of them. They put you in the leadership role you currently enjoy.

To the extent that such substantive matters are discussed – for instance, in the chapters entitled "Risk and talent assessments" and "Culture" – it will primarily be done from an internal perspective of the legal organisation. There are two important implications that flow from this that need to be established up front. First, this book is intentionally written with an inward, legal team, focus; it does not address in great detail the critical company-facing role that the GC and the legal department play in the smooth running of a corporation, including how to cultivate good relationships with the board, the CEO, and other business leaders and staff.

Secondly, this book does not discuss in detail the vital role that the GC has in establishing and maintaining relations with key stakeholders and actors outside the corporation.

Both of the foregoing dimensions are critical to an inside lawyer's success, and their importance should be acknowledged up front. But while these are essential aspects, they are not the focus of this book. Here, we will focus almost exclusively on organisational issues and, in particular, how to build an outstanding legal team – a vital, but often neglected skill.

Frequently, lawyers get to the GC position precisely because they are great, even outstanding, lawyers. But what they sometimes lack are the other skills they need to succeed as GCs in today's environment: how to design and build a world-class team; how to develop a culture and nurture human capital; and how to manage budgets; how to select smart technology and professionalise service delivery systems – all while formulating a compelling strategic framework and managing through change.

This book focuses on these aspects, drawing upon my decades of experience in building and leading global teams, as well as the collective experience of a wide-range of people – all experts in their fields – who have contributed to its content. It is written from the perspective of the general counsel, but it is my hope that the model outlined here will be useful for any legal department leader.

The principal discussion is divided into three main parts, set between some introductory considerations (Part A) and some concluding remarks (Part E):

- Part B opens by dealing with the 'hardware' – ie, the hard, operational components that are needed to accelerate towards Heineman's newly defined global legal organisation of the future. These include aligning your operating and service delivery models with your core legal risks, appointing the right leadership team, restructuring your relationships with external providers, rolling out powerful new technologies, controlling your budget and optimising your internal to external spend ratio.

The hardware discussion is important because inside lawyers are often not good at these tasks and many do not like doing them. There is a certain tension between managing the substance and managing the hardware. A general counsel sometimes neglects the latter. It may be because he lacks the training to do it properly, but it might also be because he lacks the time. GCs must focus on a seemingly infinite number of substantive issues that necessarily distract them from the business of running a department – and the substantive side of the role exerts a powerful pull. Moreover, even with the best operational support in the world, evaluating the appropriate cost of a matter will, to a certain extent, depend on the GC's substantive knowledge of the matter itself.

But it is the GC's job to navigate this tension appropriately. It is critical that a general counsel calendars time to review and evaluate his organisation with the same seriousness that he takes to perform at the highest level on legal issues.

- Part C focuses on the 'software' – ie, the softer, less tangible but equally critical components of culture and people. This book starts with culture because that is the sea within which your talent swims. If your culture is polluted or suboptimal, you will lose people, fail to attract top talent and prevent those who remain from doing their best work.

  We will consider what is meant by culture, why it is important, and whether culture can be built from the ground up. We will also examine how you can continually improve the legal department's subculture, in alignment with the broader corporate culture of the company that it serves. We will then move on to consider the challenges associated with leading and motivating people across generational divides, as well as the skills you need to seek out and nurture in your leadership.

  One question that sometimes comes up is whether the hardware phase needs to precede the software. My view is that it usually should, because it is generally easier to develop structural elements than it is to build culture and develop people. Tackling the hardware successfully will give you the credibility you need to take on the software. Of course, in the real world, there can never be precisely delineated sequencing; you will likely need to do some of each interchangeably. But by emphasising the hardware first, you will obtain results you can use to convince others of the direction that you want to take things.

- Part D considers two highly significant threads that will wind their way through your transformational journey. The first is change management. Ignoring the emotional and other impacts that profound change can have on an organisation is a sure-fire way to blow up your team, your change effort, or both. The second thread is strategic direction: making sure that at all times you know where you are heading. No one should set off into the great wide world without having a clear understanding of what their destination is and a decent roadmap of how to get there.

  Volumes have been written on these two threads, and space is too limited to do them full justice here. But the key elements are presented to help you build awareness about the themes that will impact your initiatives. Before you embark, you should gain an understanding of the importance they will play in your success.

Like all models, this one is merely a framework. It will be your job to put in the plasterboard for the walls and build the house. It is also my hope that this book will give you an appreciation of the multitude of variables that will impact your ability to create a world-class legal organisation of the future. Each area will provide you with food for thought as to how it might apply to your specific circumstances, so that you can accelerate your journey toward building the best, most sophisticated and highly valued department possible. Leveraging this framework to develop your team may free you to focus on being the best leader that you can possibly be.

The changing context

*The key is to embrace
disruption and change early.
Don't react to it decades later.
You can't fight innovation.*
(Ryan Kavanaugh)[1]

The general counsel's role has become one of the most complex, intense and challenging in the corporate world, because of changes that have occurred in the macroeconomic environment and in the legal profession itself. Today's general counsel must perform at a much higher level than before. What was once considered world class is now the baseline.

Before we embark (in Parts B–D) on how to build a world-class team to accelerate performance in today's multifarious and fast-moving environment, it is helpful to consider the changing landscape and the implications it has for the GC's role. We need to examine this change before we can consider how best to adapt.

Macroeconomic changes

Foremost among the macroeconomic factors that are shaking up the broader corporate and commercial landscape within which many GCs operate, are regulatory expansion, globalisation and risk convergence.

Regulatory expansion

Government regulation has increased worldwide, especially between 2001 and 2016.[2] Much of this global growth has occurred in response to the expansion of the US regulatory framework.[3]

US Federal regulations grew from a total of 9,745 pages in 1950 to more than 178,277 pages in 2015.[4] The 2010 Dodd-Frank Act alone encompasses a staggering 2,300 pages.[5] Despite having published more than 22,000 pages of new regulatory content, by 2015 the agencies charged with Dodd-Frank rulemaking had had finalised less than two-thirds of the rules that Congress had tasked them with implementing.[6]

While the growth in US regulations has been on the upswing for decades, much of the recent growth can be traced to four main factors: increased money laundering controls following the 11 September 2001 terrorist attacks on the United States; strengthened anti-fraud rules in the wake of the Enron collapse in 2001 and the 2008 global financial crisis; the increased use of sanctions as a foreign-policy tool; and the growth of anti-bribery and anti-corruption rules globally.[7]

As the United States has passed rules in these areas, often with extraterritorial impact, other nations have followed suit.[8] As global finance journalist Valentina Pasquali notes:[9]

> What began as a US-centric trend to increase regulatory reporting and related requirements ... has been taking hold in the rest of the world. This global surge has been driven in part by the US authorities' embracing of the notion of extraterritoriality [the application of US jurisdiction and regulations outside the borders of the United States] to mount enforcement actions against foreign entities, causing a rush of similar legislation to be passed in response.

The net result is a bewildering array of rules that companies must comply with in each jurisdiction. In some cases, these rules are inconsistent across – or sometimes even within – markets. In the international context, for example, the US Foreign Corrupt Practices Act permits companies to make facilitating payments (eg, payments made to government officials to perform or speed up the performance of an existing duty, such as delivery of mail), whereas the UK Bribery Act bans such payments.[10]

US data privacy laws provide a further example of this inconsistency. The absence of a single, comprehensive, national data privacy law has left a patchwork of overlapping federal and state laws and regulations that sometimes dovetail and sometimes contradict each other.[11] In addition, regulators leverage a plethora of agency and self-regulatory best-practice guidelines in the enforcement context, further complicating the GC's ability to provide clear guidance to her business partners.[12]

Along with the growth in regulations, there has been a marked increase in enforcement, particularly in the antitrust and anti-bribery areas. In 2015, for instance, antitrust fines imposed by Chinese authorities increased by 280% between 2014 and 2015 to $1.12 billion, while in the United States the Department of Justice imposed a record $2.85 billion in antitrust fines in 2015 – more than twice its previous high and more than three times greater than it imposed in 2014.[13]

The severity of penalties and sanctions in individual cases has also increased, as has the cost of managing them. It is no longer uncommon to see fines in the hundreds of millions of dollars, and sometimes even in billions of dollars, imposed on companies for violations of anti-bribery and antitrust laws.[14]

This rise in regulation and regulatory complexity has not only raised the stakes for getting it wrong. It has also imposed a remarkable burden on legal teams, who are often understaffed and under-resourced, but are under pressure to pre-empt regulatory enforcement by putting in place robust and comprehensive compliance programmes.[15]

That burden is particularly heavy in specialised industries, where there may be fewer experts in the law firm market with the requisite expertise to advise in narrow regulatory areas. In such cases, the best experts may already be in-house, making it hard for small players to navigate the rules.

Globalisation

Globalisation has significantly increased the difficulty of running a legal department, at both the organisational and individual levels. In previous decades much of what defined globalisation was made up of the global trade in goods. While that has levelled off in recent years, cross-border data flows have increased by a factor of 45 over the past decade and they are projected to grow by a further 900% by 2020.[16] Data flows now make up the largest single value component in global trade flows, whereas 15 years ago they barely registered.[17]

At the organisational level

At the organisational level, virtually every major legal matter now has cross-border ripple effects that must be considered. Whether dealing with a commercial arrangement, a regulatory investigation or a contract dispute, problems rarely remain in one jurisdiction.

Like a watch, there are many moving parts; manipulating one piece will inevitably impact the others. These moving parts are increasingly difficult to manage, particularly in an environment where enforcers and litigants are networked and globalised, and transactions are financed and negotiated worldwide.

High-profile antitrust/competition investigations are illustrative of some of these challenges. In 2006, for instance, the US Department of Justice and the European Commission launched coordinated, worldwide raids on 23 major air cargo carriers, alleging that they had conspired to fix international cargo rates and surcharges.[18] Nineteen of the carriers pleaded guilty in the United States, resulting in fines of more than $1.7 billion, while the European Commission imposed fines of more than €799 million on 11 of them.[19] Regulators in other markets jumped in, conducting their own investigations that resulted in significant fines, while third-party private litigants filed damages actions against the airlines.[20]

Steps taken in one jurisdiction in the competition law context need to be carefully considered for their potential impact elsewhere. For example, many jurisdictions provide lenient treatment for the price-fixing cartel participant who first comes forward to report the cartel.[21] While regulators often promise that incriminating documents and other evidence provided in such an instance will be kept confidential, there is always the risk that the information might end up being used against the company by private litigants or regulators elsewhere. Determining the right course of action for the company requires the GC to consider the implications of such a step, often under severe time pressure, as other cartel participants may be racing to come forward first.

Cross-border acquisitions also present GCs with many moving parts to manage, ranging from political and cultural obstacles, to legal and regulatory barriers. Complying with US law can be especially difficult, given its long reach.[22] Foreign targets may have conducted themselves in ways that violate US legislation, such as the US Foreign Corrupt Practices Act, or various export and sanctions laws.[23] Sarbanes-Oxley, SEC rules and stock exchange requirements pose additional challenges in the transactional context, including those relating to director independence, internal controls and loans to officers and directors.[24] Conflicting labour and employment laws, tax and accounting rules, and merger clearance standards are other examples of frequent sources of friction and complexity that can arise.[25]

At the individual level

At the individual level, globalisation means that many GCs – and not just those who serve the largest multinationals – must now lead, unify and inspire diverse teams of people in very different parts of the world. Digital technologies are increasingly allowing businesses to globalise in a leaner, more efficient way, selectively hiring expertise in remote locations.[26]

These trends have expanded the complexity of managing global operations from the legal perspective. Managing global teams and clients calls for a unique set of skills, including cultural intelligence, subtlety, diplomacy and a fine nose for when to 'go local' (and when not to). Gone are the days when the legal team and its clients were based in one or a handful of locations, sharing one or two sets of cultural norms. Diversity is in all respects a huge competitive advantage, but it introduces complications that need to be bridged.

Risk convergence

'Pure' legal matters have become about as common as pink unicorns. Today, the legal, economic, reputational and political dimensions of risk are blending together. GCs must carefully weigh the non-legal implications of legally appropriate courses of action. For example, even if a company has a legal right not to self-report an environmental infraction, it must consider the potential reputational and political implications of exercising that right if the infraction were ever to be made public.

The speed and impact of reputational harm in an era of social media can be breathtaking. One need only consider the travails endured by Toyota during its sudden-acceleration crisis, BP during the Deepwater Horizon disaster, or Samsung following news of its incendiary Galaxy Note 7s, to feel the heat. News on Twitter travels more quickly than any legal response can follow, imposing real harm to a company's social and economic capital, irrespective of the merits of underlying legal positions.

This reality makes it more important than ever to solve problems holistically. There is a significant need to develop people with a broader overview.

Cost pressures

Corporate legal departments are under increasing economic pressure. Like CEOs, with every passing year GCs must do more with less. This relentless focus on cost cutting has coincided with a rapid expansion in the range of topics in which the legal team is expected to involve itself.

Companies are facing increased market volatility, including industry disruption and tightening profits that increase the need for legal resources. As Martin Reeves of the Boston Consulting Group and his co-authors noted in a 2016 *Harvard Business Review* article:[27]

> *Public companies have a one in three chance of being delisted in the next five years, whether because of bankruptcy, liquidation, M&A, or other causes. That's six times the delisting rate of companies 40 years ago. Although we may perceive corporations as enduring institutions, they now die, on average, at a younger age than their employees. And the rise in mortality applies regardless of size, age, or sector.*

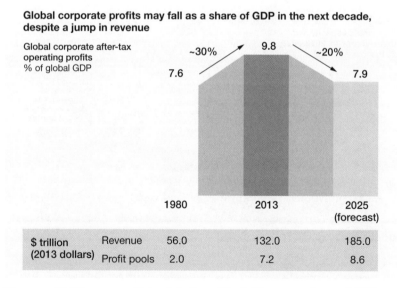

Global corporate profits may fall as a share of GDP in the next decade, despite a jump in revenue

Figure 1: McKinsey predicts global profits falling as a share of GDP
(Source: McKinsey Global Institute, "The New Global Competition for Corporate Profits", September 2015. © 2017 McKinsey & Co (www.mckinsey.com). All rights reserved. Reprinted with permission.)

This volatility is coming at a time when corporate profits are in decline. McKinsey has reported that the global corporate-profit pool, currently valued at approximately 10% of global GDP, may shrink to less than 8% by 2025, undoing in the next decade nearly all of the corporate gains made relative to the world economy over the past three decades (see Figure 1).

This increased volatility and downward pressure on corporate profits is increasing pressure on companies to achieve sustainable growth by transforming themselves. KPMG reports that 93% of US-based multinationals are currently at some stage of undergoing or preparing for a business transformation.[28]

The workload that this drive is imposing – and will continue to impose – on legal departments is outstripping capacity. A recent study by best-practice technology company CEB indicates that the growth in demand for in-house legal services is expected to outstrip capacity by between 10% and 30% by 2020 (see Figure 2).

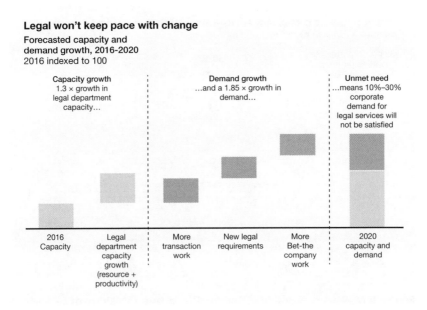

Figure 2: Demand for in-house legal services will outstrip supply by 2020

(Source CEB, The New Legal Operating Model (2016), pp11, 12 and 56. Reproduced with permission.[29])

To meet this increased demand for in-house legal services and remain sustainable, cost-cutting efforts must be sophisticated and nuanced. GCs need to shelve the financial machete that they used in the outside counsel consolidation process and learn to work with a scalpel, leveraging sophisticated procurement techniques that previously were only used by purchasing experts. They have had to become far savvier consumers, stratifying needs across different types of providers, crunching numbers to identify opportunities, rolling out technologies and tools, and tirelessly improving transparency and strategic partnership principles.

GCs have also had to become much more refined in how they communicate legal costs, risks and benefits to their business partners. In the same way that their business partners most frequently think in numbers, charts, trends and projections, so too increasingly must their lawyers if they are to hope to persuade them to give the legal department sufficient resources. This requires financial acumen, a deep understanding of the business, communication and persuasion skills, and political talent.

The twin revolutions

In addition to the above-noted macroeconomic trends and cost pressures, the legal profession itself is in the process of significant disruption caused by two revolutions taking place simultaneously: those termed the innovation revolution and the professional convergence revolution.

The innovation revolution

The legal profession, once a bastion of stasis and conservatism, will undergo more innovative disruption in the next 20 years than it has experienced in the preceding two centuries.[30] As Professor Richard Susskind explains, over time "traditional lawyers will in large part be replaced by advanced systems, or by less costly workers supported by technology or standard processes, or by lay people armed with online self-help tools".[31]

Some of that change has already arrived. Activities that were previously deemed to be solely in the province of outside counsel are becoming unbundled by legal start-ups. Starting in the early 2000s, new ways of providing document searches, contract management and legal advice have been disrupting the profession.[32] The legal market has also become more transparent through services that instantly connect consumers and lawyers, facilitate legal bid comparisons and document reviews, and streamline legal project management and research, among many others.[33] Indeed, Professor Susskind claims there are at least 13 disruptive technologies in law (see Figure 3).

Susskind's disruptive legal technologies
- Automated document assembly
- Connectivity tools
- Electronic legal marketplace
- E-learning
- Online legal guidance
- Legal open sourcing
- Closed legal communities
- Workflow and project management
- Embedded legal knowledge
- Online dispute resolution
- Intelligent legal search
- Big data
- Artificial Intelligence-based problem solving

Figure 3: Susskind's 13 disruptive legal technologies
(Source: Richard Susskind, Tomorrow's Lawyers: An Introduction to Your Future, Oxford University Press (2013), p616 in e-book edition.)

Two big trends are driving the innovation revolution: unbundling services and technological disruption. Each is described further below.

Both of these trends will have profound implications for how lawyers work, what they work on, and how GCs source their needs. Most of these implications will be a net positive for in-house departments because they will enable them to apply a more effective approach to sourcing. In a world of alternative legal service providers and technology-enabled process improvement, outsourcing and analytics solutions, it is no longer appropriate to default to law firms alone.

Unbundling services

The first is what might be termed 'the great unbundling'. Much of the work that used to be performed by law firms is shifting in-house. GCs have realised that it is both more affordable and more efficacious to bring expertise in-house and handle core risk areas proactively and pragmatically. Additionally, the traditional model – in which the law firm was a one-stop shop for all of a company's legal work not handled internally – has come undone, leaving law firms to compete over a much smaller volume of work that they are uniquely qualified to perform. At the same time, globalisation and technology are enabling in-house lawyers to break down and disaggregate what remains into ever-smaller pieces, farming each part out to a competing array of increasingly efficient alternative providers. There are numerous examples – Susskind identified 13 back in 2013, and new ones are arising all the time.[34] Some of the weightiest ones include the following:

- *Offshoring* has made deep inroads, particularly at the 'commodity' end of the spectrum. Teams of competent lawyers in India, South Africa and similar countries are doing a significant amount of the work that historically went to associates at law firms in the United States and Europe. While work conducted offshore used to be mainly at the basic end of the spectrum (primarily document reviews and document processing), it is increasingly moving up the scale to encompass higher-margin work such as contract negotiation and transaction support.
- *Near-shoring* provides another alternative, particularly for mid-level work where clients may prefer qualified attorneys in their own jurisdiction and time zone. These attorneys work offsite, mainly through third-party law firms or agencies that run such business ventures in lower-cost locations. In the United Kingdom, Allen & Overy, Ashurst, Herbert Smith Freehills and Hogan Lovells are examples of firms that have established captive service centres in cities such as Belfast, Glasgow and Birmingham.[35] The firm of Dorsey & Whitney exemplifies this trend in the United States, where its LegalMine™ document review business, housed out of offices in Minneapolis, provides review services that take advantage of its cost-competitive location.[36]
- *Staffing* involves the retention of highly qualified lawyers for non-

permanent engagements in the legal department, often on a project-by-project basis.[37] The lawyers who undertake this work are typically employed by or through alternative legal service providers (such as search firms or alternative law firms) that do not have the same high brick-and-mortar overheads of traditional law firms. Those lawyers may have been trained at the best schools and law firms but have chosen to work independently, and prefer working on a project-by-project basis to best balance their work and personal lives.[38] This provides a viable and cost-effective solution for longish but non-permanent demand spikes. The days are over of having to choose between eye-watering hourly rates for full-time associate support or the fixed costs of additional headcount. You can now have an experienced, specialist attorney embedded in your operation for weeks or months at reasonable cost – and only for as long as you have need.

- *Subcontracting* is yet another solution that is gaining ground. Pieces of a transaction, investigation or dispute that is being handled internally or by a law firm may either be subcontracted to multiple, smaller law firms or non-law firm specialists, such as e-discovery legal process outsourcing firms who are able to undertake discovery work at a lower cost point, and more efficiently and effectively.[39]

Technological disruption

The second big trend that is driving the innovation revolution is technological disruption. The information technology revolution and, increasingly, artificial intelligence (AI), machine learning and networked technologies, are leveraging cloud-based solutions and what is known as 'big data' in order to develop ever more powerful tools that are transforming how we work. These tools fall into a number of categories, as follows:

- *Communication and productivity-enhancing tools* have reduced the need for people to be based in centralised locations. Instead, they can operate from wherever they are most cost-effective or needed. Telecommuting also empowers people who might not have otherwise been as mobile, including single parents and the disabled, thereby boosting diversity.

- *Self-help tools*, such as Practical Law from Thomson Reuters (know-how, including standard documents, checklists, legal updates and how-to guides), and other products and services from CEB (best practice, insights and technology solutions), LexisNexis and Westlaw (content-enabled workflow solutions and online legal research) allow in-house attorneys to independently pull top-notch off-the-shelf documentation providing basic introductory information and legal templates, leverage best practice and insights from numerous other companies, and conduct sophisticated legal research, all without going through outside counsel.

- *Efficiency tools* such as contract management, e-discovery and matter management systems provide powerful, innovative tools to perform cheaper, faster and better. Many of these tools are cloud-based, eliminating the need for significant up-front investment costs and harnessing enormous power. And they are getting better by the day.

- *Transparency tools*, including e-billing software and on-line bidding platforms, are giving legal departments the analytics that enable them to 'x-ray' their invoices against billing policies, negotiate better rates, eliminate waste and secure the best deal among competing firms at any given moment.

- *Artificial intelligence and machine learning:* AI technologies, as embodied by Ross Intelligence, are undertaking increasingly high-value work, including cross-disciplinary legal thinking, pattern spotting and legal analysis. And machine-learning-based legal solutions is undoubtedly just around the corner.

Corporate innovation

To take advantage of these innovation trends, legal departments have needed to become far more sophisticated in optimising their internal workload allocation, execution and procurement strategies. Three broad strategies stand out in this regard:

- *Service menu optimisation:* Legal departments are leveraging innovative strategies to identify which legal services they have a comparative advantage in delivering in relation to external providers. This involves inventorying and categorising all of the work done by the department, to determine which elements of their work should be internal priorities based on value, risk and competitive advantage, and then outsourcing the rest. This enables them to provide internally at fixed cost only what they know they are best positioned to undertake. And outside counsel is hired only when needed for its expertise or its ability to quickly staff up a major matter.

- *Service delivery optimisation:* Once they have identified what they are best placed to do internally, legal departments are getting more effective at determining how to optimise their delivery of those services. Legal departments are increasingly using process mapping and 'lean law' methodologies in order to break up the remaining work into steps, identifying the steps that add value and eliminating those that do not.[40]

  They are streamlining their processes, and formalising how they make decisions and allocating work. This ensures that the best-placed resources do the work and that the business partners who generate that work are able to identify the right people to contact when they have legal work that needs to be done. Establishing accountability for the work in this way also ensures that the performance of those who undertake it can more easily be measured.

- *Procurement optimisation:* When legal departments have identified what work they will outsource, they increasingly employ more sophisticated procurement concepts to determine which partners are best positioned to undertake which pieces of work. One procurement concept is to pilot a particular process (or processes) with alternative service providers so as to determine which provider can most efficiently manage a given type of work. Another common procurement concept is to establish formal processes for selecting law firms, negotiating favourable terms and securing mutual investment and transparency in the relationship.

The professional convergence revolution

The general counsel's role is also being transformed by a second major revolution that is under way: the professional convergence revolution. Breakthrough innovation mostly happens when diverse groups of people, with different skills and ideas, bump into and learn from each other.[41] Or, as Matthew Ridley, a British journalist, businessman, author and Member of the House of Lords, more colourfully puts it in his excellent book *The Rational Optimist: How Prosperity Evolves*, human progress through innovation happens when "ideas have sex".[42]

If, as Ridley argues, exchange is to cultural evolution as sex is to biological evolution, innovators must be open to new ideas, be willing to learn across formal academic disciplines and then build upon existing ideas with contributions of their own.

The drive to generate such innovation is causing people with very different professional skills to come together like never before, in ever-denser working groups. Sarah Parcak, a renowned archaeologist, is working with satellite technicians to develop the emerging field of space archaeology, in which satellite imagery is used to track and identify archaeological sites that are not visible from the ground. She and her cohorts are now leveraging a digital platform to enable crowdsourcing, turning all of us into archaeologists.

This convergence of professions, which were previously separate and unconnected, is happening because of a simple rule: the more networked we become, the smarter each of us gets; and the smarter we get, the more innovation is generated.[43]

The demand for 'T-shaped' people

The professional convergence revolution is creating a demand for so-called 'T-shaped' people – ie, those who combine deep cognitive, analytical and/or technical skills in a specific discipline with broad multidisciplinary and social skills.[44] Such people learn by linking up their expertise with multiple perspectives from different areas.[45] IDEO chief executive Tim Brown has described the concept as follows:[46]

> *The vertical stroke of the T is a depth of skill that allows them to contribute to the creative process. That can be from any number of different fields: an industrial designer, an architect, a social scientist, a business specialist or a mechanical engineer. The horizontal stroke of the T is the disposition for collaboration across disciplines.*

The concept of T-shaped individuals was introduced more than 20 years ago, but the importance of such individuals to organisations has been growing.[47]

GCs are naturally T-shaped professionals by virtue of their deep legal expertise and simultaneous role as central connectors. Lawyers touch almost every part of the company – they are the proverbial spiders in the web, coordinating with human resources, finance, marketing, research and development, corporate affairs, government relations, compliance and the board, to name only some. And since they are a relatively small and cohesive group, they communicate effectively with each other through dense networks.

The need for the GC to be T-shaped is in some ways even more important than it is for other influential senior executives, because the GC is accountable for managing risks that are themselves converging. In the era of social media and instant messaging, the legal, reputational and business dimensions of risk are one.

All of this makes it more important than ever for experts to solve problems holistically. Yet we often continue to work in silos. As Gillian Tett, a British author and journalist at *The Financial Times*, notes in her 2015 book *The Silo Effect*,[48] the traditional way of organising things around functional departments can cause institutional blindness because it limits information and restricts thinking. The GC serves as a critical connector in the risk mitigation context.

Role overload might arise

To succeed in this 'new normal', the modern GC must successfully navigate a host of new, often contradictory and non-legal roles, in addition to being a first-rate professional legal adviser and guardian of the company's integrity and reputation. These new roles include:

- *Senior corporate executive and strategist*, who is deeply knowledgeable about the company's business and fluent in many other functional areas (such as finance, human resources, corporate communications, security, technology and procurement), and who can act as a strategic connector, proactively bringing together these diverse strands in interactions with other senior executives;

- *Leader and communicator*, who can define and articulate the department's purpose and value to the executive leadership, and inspire, coach and mentor a team of demanding, highly autonomous professionals, often with big yet fragile egos;
- *Ethics officer*, who has the courage and foresight at all times to act as a primary strategist of, and voice for, governance and compliance, encouraging senior management to openly advocate for, and model, an ethical climate;
- *Public voice*, who, together with other parts of the corporation, is able to act as a face of the company, inspiring both internal and external audiences;
- *Diplomat and politician*, who can effectively persuade multiple constituents, able to justify increased legal spend, and balance the needs and commercial objectives of the company with the constraints imposed on it by the regulatory and legal landscape;
- *Project manager*, who sponsors, supports or leads a diverse array of initiatives across the company;
- *Crisis management guru*, acting as a key leader at times of crisis and a team member involved in developing response procedures;
- *Organisational design expert*, who can develop and implement a superior service delivery model for the legal department;
- *Chief operating officer*, who can manage the administration of a large and sometimes globally dispersed department, track and manage organisational spend and act on metrics in order to ensure operational effectiveness;
- *Procurement expert*, able to nurture first-class cost-effective relationships with outside law firms, alternative legal services providers and other suppliers; and
- *Technologist*, who understands and can roll out world-class technology solutions.

In addition to this long list of informal roles, many GCs are also asked to take on additional formal roles, including leading the compliance function and the corporate and secretarial functions, as well as other areas ranging from human resources to security and from government relations to aviation. Thus, they are sometimes expected to not only be T-shaped, but 'Pi-shaped' or even 'Comb-shaped' – ie, to have not one area of deep functional expertise but two or more, in addition to being a socially-connecting generalist across other dimensions (see Figure 4).

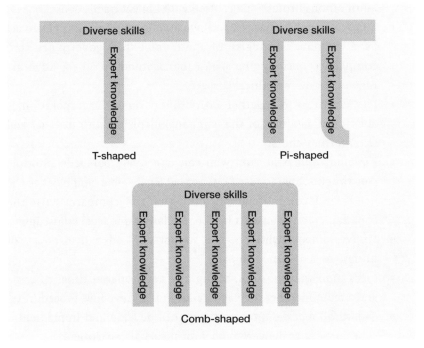

Figure 4: From T-shaped to Pi-shaped to Comb-shaped

As a consequence of these demands, the GC's job is increasingly laden with what organisational psychologists might call 'inherent role overload', where the nature of the role itself is too demanding for any one individual to carry it out successfully.[49] And yet, given the nature of the position and the way modern corporations are structured, it really is not possible to break the role into smaller portions.

At the same time as the GC is tasked with performing these new roles, she must never forget to perform her core function as legal guardian of the company's assets and reputation. She must never let these other roles obscure that obligation. If she does, the company's board, its shareholders and society at large will hold her to account.

The GC as chief executive

As the world that the GC inhabits becomes increasingly complex, she needs in many respects to become her own chief executive, tackling many of the same issues in her legal department that the CEO must tackle for the corporation as a whole. This requires an entirely additional set of skills to those she learned in law school, including developing and executing a strategic plan, building teams, leading and inspiring people, managing complex global budgets, securing partnerships with an ever-growing list of external vendors, interfacing with government officials, the press and interest groups, and managing investments and technology transformations.

To succeed in this environment, the GC must work seamlessly with her team. Indeed, to succeed, she needs her team to be world-class. That is where the model we now embark on examining comes in. What follows is an effort to give GCs the framework they need in order to develop their organisation, culture and people so as to be in a position to tackle the challenges described above and stay in front of change, accelerating toward world-class professionalism.

Part B:
The hardware

Talent and risk assessments

Things which matter most must never be at the mercy of things which matter least.
(Goethe)[1]

On the hardware side of your transformation, the first step that you need to take is to assess the talent available to you and identify your firm's core legal risks.

A continual process

It is important to realise that you are about to embark on a continual process of transformation. There is no final destination, no final moment of perfection. Instead, there will be constant change. After you scale the first mountain in front of you, there will be other vistas to tackle.

What they may involve is difficult to predict. If you are successful in working through the model outlined in this book, you will have created a framework that is resilient and able to adapt to change.

This model will mould your organisation so that it can keep evolving, long after your immediate transformation has been effected.

Start by thinking

Before you do anything, give yourself some time to think. A general never enters into battle without a plan; nor should you.

Do not underestimate how hard it is to find time to really think things through. As general counsel, you are continually confronted with a daunting number of priorities that require your urgent attention and pull you in different directions. And yet, to succeed, you must separate the daily grind of crises and urgent triage from your longer-term, strategic challenges.

Why is it so important to spend time thinking?

In the midst of a busy routine, matters that are truly important for the long-term health and success of your organisation can be difficult to spot, and they only become clear if you invest the time it takes to ferret them out. There is typically no time to think about transformation unless you consciously commit to doing so.

To get beyond stasis, block out time in your diary for structured thinking, and actively use that time to plan how to implement the model outlined in this book, starting with organisational design.

When is it best to do your initial focused thinking?

The most opportune time to give some thought to your strategic challenges is at the very beginning of your tenure, *before* you get pulled in a million directions. Do not despair if you are already long past your first 100 days; there is always time for a reset.

There is no single answer for when in the day it is best to do structured thinking. For some GCs, it will be very early in the day, before the madness begins. Others find it best to think in the quiet of the evening. Whatever time works best for you, block it off and make a habit of it. As Aristotle noted, "Quality is not an act; it is a habit."[2]

Some GCs block out one day per week, when internal legal department meetings are banned from the department calendar and attendance at other non-essential non-departmental meetings are discouraged, giving everyone time to catch up on work – and time to think. If this plan seems unfeasible, you might aim at spreading out your thinking time in smaller blocks of 45–60 minutes on several days in each week. As your thinking evolves, you can work the actual projects that arise into your day and delegate some tasks to others on your team.

Weekly and annual focused thinking

You should engage in two types of focused thinking: weekly scheduled time that is shorter in duration, and annual 'away days' for a longer period of uninterrupted thinking.

During your weekly thinking, calendar your time, do not allow for interruptions and conduct it outside the office. For your away days, travel somewhere peaceful and quiet, where you will be uninterrupted. Even spend a weekend alone, thinking through your long-term strategy and the implications of your ongoing assessments and actions.

If you find these suggestions unrealistic, given your schedule, then you may want to start by focusing on time management. Tackling that before all else may be the single most important investment you ever make. One good place to start is *Time Management Magic: How to Get More Done Every Day – Move From Surviving to Thriving*, a book by former Disney executive Lee Cockerell.[3] It is a quirky, entertaining and easy read that will nonetheless provide you with helpful tips on how best to prioritise your time each day.

Developing your foundation

In whatever manner you tackle your time management challenges, as you begin to think about how best to upgrade your organisation you will probably find that your list of strategic challenges is nearly as long as your list of daily triage activities. There are so many aspects that you might tackle up front, including people issues, technology decisions, outside partners, budget shortfalls – the list is seemingly endless.

Fortunately, there is a logical flow to the order in which you should tackle these challenges.

Assess the company and your team

Similar to building a house, the order in which you analyse an upgrade is critical to your success. If you attempt to build a house by putting up the walls before the foundations, you will fail. When accelerating the performance of your legal team, you also need to start with the foundation, and then build methodically and sequentially from there.

If you are new to your organisation, the first step in designing your foundation is to stop, look and listen, making sure you take time to preliminarily assess your people and get your bearings. You need to take sufficient time to understand how the organisation works, who your people are, what their skills and limitations are and what motivates them.

Identify your core risks

Once you have a clear understanding of your situation and have inventoried your talent, you will be ready to identify your company's core risks. Ideally, you will want to do this before you assemble or make changes to your team: if you start designing your team without fully knowing what your major risks are, you might well end up with the wrong set of talent focusing on the wrong set of problems.

This may not necessarily be apparent at first. You could fully staff your organisation with business-oriented commercial lawyers who help move projects forward. That will seem fine at first; but unaddressed material risks will lurk below the surface of your successful team, waiting to emerge later. You need to know your risks first, so that you can navigate around them by applying the right resources to plug them.

Design an integrated team structure

Once you have conducted a basic assessment of the company and your team, and figured out what your core risks are, you will be able to assess whether the capabilities and areas of expertise that your team possesses are sufficient for the task at hand.

You can then organise your team into subject-matter specialists (who focus principally on your core risks) and legal generalists (who focus principally on partnering with the business). At this stage you should also appoint your leadership team, before mapping out the rest of your organisation under them.

These steps will be considered in greater detail in the next chapter but are summarised in Figure 5.

Building a solid foundation through organisational design:
- Get your bearings and evaluate your talent.
- Identify your core risks by conducting a thorough audit.
- Organise your team into specialists and generalists, identifying gaps you may have based on your risk study.
- Appoint your leadership team with one leader for each specialist area, core business partner and enabling function partner.
- Map the rest of the function under each of your new senior leaders.

Figure 5: Building a solid foundation

If you are new to your role and have inherited a team, make time to consider your surroundings, evaluate your team and assess what each of your team members brings to the table. Few GCs have the luxury of designing an organisation entirely from scratch. Usually, they inherit a team of people from their predecessor, with a structure already in place.

There will undoubtedly be things you will want to change, but there is a 'sweet spot' in terms of when it makes sense to do so. If you move too quickly, you will have insufficient information, either about the organisation or the underlying competencies of your people, to accurately assess the situation. However, if you wait too long, it will be far harder to make fundamental changes to the status quo. Gradually, as you settle in, you will begin to 'own' the existing environment.

The optimal timing to begin accelerating your team's performance is around the 100-day mark. Spend the first several months getting to know your new company, its board, CEO and CFO, your colleagues on the executive and in senior leadership, the risks you face and the people you lead.

Your own on-boarding process

It is critical that you design and prioritise your own on-boarding process during these first 100 days. Take this very seriously because you will never again have the opportunity to ask baseline questions, view the organisation from the perspective of an outsider and define your initiatives and priorities on a blank slate. Mark Roellig, Executive Vice President and General Counsel of Massachusetts Mutual Life Insurance Company, notes that within the first 90 days "you are either heading toward a great career or it is the beginning of the end. Take this period extremely seriously".[4]

Here are some thoughts about how to structure this critical time:[5]

- *Read:* Read as much as you can about the company, including reporting documentation such as annual reports and proxy materials, board minutes, strategy papers, websites and newspaper articles.
- *Ask:* Set up a systematic interview process and spend quality time with the CEO, all of the executive members, heads of functions, and business leaders in the company, as well as the chairman of the

board and each of the company's directors. Start to develop relationships with as many of them as possible and take their temperatures on what is working well and what needs improvement.

- *Look:* Draw up a detailed travel agenda to visit as many key locations and markets as possible. Get a sense of the culture in each place and the core drivers of the business.
- *Meet:* Spend time with outside counsel, auditors, consultants, and your team of people. Do not forget your assistant, who likely has inside information about the company and individuals you will interface with.

As you go about these meetings, get a sense from each person what they think your priorities should be and what the company's culture is like. Do not judge; just listen.

These meetings are a critical time for you to establish your own 'brand' with your new team and key stakeholders. You will want to be at your best, projecting high emotional intelligence (EQ) and listening actively. First impressions really do matter.

As you spend time with your team, try and get a sense of their work quality, approach and skills. Make sure you interview as many of them as you can, as quickly as you can. If possible, depending on the size of your department, over the first 100 days you will want to spend time with each lawyer in your team. Do not label people based on current roles; focus on where they might fit within the emerging structure. Everywhere you go, listen and observe. Take careful notes.

Four times five

A useful tool as you go about this effort is the "Four Times Five" tool developed by Bobby Katz, General Counsel at Jabil, for use with direct reports at the start of an assignment. The tool consists of the following four questions, each one asking the recipient to provide five inputs:[6]

1. What are five important things you believe I should know about you personally or professionally?
2. What in your opinion are the five biggest risks facing the company?

3. No company is perfect. If you could change five things at the company, what would you change?

4. What in your opinion are five things that the company is doing successfully to a world-class standard?

This is an excellent way of framing common issues and themes, to see what is top of the agenda with your team before you really dive in.

Assessing your team

Once you have completed these initial meetings, you will be in a position to perform a 'gap analysis' for your team to determine what is working well and what may be missing. Identify also what skills your people have and what skills are missing. Try to put structure around your evaluations, categorising people's skills and aptitudes across a range of needed variables, including leadership capability, technical proficiency, EQ, courage, the ability to learn new skills, and general demeanour. This will become important as you begin to map out your priorities.

Keep in mind that any changes you make to your team will have reverberations across your organisation. Staff moves initiated by you will meet a response (positive or negative) from other people on your team, as well as business partners who work with your people on a regular basis.

Any promotions, demotions or terminations you make are likely also to have consequences at various other points in your organisation and across the company as a whole. Be aware of what these implications may be before you move on anything. Remember that movements can create multiple vacancies. As a result, you must be systematic and structured in the way you go about this aspect. Coordinate with your business partners, the company's leadership and your HR representative to ensure you align and understand the implications and follow-on decisions that will need to be taken.

If you are new to the organisation, make sure that you take the time to truly understand your new team before deciding to replicate any approach you may have used successfully somewhere else. Your new company's needs may be very different and you may end up imposing a structure that is not good for the new organisation.

Keep a very open mind during your first 100 days as you formulate your battle plan.

Assessing your core legal risks

Once you have settled in and had an opportunity to assess the talent in your team, you are ready to identify and assess your core legal risks. Without a clear picture of what your risks are, you will be 'flying blind'.

Secure alignment with top management

As the first step in this exercise, it is vital that you get proper buy-in from your CEO, senior company leadership and business partners. You may even want to express your intentions to those you meet during your interview process, including interviews you have with the CEO, to ensure there is basic alignment on your approach. Buy-in from these constituents is critical to the success of your venture. You will be digging deep into the company's vulnerabilities and engaging in a fairly robust review that will require you to interview a fairly large number of people and collate a significant volume of input. You want to make sure that the audit committee, the CEO and your senior business partners are aware and supportive of your plan, rather than being surprised by it.

If you have a risk assessment team in your company, make sure that you are building good relations with them in advance of this work. Your audit will intersect with their work, and you want to ensure you are not perceived as intruding on their area of responsibility. Assure them that your efforts are aligned with theirs. Solicit their support and advice as you begin to plan your work, and collaborate with them as your work gets under way. You will uncover legal risks that have multiple dimensions and you want to ensure that the risk team is engaged fully in the process and capturing what you are doing. Your central message should be that your work is complementary to their core expertise and will assist them in their efforts.

Decide the time frame

The length of time your risk assessment will take will vary greatly, depending on the size and complexity of your company. If your company is a small single-product/service start-up with a relatively small population of employees, the evaluation process may take only a few weeks. Should your company be a large and complex multinational with many hundreds of thousands of employees and multiple business lines, you will need to be prepared for a lengthy process that might take several months to complete. In such an event, it is advisable to hire a project manager to help organise and run the process.

In either case, do not let the process drag on too long. Identify a reasonable time frame and stick to it, or you will find yourself mired in an endless study.

Conduct a risk audit

The best way to get started with identifying your core legal risks is to conduct a risk audit. As you do this, an accurate picture of your risk profile will begin to emerge.

Depending on the size and complexity of your organisation, you may want to consider the pros and cons of conducting the review yourself as opposed to hiring a third-party consultant or other provider to do the legwork for you. If you have a large department, it is strongly advisable to hire an outside consultant, who will be able to put structure onto the process and provide neutrality in the assessment. In either case, you should personally conduct the interviews with key people such as your chairman, CEO and audit committee chair.

There are a number of steps that you should take to assess your risks, as set out next.

Interviewing

To get a proper view, you will want to gather the perspectives of significant people who have the ability to view the company from differing vantage points. You will want to ensure that you interview at least the following:

- *The board:* If you are able to, interview all of your directors. At the very least, interview the chairman of the board, the chairman of your audit committee, as well as the chairmen of any other key committees that impact reputation and risk, and a sampling of other non-executive directors.

- *Executive leaders:* Interview the CEO, chief financial officer, chief operations officer, chief human resources officer, chief technology officer, chief information security officer, group presidents, chief compliance officer, the heads of strategy, internal audit, tax, corporate affairs, and government relations, as well as those in charge of crisis or incident management, quality and R&D. Also include any other members of the company's executive team or operating committee.
- *Internal legal team:* You need to interview a good cross-section of your own team, at all levels, from personal assistants to deputy GCs. Make sure you cover all geographical areas, business units and functions. In a small department, take the time to interview everyone.
- *Internal audit, enterprise risk team, compliance, security and other key corporate teams:* Interview a sample of internal auditors, risk professionals and compliance investigators. Interview also the heads of security, health & safety, procurement, marketing etc. The specific list will depend on your particular business, but the goal is to identify those areas that are critical chokepoints for your business, its ability to operate, its legal status and its reputation.
- *External auditors:* Set time aside to meet with your external auditors – both the senior people and those further down who actually do the detailed work.
- *Outside legal counsel:* Invite several of your outside counsel who have worked with you the longest to prepare informal presentations to you of what they see as your core risks. Make sure you avoid colouring their opinions by giving them a sense of what you believe the risks are – you want to get the unvarnished truth as they see it, in order to benefit from a truly external opinion.
- *Outside consultants:* Meet with external strategic consultants, crisis management consultants and project management consultants to get their views.
- *Discussion groups:* Depending on the size of your business, you may want to consider running several discussion groups (ie, group discussions where the conversation is structured or partly structured around a set of topics or questions) of other people from cross-sections of the business, so as to qualitatively assess the

company's risks as they see them. These discussion groups could be run by you or by an outside facilitator from either your HR department or a consultancy firm.

Once you have drawn up your list of people to interview, ask each of them to list the top five legal risks they believe the company faces. Some of the answers the interviewees provide will seem naïve or completely irrelevant, but let a pattern begin to emerge before you make judgements about the merits (or lack thereof) regarding the feedback.

Collate and map out the answers you are getting into groups of risk.

The challenge of non-experts

The challenge of asking people from outside the legal department about legal risks is that they may want to talk about basic legal risks that they confront on a regular basis, such as ongoing litigation. By contrast, your legal experts are more likely to flag the strategic risks they see coming in the future.

Try to guide your conversations with the non-experts to get forward thinking. Ask about legal risks within specific time frames (eg, within the next three years and up to 20 years). In addition, have them talk about business risks, since frequently these will have legal components that they would not otherwise have considered.

Liaising with the risk assessment team

Once you have completed your conversations, check in with your company's risk assessment team (if you have one) to ensure that your emerging assessment of the company's legal risks is aligned with theirs and with their assessment of the company's overall risks.

Documentary research

Complement your interviews with documentary reviews. To that end, you will want to collect and review:

- Any disclosure documents your company may have issued in the past five years, such as annual reports, stock exchange notices or shareholder reporting documentation.

- Regulatory filings and submissions made in connection with various licensing or permit applications in key parts of the business.
- Internal documents from the board and executive on company strategy, risk and risk appetite, and commercial priorities and challenges. These might include business plans – both short- and long-term versions for the various markets, as well as an overall corporate plan.
- Legal department memos on strategy and risk, including any business plans.

Look for sections in these documents describing key risk factors, management discussions and analyses, legal reporting, financial controls etc and begin to map out the areas of commonality and difference in terms of how they describe company and industry risks.

Walk the beat

Get out of corporate HQ and visit your main markets, including any intuitively high-risk areas, such as subsidiary operations located in markets that are perceived to be at high risk of corruption (eg, those that score high on Transparency International's Corruption Perceptions Index).[7]

While out and about, meet with the local legal teams, local outside counsel and local management, as well as a sample of people lower down in the organisation, to the extent that they are accessible – for instance, language barriers may be a problem but translators are always available; plan for that need in advance.

Surveys

Risk surveys are an option. In general, broad discussions with key people are more effective in ferreting out unknown risks, but risk surveys can be helpful for drilling down on a more narrowly defined risk or risk topic.

One particularly helpful use arises if the survey is a precursor to discussion group conversations and the interviews that you run. You could, for instance, produce (or develop further) a broad questionnaire on the top five risks, and then organise discussion groups to prioritise those risks, leveraging your interview time in a more focused manner.

Pointers for a successful outcome

Set out next are five key pointers to consider when going about the tasks described in the previous section.

Pointer 1: Be broad and holistic

If you limit your reviews to a very narrow range of people, you will get a very narrow view of the risk base. Start with your department and have them tell you what they think the biggest risks are. But do not stop there; you will need to ask many other people as well, both internally and externally, to get a proper view of what's going on.

It is also important that the people you ask are not just at one level of the organisation, hierarchically speaking. People at different levels will have different views, all of which together paints a more accurate picture. Indeed, people further down the organisation ladder will often provide you with a more accurate view of the risks than those higher up. A line manager at a plant might tell you that she sees a lax safety culture where she works. A local sales representative might explain that people seem to be quite relaxed about taking or giving bribes to get things done. These can be absolutely critical perspectives to take into consideration.

Make sure that you take into account the perspectives of people who are outside the company but know the organisation well, including outside counsel, external auditors and consultants. Ask several from each category – but only those who have worked with the company for many years – to provide their ideas on what the company's material risks are.

Be careful not to feed them your own views in advance. It is much better that they provide their input with minimal influence from you. This may require you explaining what you are doing up front, to avoid any of them feeling as though you are testing their knowledge. You are not trying to see how much they know; instead, you are using what they provide to you as a thread among many threads that you will be weaving into the tapestry of risk in front of you.

Pointer 2: Be both qualitative and quantitative

It is important to conduct both quantitative and qualitative research as you go about conducting your risk assessment. By using both quantitative and qualitative methods, you will end up with a more nuanced and holistic view of your risks. For instance, you might send out a survey to the entire population to understand the broad trends, patterns and categories of risk, and then follow up with structured conversations around those trends and patterns with smaller groups of representative people from across the company.

Do not just circulate a questionnaire and tabulate the results as they come in. Much of the value of this exercise comes from the nuances and comments that get added in the qualitative discussions. People may reveal as an aside (when describing something else to you) a much more significant risk that they had not even considered. Furthermore, the subtext that floats in the air can be a critical thing to pick up on in many cultures, particularly in Asia. People may be saying one thing but signalling something entirely different.

Of course you want to make sure you ask people the same questions in your qualitative assessments, but you also want to make sure that you are structuring the conversations in such a way that people can express their views through open-ended questions that enable you to pick up on what might not be included in the list of questions you think are relevant (eg, "How would you describe the risk environment?" and "What do you see as our biggest threat?").

You might have your subjects rate the risks they identify by both likelihood and impact. The scales set out in Tables 1 and 2 on the next page might be a place to start.[8]

Pointer 3: Take the long view

Ask about both the current risks *and* how the company's risks have evolved. What were the risks five years ago? What will they look like five years from now? Try to get a sense of where the risks have historically emanated from and where they are likely to go next. Your goal is not to just get a snapshot of the risk profile at a particular moment in time but,

Table 1: Scaling risk by likelihood

Rating	Likelihood	Criterion
5 – Almost Certain	>90%	Event will probably occur in most circumstances or is occurring regularly now
4 – Likely	66%–90%	Event likely occur at some time
3 – Possible	36%–65%	Event could occur at some time
2 – Unlikely	10%–35%	Event could occur in rare circumstances
1 – Rare	< 10%	Event could occur only in exceptional circumstances

Table 2: Scaling risk by impact

Impact	Description
Severe	Could shut down the business operation. The majority of business objectives would not be achieved
Major	Significant impairment of the ability of the company to pursue its mission, goals and strategic initiatives
Moderate	Moderate impact; key business objectives not achieved
Minor	Noticeable impact; some business objectives not achieved
Insignificant	Low impact; most business objectives met

Source: Tables based on data provided by Pearson plc

rather, a sense of where the 'river of risk' has been and where it is likely to flow next.

Pointer 4: Take the broad view

People may mistake legal from non-legal risks or describe something as a commercial risk when in fact it has significant legal aspects to it. As discussed earlier, you need to make sure you are actively breaking down the silos between legal and non-legal risk because in many cases there are multiple dimensions of risk in any one category of risk. Lax environmental compliance at a manufacturing facility, for instance, may involve legal, reputational, government relations, employment and financial risks, among others.

Focusing too narrowly on any one sliver of information will cause you to miss the bigger picture. As noted earlier, as you begin to uncover risks that have both legal and non-legal dimensions, make sure you are coordinating with, and reporting back to, your company's risk team, who will likely have an in-depth understanding already of some of these risks.

Pointer 5: Keep conversations confidential

People will be much more likely to be frank and open about their views if they feel safe and confident that their opinions will not be relayed back to their managers or others.

You want people to be as candid as possible and that requires them to open up. Therefore, do not interview them in large groups, and avoid interviewing people at the same time and place as you interview their managers. Where possible, have people from the same culture and speaking the same native language conduct the interviews to ensure they are able to pick up on subtexts, cultural or linguistic nuances.

One thing to be aware of is the potential audit or discovery trail that might be created through these conversations and the output created. Depending on the jurisdiction you are in, you will want to structure these in the most protective manner possible, securing legal and professional privilege wherever that is possible.

One positive note in this respect from the regulatory perspective is that the trend is to give companies credit for taking a proactive approach to risk assessment, so long as something is done about it once the risks are identified.[9]

How to assess the materiality of risk

Once you have conducted your risk audit and gathered the necessary information from inside and outside the company, you will be left with a long list of risks and impressions. Try to group the risks together into categories, ideally in visual representation.

Your next challenge is to filter those risks down to a core of not more than five or six key risks. But how do you determine which risks are core risks and which ones are not?

There will likely be a number of outlier risks that are perceived as central only by a small minority of people and then there will be groupings of similar risks that a large number of people see from different vantage points. Does the majority view rule? If a large group of people from different vantage points has identified the same risk or very similar risks as material, might it be worth paying more attention to them? Should you ignore the outliers that only a few have identified? Not necessarily: for all you know, they may be the most material risks.

There is no ironclad and universal way to determine how to approach narrowing down your list. Risks flow and evolve and have permeable boundaries that make them hard to define and categorise with any amount of certainty.

You can consider risk from many different angles: some risks are highly unlikely but would have a massive impact if they were to occur. Others may occur with regularity but be more benign in terms of their impact. Some of these risks that are benign in the individual sense may become material in the aggregate. At heart, whittling down your list is a practical determination that is more art than science. You will need to configure the definition of what is material in a manner that is most suitable for the particular business you are in – and you are doing so with an eye to determining how to allocate your scarce resources.

One way you might begin to approach this is to piggyback on work undertaken by other experts in your company. Talk to your colleagues in internal audit, compliance and finance. Consider the materiality thresholds that are used by your organisation in other contexts. Talk to the team in charge of risk analysis for your board and leadership. Consider the views of other members of your company's executive team and ask them how they have arrived at their own views on the issue. If you work for a publicly traded company, you might also consider the materiality standards that apply to your disclosure obligations.

Use these approaches as a starting point rather than as boundaries. Keep your mind open but try to focus on narrowing your list to those legal risks that you believe could have a major impact on the company's operations, reputation or financial condition, taken as a whole.

Impact and likelihood
Both the impact and the likelihood of each risk will need to be considered (see Tables 1 and 2 above). But keep in mind that, at the end of the day, you are using this analysis for the practical purpose of trying to determine how and where to allocate your scarce resources.

If you face a very small possibility that a particular legal risk could unleash a major catastrophe that would wipe the business out and, in contrast, a very significant possibility of a somewhat less disruptive but still significant risk happening, and you can only afford to hire in-house resources to cover one of them, which will you choose? There is no clear answer that applies generally in all cases and to all companies. That is where your substantive skill as general counsel comes into play: your determination, while imperfect, will need to balance both impact and likelihood. The company is paying you to exercise your judgement on issues like this.

Relevance
You will also need to filter out the risks based on relevance – those that are principally legal risks from those that are principally non-legal, even if there may be legal aspects to them. This should not in any way be taken to mean that non-legal risks are somehow less important; only that there

needs to be a determination as to who is primarily accountable for managing the risk.

To the extent that the risk is not principally a legal one, it is best led by the experts most suited to manage that exposure – for example, your partners in finance and public affairs, with your support, rather than you or a member of your team.

Ultimately, you need to configure your definition of materiality and relevance based on the individual circumstances that you face and make the best judgement you can under the circumstances, leveraging the work that has gone on before you by your accountants and securities lawyers.

Your shortlist of the five or six core legal risks – the most significant risks that, based on your extensive review, pose the gravest threats to the company's material well-being – are the ones that you will be focusing on as you build and organise your team and allocate your budget.

Mapping your risks

Once you have completed your interviews and questions and determined which risks are both relevant and material, you will want to map them out to get a clearer visual picture of what your risk universe looks like.

One example of what that might look like is the chart in Figure 6. The y-axis measures the potential reputational, financial, strategic or operational impact that the risk might have on the business, ranging from insignificant to severe, while the x-axis gauges the probability of the event occurring, ranging from rare to almost certain.

A box on the side labels each risk and articulates with more specificity the nature of the risk and the mitigation status using a colour-coded score ranging from black (requires a substantial number of urgent actions) to pale grey (requires a small number of minor actions).

The visual representation allows you to consider your material risks in terms of both likelihood and potential impact. This in turn may help you to determine which of those risks deserves a disproportionate amount of

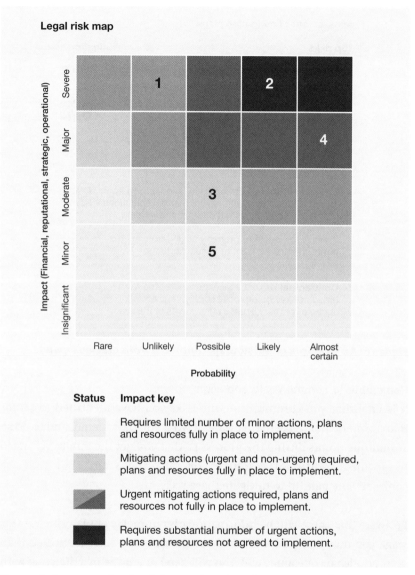

Figure 6: An example of a risk map *(continued on next page)*
(Source: Chart design used with permission from Pearson plc. The information contained in the chart is purely hypothetical.)

your scarce resources. If your company already gauges risk in a specific way and incorporates legal risk into its assessment process, you can just use that as your approach. The important thing is to ensure that you have something with which to visualise your risks.

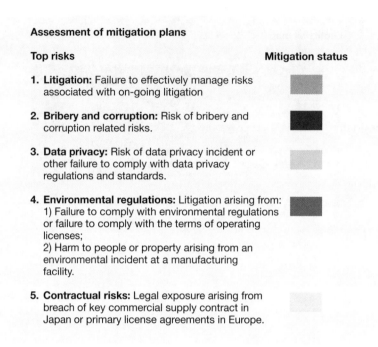

Assessment of mitigation plans

Top risks   **Mitigation status**

1. **Litigation:** Failure to effectively manage risks associated with on-going litigation

2. **Bribery and corruption:** Risk of bribery and corruption related risks.

3. **Data privacy:** Risk of data privacy incident or other failure to comply with data privacy regulations and standards.

4. **Environmental regulations:** Litigation arising from:
1) Failure to comply with environmental regulations or failure to comply with the terms of operating licenses;
2) Harm to people or property arising from an environmental incident at a manufacturing facility.

5. **Contractual risks:** Legal exposure arising from breach of key commercial supply contract in Japan or primary license agreements in Europe.

Figure 6: An example of a risk map *(continued from previous page)*

Remember to communicate and align

It is vital that you communicate the risks you have identified to senior management and make them aware of what you have found, and to do so at multiple points during the process so that you get the buy-in you need to acquire additional resources or take the steps that may be commercially painful to mitigate these risks.

Be aware that there will be information dissymmetry at play since at this stage you may know a lot more about the risks you have identified than your non-legal colleagues will. You will need to engage in a dialogue with them as your own assessment evolves. If you fail to do this, you may end up being perceived as 'crying wolf' and being overly sensitive about the nature of the risks you have uncovered.

The more you engage with them early on in your analysis, the more likely you are to secure their buy-in for difficult measures that may be needed to plug the risk. Make sure you show them the thoroughness that you have had in your approach, so that they get a sense of the validity of your assessment. To engage properly, start by holding individual meetings with key stakeholders to introduce them to the risks you have uncovered, explaining your methodology and reasoning. Take seriously their comments and input over a period of sessions.

Mitigation plans and accountability

Once you have aligned your findings with key stakeholders, you are ready to introduce your risk assessment to your executive and board. Be prepared to explain your mitigation plan and outline what resources will be needed, as well as the timing and impact that your mitigation plan will have.

The risks you have identified will very likely shade from legal into non-legal areas. For instance, if you have identified data privacy as a risk, it will have both legal, technological and reputational implications.

Once you are into the process of obtaining buy-in from relevant colleagues, make sure there is clarity on who is accountable for dealing with what aspects of the risk. You need to obtain clarity on accountability and, based on that, who will drive action planning for risk mitigation. This can be a difficult and time-consuming process, especially when you are also trying to secure general alignment. But without clear accountability, it will be hard to accomplish significant change or assess whether and how risk might be mitigated.

When considering mitigation, try to integrate your efforts with those who are accountable for other aspects of the same risk. For instance, you might seek to align with your technology and information security colleagues on the kinds of due diligence that need to be run on third-party partners in the data privacy and security areas. The broader objective is to leverage the organisation to help you manage the legal risk by piggybacking on the efforts that others will need to take. Do not try to do it all alone.

The three golden rules of risk

Clearly, the question of risk and how to identify it, manage it and prepare for it is a massive one. Reams have been written on this topic, from both practical and philosophical perspectives, and a consideration of the topic that would fully do it justice is clearly beyond the scope of this book. But that said, there are three (somewhat philosophical) 'golden rules' on risk that are worthy of consideration before moving on.

Rule 1: Guard against untested assumptions and groupthink

You may think you have a good grasp of what your core legal risks are, particularly if you have been in your role for a while. But be aware of untested assumptions: unless and until you have considered risk in a thoughtful and structured manner, how can you be sure that your assumptions are even remotely correct? You could be operating on outdated or incorrect information or the untested wisdom of others – in which case, you might as well be flying blind.

Be particularly aware of the dangers of groupthink – do not just go along with conventional wisdom. If you are a newcomer and organisational groupthink has long ago defined what everybody thinks the organisation's material legal risks are, take advantage of the fact that you are still 'too green to know better'; you can more easily afford the political cost of upsetting the status quo with scepticism and probing questions.

The risk of groupthink can be great if you have been in your role for many years. You need to stay fresh and alert to evolving risks. It pays to be slightly anxious.

> *When groups ultimately do well, it is often because they have anxious leaders ... Groups need a little anxiety, maybe even a lot of it. They need a culture that enables them to find out what they need to know.*
> (Cass Sunstein and Reid Hastie)[10]

One way to guard against internal groupthink is to get company executives to talk with their peers in other businesses about the challenges they are facing. This can be done through a conference or trade association. You clearly need to be careful not to share confidential information and you will generally want to avoid get-togethers by executives within the same industry for competition law reasons, unless lawyers are present and safeguards put in place. But getting your executives to think outside the company box and listen to the thoughts and concerns of peers in other companies can be enormously helpful in broadening their perspectives.

Your non-executive directors can also provide helpful perspective in this regard. Consider holding a broad risk discussion at a board meeting, or even better at a board away day where the rest of the executive might be in attendance.

Rule 2: Risk is not static

Risk is like a living creature that organically evolves as your business and operational environment grows. The core legal risks that your company faced five years ago are not necessarily the same ones that it faces today. A true assessment of risk requires subtlety and careful consideration.

There is also risk velocity. If a risk emerges, how quickly will it materialise from a risk to crystallised event? Some things can change overnight, while others will emerge slowly. You should try to consider this quality in your identified risks, and ensure that you have the contacts and the networks to respond appropriately.

The above will hopefully convince you that risk assessment is complex and fast moving. For that reason, you should conduct a structured legal risk assessment on a reasonably routine basis, so that you are always on top of your core risks and in a position to determine what resources to deploy to keep the company safe.

If you get pushback, remind everyone that you are paid to worry about things.

Rule 3: Always try to see the forest from the trees

In recent years, the general level of understanding about risk has evolved significantly in the corporate world. Enterprise risk management is now a stable part of the landscape. New standards such as the new UK Corporate Governance Code[11] are raising the bar on assessing and managing risk and risk appetite.

Consequently, many companies today employ a chief risk officer, whose job it is to focus exclusively on enterprise risk. Others will also have important roles to play in assessing risk, including the chief financial officer, the chief technical officer, the head of public affairs, the chief operating officer and others.

So how should your approach to legal risk interface with the risk management duties of other senior leaders within your company? At one level, it may seem obvious which risks relate to legal matters and which do not. But as British author and journalist at the *Financial Times* Gillian Tett has so eloquently written about in her 2015 book *The Silo Effect*,[12] people working in large modern institutions often act in ways that seem, with the benefit of hindsight, patently stupid because of the effect of silo'd thinking – that is to say, thinking that is constrained to the confines of a specific area of expertise or responsibility, as opposed to a broad and holistic perspective.

In her book, Tett discusses how both risk managers at UBS and their Swiss regulators failed to see the cumulative risks associated with the bank's trading activities prior to the 2008 financial crisis because they were focused on specific parts of the whole, rather than thinking holistically about risk. No one was tasked with thinking broadly about the risks that the company faced.

Your job as general counsel is to do just that by 'connecting the dots' across risk categories. You are uniquely well positioned to do so because the legal department is embedded across the enterprise, working with and understanding the risk profiles within HR, finance, corporate affairs, compliance, security and other functions, as well as each corner of the business. You need to be able to step back and see the whole picture and not just the legal risk.

Risks have soft and permeable boundaries that cross easily from one artificial, human-constructed category (such as legal or technological) into another (such as reputation). There is the court of law – but then there is also the court of public opinion. If you only view risk through the lens of the one over the other, you will run the risk of winning the battle but losing the war.

That is not to say that you, as general counsel, are responsible for managing all aspects of every risk. You are not, and your chief area of focus needs to be on legal risk. But you need to be aware of risk in a holistic sense, and you must always analyse risk holistically, whether you are assessing what the core risks of the company are or providing input on whether to proceed with a particular action.

Designing an integrated team structure

Great things in business are never done by one person. They're done by a team of people.
(Steve Jobs)[1]

Once you have determined your core risks and assessed the capabilities of your team, you can organise your team into subject-matter specialists (who focus principally on your core risks) and legal generalists (who focus principally on partnering with the business), appoint your leadership team, and map the rest of your organisation under them. You will also be in a position to organise your budget. We discuss these topics in this chapter.

Appointing specialists and generalists

As you begin your design strategy, you will need to determine whether you have the internal and external resources in place to fully address your core risks and plug any deficiencies you may have in servicing your commercial and enabling-function partners. To do that, you will want to divide up your universe of talent into two groups: specialists and generalists.

Specialists

The primary function of your specialists is to cover each of the core risks you have identified and provide internal expertise that can be leveraged by the rest of your legal team, as well as your business and enabling-function partners. The specialists are primarily responsible for servicing the other lawyers but they will also interface directly with the business.

You may be wondering whether this kind of highly specialised and technical expertise should not best be covered by outside counsel. Law firm lawyers will certainly have a critical role to play in helping advise you on your core risks, and you will want to ensure that you select the very best advisors to do so. However, to the extent that you have the capacity to recruit internal specialists to focus on these core areas of risk, you would be well advised to do so. Remember, these are your core risks, not peripheral ones. Internal resources can be a vital part of managing them appropriately.

There are three key reasons for this:
- *Preventive advice:* You need to address your core risks in a

preventive manner. Outside lawyers are a great resource to tap into once you have a major problem that you need to solve. But by then it may be too late and the material damage is likely to have already been done. You want to have someone who is on the inside – who can be pragmatic and help reduce the likelihood of the risks materialising in the first place by providing general guidance, conducting audits, putting in place preventive and remedial measures, rolling out policies, educating and informing colleagues across the business, and shaping the company's actions. An external advisor, by contrast, will be very proficient but can do little, if any, of the foregoing measures with anything like the effectiveness that a good internal resource will bring.

- *Pragmatism:* You need your chief advisor here to be pragmatic. Only someone sitting on the inside, who is privy to the conversations and who has 'a seat at the table' can modulate advice so that it is tailor made for addressing the specific circumstances that the business may find itself in. Good internal specialists will also be able to filter and digest external advice, enabling the business to benefit more effectively from the nuggets of wisdom being dispensed by discarding extraneous or irrelevant aspects and evaluating the level of risk that is appropriate under the specific circumstances. These things are much harder to do if you are an outside lawyer, unfamiliar with all of the aspects of the matter, the personalities involved and the broader objectives at stake.

- *Cost effectiveness:* An internal specialist will be far more cost-effective than a situation where the firm is relying purely on external counsel. This will allow you to reduce your primary exposure at a substantially lower cost.

The efficiency you generate by having specialists on your team is not just about saving on the legal fees you pay. It is as much, if not more, about the indirect but equally real gains you make putting the right resources to work on the right tasks. Excellent outside counsel are most certainly an important part of your mix. But good internal specialists can save you enormous sums via the strategic input and the value they bring to the management of external counsel.

How many specialists do you need? Depending on the size of your legal team and company, the number of specialists in each risk area can range from one person to dozens, or perhaps more in large companies in highly regulated areas. But you can certainly save enormous expense and generate far better outcomes in your core risk areas by in-sourcing specialists to help lead and manage your efforts.

Generalists

The generalists in your organisation are those lawyers whose primary focus is to interface with your business partners. They are the lifeblood of your practice and the face that most of the non-legal colleagues within your organisation will see. They may come from either a specialist or a generalist background. People in the company will judge your competence in large part based on how good your generalists are at handling issues, interfacing with clients and being pragmatic, effective, efficient and resourceful.

Most generalists will lack the deep technical expertise that a specialist will bring within a narrow area of law. Yet, they need to be equally outstanding legal professionals, with deep legal competence that has been honed through many years of practice – ideally in a mix of law firm, government and corporate settings.

They must possess outstanding legal skills and be highly competent analysts. But more so than the specialists, the generalists must also possess the qualities of a good general counsel, including the ability to manage a business partner relationship, demonstrate rock-solid judgement and be comfortable in navigating across a broad spectrum of issues, many of which they will not be expert in themselves. They must also have the deep commercial competence, solid communications skills and the high EQ necessary to thrive in a high-pressured leadership role within a business unit.

The fundamental structural principle that should underlie your organisational design when it comes to generalists should in all events be accountability for a specific part of the business. Every generalist lawyer must have a designated client or group of clients and every client or group of clients must have a designated generalist lawyer. This accountability ensures that the generalists develop personal relationships with their key business partners and that their business partners feel an obligation to educate and develop their lawyers, much like they do with anyone else on their teams.

Enabling-function lawyers: specialists or generalists?

One question that will arise as you develop your organisational structure is whether the lawyers you employ to support the other enabling functions (such as HR, finance, public affairs and procurement) should be specialists or generalists.

The answer is that they will be a mix, depending on the function they support. Your HR lead will likely be an employment specialist and your finance lead will probably be either an M&A or a capital markets lawyer. On the other hand, in other enabling-function contexts, generalists may be best positioned to take the lead – such as, for instance, in public affairs and communications, marketing or procurement – perhaps supported by specialists elsewhere in the legal department.

In some of these hybrid contexts, you may have more flexibility in terms of whom to appoint; in others, the technical skills needed are sufficiently specialised that you will need to consider only those who come from a narrower pool of candidates.

Who decides: specialists or generalists?

One question that often arises within the legal department is who has the final say on a matter: the generalist or the specialist? If a specialist warns the generalist and his clients of the risks inherent in proceeding with a particular course of action but the generalist believes that the risk is worth taking, who decides what action should be taken?

There is not necessarily a stock answer that will suffice in all cases for this dilemma, which is bound to arise on numerous occasions. But there are two general guidelines you can put in place. First, if the matter is black and white – eg, proceeding would be in violation of law or company policy – the specialist's view must prevail. If, however, the matter is not clear cut, you need to proceed with the same careful consideration of the facts as you would in any situation. You might consider letting the business partner decide, taking into account the views of both the specialist and the generalist. Or if the matter is sufficiently material, as general counsel you may want to articulate a view or intervene and decide for yourself.

Some large legal departments have put in place internal policies or directives setting out some basic rules in this respect. This is discussed further in the next chapter; but depending on your situation, you might consider putting such guidance in place so as to ensure that disagreements are resolved in light of certain core principles.

The optimal ratio of specialists to generalists

What is the optimal ratio of specialists to generalists? That can be a difficult question to answer because it depends on the particular circumstances you face. Generally, unless there is a strong need for highly specialised legal knowledge because of a heavy regulatory environment, most companies tend to end up with far more generalists than specialists.

To a certain extent there is an overlap between the two categories, which makes this analysis difficult. Outstanding generalists typically will have had a specialist background at some point in their career; however, as you approach the very top end of the talent pool the candidates may possess both excellent generalist and outstanding specialist qualities.

In his book *The Inside Counsel Revolution*, Ben W Heineman Jr notes how, at the beginning of his tenure, he recruited lawyers almost exclusively from law firms and government because the pool of highly qualified in-house lawyers was not as deep as it would later become.[2] In some cases, particularly in many of the highly regulated industries, generalists inevitably also needed to be specialists. But he was able to pay top rates for the very best lawyers in the market.

That might be challenging for some GCs to achieve. A specialist who also possesses the skills to be a generalist is a rare and valuable gem. The pool of such candidates, who possess the skills to be both an outstanding specialist and an outstanding generalist, is far smaller than the pool of candidates for roles that rely on qualities that fall primarily on one side or the other.

Moreover, the pool of generalist in-house talent today is far deeper and more capable than it was even a few years ago. Not only is there little need for a firm to restrict itself to pools of talent within law firms, but doing so would also be counterproductive. The qualities of a good law firm lawyer can be very different from those that make a good in-house counsel. If you recruit only from law firms, you will largely be looking in the wrong place, particularly when it comes to generalists.

The rise of the legal operations officer

Over the past decade or so, a new profession has arisen within the legal industry: the legal operations officer. These specialists have varying responsibilities depending on the legal department they belong to; but at core they are, like a company's chief operations officer, responsible for ensuring the smooth operation of their organisation.

The Corporate Legal Operations Consortium describes the role thus:[3]

> *Corporate Legal Operations Officers bring the leadership, knowledge and experience necessary to drive peak in-house legal department performance. They offer a deep understanding of the industry; expert knowledge of best practices and enabling technologies; team development skills; and core competence in implementing policies, processes, and technologies to increase value to the Company while driving down costs and fostering a globally connected culture.*

There are innumerable tasks that can be assigned to a team of legal operations officers, but some of the more common ones include the following:

- *Metrics:* developing, tracking and managing metrics and key performance indicators (KPIs);
- *Technology and tools:* identifying, selecting and implementing efficiency and effectiveness technologies, such as e-billing software, contract management systems;
- *Policies and processes:* formulating, rolling out and enforcing

department-wide policies and processes, including outside counsel guidelines and vendor selection rules;

- *Strategic planning:* taking the lead in formulating and implementing strategic planning for the legal organisation;
- *Legal vendor management:* establishing selection criteria and overseeing the management of relations with outside providers, including outside counsel, alternative legal services providers, consultants, and vendors of technology and other products or services;
- *Budgets:* tracking and managing all department-related budget initiatives;
- *People and culture:* taking the lead in formulating staff development and culture initiatives;
- *Communications:* managing and formulating department-wide communications initiatives, including managing and setting the agenda for regular leadership meetings, company-wide meetings and other gatherings, as well as the maintenance of related tools, such as the company's intranet and blogs;
- *Litigation support:* supporting the litigation department with technology or process-driven solutions, including e-discovery and document review; and
- *Contract management:* handling or overseeing contract management teams who negotiate, draft and process contracts.

These are just some of the possible areas that may be included within the ambit of the legal operations officer role. The exact structures and components will depend on the nature and structure of the organisation. Some legal departments will divide the above list of tasks among various groups, with the legal operations team taking the lead on metrics, technology and tools, budgets and contracts, with other groups or teams handling the other areas in parallel, because that is what works best organically given their structure. There is no single correct way to carve up the role.

Do you need a legal operations team?

A 2016 survey revealed that 68% of general counsel had seen the need for a greater emphasis on legal department operations over the previous two years, including the need for metrics and software solutions. As is evident from the chart in Table 3, the percentage of legal departments that now employ between one and nine legal operations professionals more than doubled, from 20% to 43%, in 2015 alone.[4] This explosive growth reflects the increasing need that GCs have to manage and run their legal departments as efficient and effective business operations in the wake of the pressures they face.

Table 3: The growth in legal operations teams

Year	Number of legal operations positions					
	0	1–9	10–24	25–49	50–99	100+
2015–16	51%	43%	3%	1%	1%	<1%
2014–15	79%	20%	1%	<1%	<1%	<1%

(Source: www.law360.com/articles/751500/gcs-embrace-of-legal-ops-refocuses-in-house-departments/)

Regardless of the specific tasks they are given, medium-sized and large legal organisations can benefit greatly from having a full-time operations person or team. The work that such a person does is critical to driving both quality and effectiveness into and across the function. Doing this well is a full-time job for seasoned professionals who can bring their financial, planning and project management skills to the task that lawyers may not possess.

This will only become even more important in the coming decades as so-called 'big data', cloud computing, artificial intelligence and network effects begin to have a greater impact on the operation of the legal team. You can benefit from having professionals who understand these developments supporting you in your endeavours.

Legal operations professionals can either be lawyers who migrated to the role or non-lawyers who come from other backgrounds, such as finance, project management, procurement or technology. There can be pros and cons with each. Lawyers will typically have credibility with the rest of your team. This can be helpful when trying to push through new initiatives that require changes in behaviour. However, they are likely to lack the technical and planning expertise that the non-lawyers bring to the table. The best would be a combination, such as a former lawyer who has been in the role for many years, combining technical and operations skills with legal experience and the credibility that brings.

Good legal operations professionals, including chief legal operations officers, will pay their costs many times over in the savings and efficiencies that their work will generate, and will free you up to focus more of your time on legal work. You absolutely need these people as soon as you begin to have any level of scale and complexity in either your organisation's size or workload.

Smaller departments that cannot afford a full-time legal operations person might consider retaining them on a temporary basis through an alternative legal staffing company. They can be hired for shorter periods, either to work on discrete projects or to help you put together a strategic plan for the area.

Whom should a chief legal operations officer report to?

Just as there is no single perfect answer to the question of what roles the legal operations team should take on within a given team, the optimal reporting line will depend on the circumstances.

If the chief legal operations officer (CLOO) is handling a broad range of matters, including strategic planning, budgeting and vendor management, you will want to have the CLOO report directly to you as general counsel because not doing so will remove you from some of the most critical decisions that you should be making in terms of your team's operation. If the scope of the CLOO role is defined very narrowly – for example, having it mainly focused on the implementation and management of technology solutions – it could be delegated to another senior person on your team.

You need these professionals and you want to stay close enough to what is happening in their analyses and operations to set the overall department direction and ensure that what is being implemented is in accordance with your strategic priorities.

Appointing your legal leadership team

Once you have assessed and appointed your team members, you will be in a position to begin to think about how you want to organise your leadership. This is the critical first step in building your organisational design and you will want to do this within, or very shortly after, your first 100 days.

This is a task that is being undertaken on a continual basis because your organisation and your team keep evolving. But it needs to begin on day one. There are three key reasons for this:

- *Wise counsel and input:* You will benefit greatly from having your leadership in place as you think through how to structure the broader department. It will be an excellent sounding board and, if you go about things in the right way, you will benefit from calibrating your initial thoughts with theirs. Trying to determine the design structure of your new organisation entirely on your own and in a vacuum is suboptimal.
- *Persuasion:* Appointing your leadership team up front will give you the opportunity to persuade them first about your views. Persuading a smaller team of highly motivated leaders to share your viewpoint is far easier than trying to persuade everyone at once. Of course, that is a two-way street, but as you collectively settle on your direction and goals, you will have a built-in first generation of supporters who will spread the word to the broader community. Without their assistance and support, it will be you alone trying to influence your world, rather than you and your leadership doing that.
- *Legitimacy:* By including your leadership into the decision-making process, you will instantly reap the benefit of more legitimacy than if you alone, without the benefit or formal input of those who have been there for a long time, make radical or not-so-radical decisions about where the team needs to head in terms of structure. Your

decisions will be backed up by a group from within the team who is familiar with who they need to focus their persuasive efforts on, what communication style and message is likely to be most impactful and how implementing the new design is best likely to succeed.

Team size and composition

There is no clear answer to the correct size for your new leadership team, because that will vary radically depending on the size of your company and your team as well as the complexity of the business you are trying to cover, the geographical spread and other factors.

The Goldilocks principle

There is an inherent tension between ensuring that you have full representation on your leadership team and spreading yourself too thinly by having too many people on it.

If you have too few reports, you will end up isolating yourself. But if you have too many, you will have no time to devote to matters of importance outside of the team and insufficient time to devote to your reports. Like Goldilocks, you need to find a leadership team size that's not too big, not too small, but just right.

So what size is 'just right'? Generally speaking, you want to have the right spread for your circumstances. This should be between, at one end of the range, full coverage and connectivity, and, at the other end, the group being small enough that the team is able to deliberate and make effective decisions in an environment where everyone can be heard and confidences can be shared.

The layered leadership approach

If you need to have a leadership team that is larger than four to six people because of the size or complexity of your organisation, you may want to consider adopting a 'layered leadership' approach. Under this model, you put in place not one, but several leadership organs, each with its own well-defined mandate. That will enable you to have one larger 'senior leadership team' consisting of leaders representing all areas of material importance to your team, as well as one or two smaller committees consisting of a much smaller group of four to six leaders to make strategic decisions regarding the legal department and your legal practice across the company.

A layered leadership structure could be as follows:

- *Operating committee:* At the core of your leadership model could be an operating committee consisting of, for example, four or five direct reports. The committee advises you on all aspects relating to the 'hard wiring' of your department, including:
  - financial condition, operational effectiveness and morale;
  - overall strategic priorities;
  - monitoring, setting and allocating of budgets, headcounts and other resources;
  - evaluating and developing top talent; and
  - establishing and monitoring the effectiveness and adequacy of department-wide policies and procedures.

- *Field committee:* Alongside the 'hard wiring' focus within the operating committee, there should be a 'front-facing' field committee, consisting of the top three or four lawyers in your field operations, all of whom are also direct reports. This group is responsible for reporting to, advising, and aligning with you on:
  - material legal and commercial issues;
  - material litigation;
  - key business decisions and priorities, including decisions or discussions taking place at the leadership team levels of major business partners;
  - core or emerging risks;
  - compliance and government relations matters;
  - governance structures;
  - budgeting and resource priorities; and
  - the evaluation and development of 'in-field' talent.

- *Senior leadership team:* Finally, at the broadest level, you might have in place a senior leadership team (SLT), consisting of people who both report directly to you as the general counsel and other senior lawyers with material remits who report to your direct reports, including members of the operating and field committees. This group should comprise no more than 15–20 people.

The purpose of this group is to regularly communicate, act as a sounding board and align with you on the status of a broad range of topics relevant to the operation of the department, including:

- strategic or operational issues that have been considered by you, the operating committee or the field committee;
- key business or operational initiatives under way at the corporate or field levels;
- IIR or finance updates or initiatives of relevance to the department;
- personnel, talent and department morale; and
- policy, process or other governance initiatives.

The SLT acts as a forum for airing and coordinating these and other initiatives prior to implementation or broad dissemination across the department.

To ensure that there is 'cross-pollination' between the operating and field committees, one member from each rotates as a guest member on the other committee at all times.

This layered approach to governance will be overkill in a small department. But in a large one it may just strike the best balance between maintaining involvement and clear communication across a broad leadership group and securing a more intimate and confidential team that is small enough that it can make effective decisions in key areas.

Insiders v outsiders

One question that may come up as you begin to appoint people to your leadership team is whether you should appoint people from within your organisation or from outside. The answer depends on the depth of talent and the range of skills that your existing team possesses, which in turn may depend on how large it is.

Generally speaking, appointing from within your existing team is good on many levels for your department. It will send a strong signal to your people that you have confidence in them and that there is room for people to grow and thrive in the department. Appointing from within also creates a core group of people in your department who owe their position to you and who therefore are presumably loyal to you and supportive of what you are seeking to achieve.

Having people from inside the existing structure trying to put into effect your new direction will also make doing so much easier because they already know how to navigate within the organisation and how to communicate your decisions more broadly and with best effect. If you are new to your department, you will be unfamiliar with the legacy legal team, their talents and weaknesses and the pitfalls of the organisation. If you appoint a new leadership team that includes at least some legacy leaders, you will benefit from their institutional knowledge, including the department's pitfalls. Of course, the legacy leaders you appoint to your leadership team might have biases – be wary in particular of personality discussions, as it will be hard at the initial stage of your tenure to determine truthfulness from jealousy and fear. It will be up to you to rely on your own emotional intelligence to ascertain who among them seems best suited to remain as part of your leadership.

There will be times, however, when you simply lack the right capabilities or skills from within, or where your vision is inconsistent with those of the existing potential candidates. In such cases, you will need to go outside to appoint people. Bringing in new talent can be a positive experience for the team as a whole, provided you do so in moderation because otherwise your existing talent will begin to feel that there is an 'alien invasion' under way and that they no longer have your support or confidence.

One or two senior people from outside the existing organisation can provide fresh blood and a new way of thinking. They will also be extremely supportive of what you are doing and the changes that you would like to bring. In particular, where such new talent is bringing in skills that people in the organisation lack, they will be generally well received.

Mistakes will be made

When appointing a new leadership team, you need to resign yourself to the notion that some of your choices will prove to have been a mistake. You will be unable to perfectly know everyone's skills, personality traits and motivational drivers within the first 100 days. But you must move forward nevertheless. A perfect 'dream team' will always remain elusive; at any given time, parts of your team will function flawlessly, while others will struggle.

Do your best in trying to appoint the right team members to leadership positions up front and then calibrate as you go forward, replacing the ones that were not placed in the right roles. Accept from the beginning that this will happen. After you have promoted people into their new leadership roles, monitor their progress carefully with your business partners and their reports to ensure that things are working. If they are not working well, do your best to provide coaching and support.

If your team is not optimal, act quickly to strengthen it. Your own credibility will rise and fall with the performance of your new team, so if you wait too long to address the problems of others on your team, you yourself will come to own those problems. Two of the biggest mistakes managers make is hiring the wrong people and then keeping the wrong people too long.

What to look for in potential leaders

As you think about who is best positioned to take the senior leadership roles in your department, you should read and consider the chapter below entitled "Leadership skills". The primary considerations to mention here are twofold.

First, the skills of the team members needs to be considered. As the legal profession changes amidst the disruption outlined in Part A above, your leadership will require a host of non-legal skills in addition to being excellent legal professionals. In reviewing what skills you have in the team, take account of the notes made and impressions gained during your initial meetings in order to help evaluate who might be the best fit.

Secondly, you need to consider diversity. As you identify leaders from internal choices and new hires, do so with a view to building a diverse team of people who are capable of viewing things from different perspectives. Diversity is essential for optimal decision-making. As Mark Roellig, Executive Vice President and General Counsel of Massachusetts Mutual Life Insurance Company, observes:[5]

> *Only a diverse team will give you the different perspectives you will need to be successful. It also helps to establish a visible culture of opportunities based on performance, not on other factors.*

To get the full benefit of diversity, you should aim for not only racial and gender diversity, but diversity in a broader form, including age, background, disability, national origin, ethnicity and point of view.

Unless it already exists, you may want to consider creating a diversity committee, headed up by one of your senior leaders, to ensure that diversity gets embedded and emphasised across the department and not just in your leadership team.

Validate your choices

Once you have settled on a group of leaders, make sure you validate your choices with key business partners, including your CEO. They will be interfacing with these people, who will wield significant influence over key legal decisions, and many of them will have pre-existing opinions about them. If you meet resistance to one or more of your first-choice candidates, weigh carefully what to do and whether it is worth a battle. Your reputation will rest on the team you select. Make sure you set yourself up for success by picking people that your key business partners support.

You should also validate your selection with those business partners who will be losing their lawyer as they move from their current role to the new role within your leadership team. Make sure those partners are informed of, and aligned with, the decision and are comfortable that there is a plan for a smooth transition and handover to an acceptable successor. If you fail to do this, you may create significant tension with these partners.

Similarly, if you are bringing in talent from outside, make sure that key stakeholders interview the final candidates and broadly support your selections.

Once you have picked your leadership team, announce it broadly to the rest of the department and make sure you stay close to your new leaders in the early days, ensuring that they are embedding themselves in a careful and appropriate way with the broader team. There may be people in your department who are disappointed they did not get a spot on the leadership team (especially if they held one under the prior general counsel), and you will need to smooth some ruffled feathers and get them comfortable with their prospects for the future   or, if they are unable to adjust, you need to remove them from the organisation.

Keep in mind that every appointment to a new role will require thought in terms of how that person's existing role will be backfilled. There are many moving parts of which to keep track. Involve the new leadership in these backfill discussions and give them significant input over how their teams should be constructed and whom they want on them. This is a collective leadership task, and it would be wise to set aside a few days together for an offsite discussion early on with your leaders and HR to organise the rest of the changes and construct the blueprint for the broader department structure.

Mapping your team's organisation

Now that you have assessed and mapped your core legal risks, appointed your specialists, generalists and legal leadership team, you are ready to map the rest of your legal team under your new legal leadership. In doing so, you will need to consider a number of critical factors, including whether to put a 'dotted line' or 'solid line' reporting structure in place (see below) and how to decide who within your organisation should report to whom.

A matrix structure?

In structuring your team, you should ensure that that every lawyer has a business partner and vice versa. In the real world, this will likely be somewhat messier than simply having one lawyer for each business, with a pure hierarchical reporting structure up to you as general counsel. This is because your company might be structured in a matrix format, with vertical geographical groups (North America, Europe, Latin America, Asia, etc) and horizontal functional groups (product development, marketing, R&D, etc) that span across the geographical areas. Alternatively, you might have certain specialists who need to service a particular group of business partners in addition to just the legal team.

In principle, adopting a matrix structure may make sense or, indeed, be the only practical way to work. But if you are organised in some other way and are reorganising into a matrix structure, beware that it may cause significant anxiety. People will worry about whether it means increased workload for the same pay, who their actual manager will be, and whether you are simply trying to make large numbers of them redundant.

These fears can and should be addressed as you implement the matrix. As noted in the chapter entitled "Change Management" in Part D below, you must never underestimate the change management challenges that a transformation will bring.

You will need to constantly tweak the model as you roll it out in order to navigate the unforeseen obstacles that threaten to overwhelm the initial objective. The most common challenges when employees report to two managers include fuzzy questions of authority, which may require you to push back on old 'silo' mentalities and to sort out conflicts about what to prioritise. You will need to emphasise the bigger picture and move people away from old tribal loyalties and borders between groups. Publicly reward those who follow this approach and eliminate those who resist.

Leveraging your holistic strength applies whether you have a global team or just a domestic one. Even if you are not a global department, act like one in this situation by connecting people across groups, forming practice teams and seeking ways for people to collaborate across borders (whether real or imagined).

Solid and dotted lines
In a matrix organisation, a common current structure (despite certain

well-known difficulties) is that teams will have multiple reporting lines rather than one single chain of command.[6] In such circumstances, your lawyers may also need to operate within the matrix framework, with multiple 'solid line' and 'dotted line' reporting relationships into different legal team leaders or into the business and the legal team.

What do we mean by 'solid line' and 'dotted line' reporting? In a solid-line reporting relationship, the manager tends to have ultimate decision-making authority with respect to all of the critical levers that determine whether the employee is successful or not in his or her role, including determining the employee's compensation, setting the employee's performance objectives and evaluating the employee's performance.[7] The solid-line manager may also have the authority to terminate the employee or redirect his focus toward other roles or activities.

By contrast, a dotted-line relationship's contours remain relatively fuzzy and indeterminate, with the employee's accountability to the dotted-line manager somewhat unclear.[8] The dotted-line manager's input can vary from organisation to organisation, and from job description to job description. Typically, however, the dotted-line manager will have input with respect to the employee's compensation (particularly any variable compensation, such as annual incentive pay), performance evaluation, and personal objectives within the role (where, for instance, the dotted-line manager may have the right to include certain objectives for that manager's activity). Furthermore, the dotted-line manager may have the right to demand that a certain percentage of the employee's time be allocated to her projects.[9] Nonetheless, the solid-line manager will have the final and formal decision-making authority.

In most matrix organisations, there will be a hybrid arrangement in which the lawyers report on a solid-line basis to one person, with dotted-line reporting to another. In some cases, companies may even attempt a dual solid-line reporting structure, where the employee has a solid reporting line into two people.

Reporting lines for your legal team
One of the most critical questions you will face as you map your function,

particularly if your organisation is a matrix one, is whether your lawyers will report on a solid-line basis into you or into a business partner. How this reporting structure question ultimately gets resolved may not be something over which you have complete control. There may be a history of the business going with one or the other approach with respect to the legal function, or there may be broader political or structural reasons as to why the company would like (or needs to maintain) one or other approach.

Lawyers typically have not been very focused on what their reporting structure looks like. Those who have spent most of their time in law firms are used to a flat structure, where the formal lines of accountability are less decisive. The same goes for lawyers coming into a larger team-based organisation from a smaller environment, where there may have only been a handful of lawyers who worked in a collegial law-firm-like structure.[10]

This traditionally lax approach to reporting is a mistake. In the early days, when your legal team is very small, with just a handful of lawyers sitting together in one office, reporting lines may seem less critical. But as your organisation grows in size and scope, reporting lines will matter immensely to your ability to create a superior team. In fact, it matters so much that if you are unable to secure a solid-line reporting relationship over your legal team, you should question whether the role is one you want to take on, because you will be held accountable, either literally or figuratively, for people who are not accountable to you. If you fail to secure a solid-line reporting structure into you for your team, it could materially impede your ability to ensure good corporate governance, build a world-class culture and ensure operational efficiency.

There are several reasons why having a dotted-line structure into you can be unattractive, as described further below:
- it can impede good corporate governance;
- it may prevent you from building a high-performance culture;
- you may be unable to create a 'safe' culture; and
- it might be hard to ensure operational efficiency.

Dotted lines can impede good corporate governance

Having only a dotted-line reporting relationship may make it more difficult to ensure good governance across the company, which goes to the heart of why your department exists.

You may have to rely entirely and exclusively on each lawyer transcending their own interests to ensure that sensitive matters get escalated to you. You will need to rely on every one of them finding the courage to always confidentially share with you the concerns they have, including any relating to their solid-line manager that may have negative consequences for them. This is especially true if your lawyers are broadly dispersed across a large geographical area.

You may therefore, in reality, have created a governance structure that relies exclusively on the character and moral fibre of each person in the chain, and you will only be as strong as your weakest link. If just one lawyer feels divided loyalties or is less able to transcend her own interests to report something to you that might negatively impact on her manager and team, then you might well have failed to prevent a potential disaster from happening.

Imagine, for example, that you are a line attorney based in Kuala Lumpur, Malaysia. Your solid-line manager is the charismatic and authoritative general manager for the country and he sets your pay, decides your bonus and performance rating, and determines whether you get fired; you see him many times each day. Your dotted-line manager is the deputy general counsel in charge of international business, who sits 9,500 miles away in Baltimore, Maryland, in the United States. You see her once per year when she travels through the region, except for years when there are budgetary constraints, in which case it could be several years between each visit. You have monthly telephone conversations with her. She has a limited, informal and undefined ability to set your pay, decide any bonus payment or performance rating, or determine whether or not you get fired.

Now imagine that you discover that the local plant manager, who happens to be very close to your solid-line boss, may have failed to ensure that the plant is in compliance with local environmental laws. The laws are somewhat vague, and to determine whether an infraction exists will require a full investigation. You tell the general manager but he tells you not to worry; the practice is common and, in his opinion, it is not illegal. Moreover, it is essential to continue the questionable practice to keep costs under control and ensure that everyone makes their targets. He assures you that the problem will be fixed next year when there is more funding, and orders you to keep this strictly confidential and not to report it to headquarters.

What will you do in this situation? If you are courageous and morally upright, you will nevertheless report the situation to your dotted-line boss and trust that she will find a way to ensure no local retaliation occurs. However, if you are less than perfect, you may end up not reporting it and hoping for the best.

As the general counsel of the company, you want to avoid this situation. It can be hard enough to ensure that the lawyers in your team do the right thing and report all infractions or concerns. But you will radically improve your chances of securing that level of cooperation if they know that you are the one who holds decision-making authority over their jobs, compensation and performance reviews.

Having a structure that leaves that authority in the hands of the people whom your lawyer is tasked with overseeing could significantly weaken your ability to protect the company's assets and reputation.

Dotted lines may prevent you from building a high-performance culture

With a dotted-line structure into you, you may find your ability to create and shape a high-performance culture within the legal organisation materially impeded, because your people could be less likely to want to go where you are taking the department's culture. Their loyalties might be to the teams with whom they already work.

That can be particularly true where the lawyers are highly valued by their commercial clients. In the best case, this could be because they truly are exceptional talents; in the worst case, however, it may be for reasons that contradict the norms that you are trying to instil.

For instance, a lawyer may be popular with his solid-line clients because he is lax and loose, allowing everyone to do everything, and he is unwilling to make tough calls or stand up to things that are wrong when that would be unpopular. His behaviour has gone too far over to the 'partner' side of the partner–guardian divide. He will have little or no incentive to follow your lead, and change the way he operates to the detriment of his popularity. You will have little power to do much, other than voice your concerns with his manager, who is likely to disagree with your assessment. If you try to instil more discipline into this lawyer, he is likely to hunker down and refuse to provide you with any real insight into what is going on in his business area.

Be wary of lawyers who are wildly popular with the commercial teams they serve. It is good to be popular and to do good work – but not too popular. Being a good guardian means there will be times when you have to make unpopular calls in order to protect the business, even if that ultimately means helping your business partner arrive at an acceptable solution that is less legally problematic.

Changing cultural norms is complex and difficult under the best of circumstances. If people see no reason to follow you down that difficult path and, in fact, fear the implications of going in that direction, you risk ending up as a figurehead presiding over little of substance, with multiple teams operating in multiple cultures that have only tenuous connections to you or what you are trying to create.

Even if you have enormous powers of persuasion, you will only be able to impact those aspects that people see as being in their immediate interests. It will be like trying to persuade small children to eat less chocolate and more spinach without having any influence other than moral persuasion.

Dotted lines mean you may be unable to create a 'safe' culture
You want to instil an atmosphere in which all associates within the legal organisation feel it is safe – and, indeed, imperative – to openly and confidentially discuss how to tackle difficult situations. If those people report in on a solid-line basis to commercial partners, it could be difficult to build

the necessary level of trust. People might instinctively feel as though they are betraying their first-level (commercial) partners by breaching confidences and discussing issues openly with their second-level (legal) team.

With dotted lines, it might be hard to ensure operational efficiency

Instilling operational efficiency in your organisation will require you to push through behavioural change. That can be hard to do if the lawyers have only a dotted-line reporting relationship into you.

For example, if you want to ensure that your team spends more time on matters that are central priorities, they may have to stop devoting time to matters they may either enjoy or that the local team views as priorities.

You may need to force through use of new tools, such as a new contract management system, which are painful to learn at first. People may prefer to continue to do things the way that they have always been done. Efficiency may also require enhanced reporting of metrics, better discipline around how budgets are spent, or doing more with less. You may need to reallocate teams, terminate poor performers or give up certain resources, such as a heavy reliance on outside counsel or a top-heavy team of people.

These changes are difficult under the best of circumstances. But trying to push them through when the only tool you have is moral persuasion is nearly impossible.

Who reports to whom?

Once you have established the internal solid-v-dotted reporting structure question, you must determine the reporting chain – ie, who reports into whom. This will depend on the specific circumstances of your company and how it is structured. However, as a general rule, you will want to organise your team into groups that mirror the organisation structure that your company maintains, so that all members of a specific group report into your leadership team lawyer for that group.

For example, if your company organises itself along geographical lines, such as North America, Europe and Asia as separate areas of responsibility, have the generalists who serve the North America business partners report into your head lawyer for North America. If the company in turn has a head of certain groups of geographical areas (eg, president of international business, whose direct reports include such figures as the presidents of Europe and Asia), have your heads of those geographical regions report into your international head, with that person reporting to you.

There is no obvious rule that applies in all cases, and the foregoing should merely be a guide. You should organise reporting lines within the legal department in a way that is pragmatic and that will serve the organisation most effectively.

Flat *versus* layered hierarchies

As you structure your legal team, you need to balance efficiency with ensuring your professionals have reasonable career paths. That means maintaining the right level of hierarchy to ensure career path progression without making your structure too complicated or bureaucratic.

The general frustration in the in-house environment is that, unlike conventional law-firm career paths with partnership as the end objective, avenues for progression can sometimes be opaque. There is only one general counsel and perhaps only a handful of senior deputies, and often they tend to stay in those positions for many years.

So how do you motivate and retain ambitious professionals who want to see more progression in their careers? There is no perfect model that will guarantee an optimal mix in this context. The number of layers will vary from organisation to organisation, and also from team to team within an organisation.

If there are only three or four people in the entire department, career path layering can be difficult. You will have less ability to give people some management responsibility – but you can still create career progression for your top talent. Give them increasing amounts of responsibility, such as larger geographical or subject areas. With less bureaucracy and red tape inherent in a small team, you will have more flexibility to restructure as the business evolves, moving people into new roles.

If you are in a large department, you should be able to maintain a hierarchical structure that facilitates career progression. The key here is to ensure that you have in place a process that is fair and transparent, as well as evaluation mechanisms that ensure the best people are appropriately identified and nurtured.

For mid-sized teams, you will generally want to maintain a flattish organisational structure with not too many layers. Keep it sufficiently hierarchical to allow for career progression, but not so much as to create a lumbering machine.

Budgeting for the legal team

It is critical that as you sort out the structure of your team, you must also determine how to structure your budget.

In the same way that it is critical to have a unified legal team, with people reporting on a solid-line basis into you, you need to ensure that you also have a unitary budget. Without control over the funding, you will not have the ability to develop your team, deploy your resources and organise your structure optimally. Indeed, you will be constrained by someone else who is in control of the money – or, rather, lots of other people controlling smaller pots of money, each with his or her own agendas and priorities. In such circumstances, if you wish to bring your leadership together for an offsite meeting to develop your new operating model, for instance, the business unit controlling your leaders' funds will have the power to object.

Securing a unitary budget should be a key issue you resolve before taking on the GC role. If there is significant resistance to allowing you to have such control, you should walk away from the job. If you find yourself already in the role and have not secured a unitary budget, you will need to vigorously seek to persuade your chief financial officer (or the CEO if your CFO objects) for the right to have that.

You can start going about doing this by raising certain arguments.[11] There are no doubt others, but these will at least give you a place to start. So put forward the following as your case for a unitary budget (each discussed further below):

- A decentralised model prevents the company from prioritising its biggest risks.
- A decentralised approach is the least efficient way to control legal spend.
- A decentralised approach makes tracking legal spend nearly impossible.

A decentralised model prevents the company from prioritising its biggest risks

Unlike the business context, legal resources must be geared to protect the entire company's assets and reputation. In a world of finite resources, legal funds must be allocated where they are most needed.

Use a military analogy: most countries adopt a centralised approach to national defence because decentralising military budgets and strategy would weaken national security. A coherent national defence strategy demands that scarce resources be allocated optimally. Similarly, a unified legal budget allows for a coherent, aligned legal strategy, allocating scarce resources in the manner best designed to secure the company's overall interests. When budgets are not controlled centrally, local teams will skew priorities toward whatever seems most important to them.

In a world of limited resources, you will not be able to fully fund every initiative, which means that some constituents will inevitably feel frustrated. That is the price that must be paid for plugging your core risks. Very few people will voluntarily frustrate their own objectives in the interests of a broader objective.

Having already identified your core risks, point out where the company's true priorities lie and how the current structure will not allow you to allocate resources effectively to plug those risks.

A decentralised approach is the least efficient way to control legal spend

Multiple legal budgets are less efficient and more duplicative than a centrally controlled one. It should be fairly self-evident that 10 small pots of money, all aiming to basically do the same thing across the organisation, is likely to generate waste, duplication and inefficiency.

Your CFO might point out that there are valid reasons why your company nevertheless maintains a decentralised model. For instance, it empowers local decision-makers, enabling them to react more flexibly and rapidly.[12] You can assuage concerns about eliminating nimbleness and autonomy by arguing that the central budget will be broken into coherent units for each of your groups, giving them autonomy and accountability over their part of the global budget.

You might also argue that concerns about lumbering bureaucracy are less relevant in the legal department context than elsewhere because the team is relatively small, and thus better able to remain nimble.

A decentralised approach makes tracking legal spend nearly impossible
Without a unitary budget, you will not have a clear picture over how money is spent on legal services. If you are going to accelerate the performance of the department, you need to be able to track and control key budget metrics, including spend to budget, spend by matter type and business unit, outside and inside spend as a percentage of company revenue, and various measures relating to external rate increases.[13]

While you might theoretically be able to do this by consolidating multiple reports extracted from various budgets for different parts of the organisation, it is nearly impossible to do so on a regular and accurate basis. The technology available to you may not enable automatic extraction, requiring people to manually track and extract the data and perhaps piece it together to make it meaningful. That in turn requires multiple actors to collaborate when they may not have a vested interest in doing so – in fact, they may have a vested interest in keeping their own budgets opaque. Each such step that is added to the process makes it less likely to be usable on a real-time basis. Without being able to measure and track things, you cannot really change them.

While there are many models that can be adopted when it comes to reporting structures and budgets, having a solid-line reporting structure and a unitary budget are key objectives that are essential to ensure good corporate governance and the ability to develop an outstanding legal team.

A centralised approach will empower corporate governance

Finally, you might point out that maintaining a unified legal budget will empower corporate governance. A unified budget means a less fragmented function that is able to speak with one clear voice and act on a unified set of clear priorities. Stature, alignment, authority and leverage are likely to be the positive effects that will follow.[14] Without control of your own budget, the legal department will have less overall influence and power, and will lack 'a seat at the table'.

Law firms

Legal institutions and lawyers are at a crossroads ... and are poised to change more radically over the next two decades than they have over the last two centuries.
(Richard Susskind)[1]

Disruption in the legal profession

The legal industry is in the midst of massive disruption, at the core of which lies an apparent paradox. As we saw in Part A, the demand for legal services is rising, along with the costs of violating the law.[2] This should be a boon for outside lawyers. Yet law firms increasingly find themselves under pressure as less work flows in – demand forecasts for legal services from large law firms show accelerated declines in every major region globally between now and 2025.[3]

Graduating law students are also experiencing an increasingly difficult time finding work. In the United States, the number of entry-level legal jobs continues to decline, most recently by 6.8%, and law school enrolment continues to decline.[4] The unemployment rate for lawyers in the United States sits at 11.2%, which is more than twice the unemployment rate of the general population.[5] In the United Kingdom, the situation is somewhat better, but the trends are worrying at the larger corporate and commercial firms. For instance, the six elite City of London firms that make up the 'silver circle' intended to offer 21% fewer trainee contracts in 2016 than in 2008.[6] The same rate of decline has been observed at some of the largest national firms.[7]

There are four trends that are causing this disruption, discussed next:

- the innovation revolution;
- cost pressures;
- regulatory reforms; and
- new competitors.

The innovation revolution

The first trend causing disruption in the industry is the innovation revolution, discussed in "The changing context" in Part A above, which is wreaking havoc on the traditional law-firm model with its pyramid revenue structure and hourly billing rates, making it increasingly uncompetitive.

The surge in demand is, ironically, exacerbating the problem. As the demand for legal services increases, more and more players are making themselves available, offering clients smarter ways of working. These new players are good – and poised to devour the traditional law firm's lunch.

Recall from Part A that two trends are driving the innovation revolution: the unbundling of legal services and the rise of technological disruption. As a result of unbundling, clients are no longer using law firms as a one-stop shop for all legal work. Alternatives now abound at all ends of the spectrum, including offshoring, in-shoring, outsourcing and in-sourcing.[8]

The second trend, technological disruption, has introduced a plethora of innovative tools that have reshaped the landscape, including communications- and productivity-enhancing technologies, efficiency and transparency tools, and emerging solutions that leverage artificial intelligence. As the profession has moved from the days of pen and ink to ink-ribboned typewriters and photocopy machines, and then on to computers and today's sophisticated technology, work that once was tailor made has become commoditised. Technology has 'democratised' knowledge within the legal profession, providing more transparency. As Harvard Business School professor, Clayton Christensen, and his colleagues have noted, this has enabled GCs to disaggregate traditional law firms and "reduce costs and increase efficiency through technology, streamlined workflow, and alternative staffing models".[9]

One thing both of these trends show is how relatively infrequently lawyers actually engage in value-added, tailor-made solutions. Much of what lawyers have historically provided resides on the more commoditised end of the spectrum, where the real focus should be cost and process rather than the crafting of hand-made solutions.

These disruptive trends are pulling strands of work apart, enabling clients to strip out the less value-added work. Given this reality, clients are increasingly unwilling to pay hourly rates for anything but the highest-value work. This is borne out by a recent study, which reported 24% of law firms are currently losing work to technology solutions deployed by internal legal departments, with another 42% viewing this trend as a potential threat to their businesses.[10]

Cost pressures
The second trend driving this disruption is cost pressure. In-house teams are being asked to do more sophisticated work with ever-fewer resources.

Richard Susskind has termed this the 'more for less' challenge, noting that many GCs are being required to substantially reduce their overall legal budgets.[11] The general counsel is increasingly held accountable as a profit-and-loss owner, which is fundamentally changing how internal legal departments are structured, measured and operated.[12] As Stephen Rauf of Accenture has observed: "In-house Legal Departments have been historically sheltered from business optimization (cost cutting) programs like reducing their workforce and/or slashing budgets. Those days are over." [13]

In response, many GCs are elevating their procurement processes to a strategic level. The past few years have also seen a dramatic increase in the number of legal departments that employ legal operations professionals. In addition, the number and variety of legal consultants is growing.[14] These organisations offer equivalent sophisticated procurement advice and strategic insights that conventional consultants have been giving to the broader business world for decades.

GCs are also increasingly also 'doing less with less' by conducting root cause analyses to identify and eliminate problems at their source. For example, by finding the root cause for why certain types of litigation keep happening repeatedly (eg, a deficient process, or a sales person who continually over-promises but under-delivers), they reduce the likelihood of such litigation recurring in the future.[15]

Regulatory reforms

The third trend is the relaxation of the regulatory regimes that used to protect lawyers from competition. Under the United Kingdom's Legal Services Act 2007, non-lawyers may now own and operate legal businesses, become partners in law firms, and invest in legal businesses.[16]

Other jurisdictions are following suit to varying degrees, including Australia and several EU jurisdictions, as well as Canada, New Zealand and Singapore.[17] In the United States, the American Bar Association's Standing Committee on Ethics and Professional Responsibility has noted that legal services outsourcing is a salutary practice for a globalised economy because it enables lawyers to reduce their costs and because it can enable in-house lawyers to provide services beyond what they are able to do internally.[18] Both Washington DC and Washington State permit alternative business structures to a limited extent, and the American Bar Association Commission on the Future of Legal Services is considering the issue, having released an issues paper on alternative legal services in April 2016.[19]

New competitors

The legal services supplier market is shifting in response to the three foregoing trends, and as a result new competitors are entering that range from the former Big Four accounting firms to stand-alone alternative services providers.[20] Alternative legal services providers are moving in to fill the demand for commoditised legal work as well as legal operations and strategic consulting services; they offer innovative new models, cost-saving strategies and cutting edge technologies.

As has been the case in other industries that have suffered disruption, law firms that quickly grasp the change and adapt will thrive; but they have only a narrow window of opportunity to diversify their services and offer a broader base of options. They are nonetheless well-positioned to do so, with strong brands, a powerful network of clients and the ability to leverage insights from their existing profit streams that could translate into new services.

Law firms might consider the accounting firm context. As accounting became increasingly commoditised, firms moved across the value chain to include consulting services. If law firms fail to follow, the Big Four accounting firms might ultimately replace them. In the 1990s, the five largest accounting firms began establishing 'independent' law firm networks, four of which were as large as the largest law firms in the world by the early 2000s.[21] However, with the dot-com disaster, the dissolution of Arthur Andersen and the introduction of the Sarbanes-Oxley Act in the United States (which banned the Big Four from delivering non-audit services to audit clients), this foray into the law seemed doomed.[22] Not deterred, the Big Four have been rebuilding their legal arms, which are now as big or bigger than they were in 2001.[23] EY, for instance, now operates a legal services business in more than 29 different countries, having grown its number of lawyers by nearly 30%, to 1,100, since 2013.[24] As a recent Law Society report on the future of legal services notes, "the implications of the Big Four accountancy firms offering legal services should not be underestimated".[25]

Unfortunately, most law firms are stuck in the past, unable or unwilling to identify weaknesses in their existing models – and in particular the hourly rate. That makes them ripe for disruption. As Richard Susskind has noted:[26]

> *If a 12-year-old can see the shortcomings of hourly billing, then it puzzles me that major international corporations cannot also see the problem here. Hourly billing is an institutionalized disincentive to efficiency. It rewards lawyers who take longer to complete tasks than their more organized colleagues, and it penalizes legal advisers who operate swiftly and efficiently.*

Why is it is so hard for law firms to abandon the hourly rate model? Profitable alternative models abound, such as those that are leveraged by strategic management consultants, who typically charge on a project basis rather than on a metered basis for their input.[27]

Investment banking provides another alternative. Investment bankers frequently charge a percentage of the value of the deal, rather than the hours spent preparing and managing the offering. Closer to home, alternative legal services firms are adopting output-based pricing models, to provide a fixed level of output for a fixed level of cost, with an agreed mechanism and rate to handle peaks and troughs in volume.[28] At least one premier New York law firm has moved to this model.[29]

Yet law firms remain stuck in a medieval guild-like mentality. Perhaps, as Susskind notes, it is "hard to convince a group of millionaires that their business model is broken".[30] Too many law firm partners remain convinced that what they do and how they do it is unique and irreplaceable.

The truth is that, as technology continues to evolve, and as alternative providers are given ever more leeway to move their service offerings up the value chain, more and more law firm work will prove to be scalable and replicable.

The law firm's competitive response

Some law firms are responding admirably to this growing market disruption in various ways. For instance, some are offering corporate clients more services than were previously available, including (for example) free technology tools and efficiency enhancements. Others are giving away basic legal advice for free, or combining the two by offering tools that allow customers to generate and print out memos and briefs on basic legal concepts using a client portal. Others are using technology more effectively to find new marginal opportunities or to encourage clients not to unbundle their work.

Additionally, some firms have begun to transform the basic law-firm pyramid structure – where a small group of high-fee-generating partners sit at the top of the pyramid, with a large mass of hard-working associates at the bottom – with more effective work allocation models that leverage contract or other professionals based in low-overhead locations, IT specialist workers, or temporary lawyers. In Europe, for example, law firms are partnering with contract lawyer agencies or opening temporary lawyer divisions, supplied by their own lawyers who have left the partnership track.[31]

Finally, reflecting the professional convergence revolution that was discussed in "The changing context" in Part A above, some law firms have been moving into territory traditionally occupied by professional services providers such as the Big Four accounting firms.[32] In 2010, for example, Eversheds launched Eversheds Consulting, which "seeks to move Eversheds beyond the traditional practice of law by providing a suite of consulting services in areas like strategy, technology, human resources and financial services regulatory compliance".[33] Other global firms that have recently been moving into the consulting or corporate advisory space include Mayer Brown and DLA Piper.[34]

Competitive responses by general counsel

Set out next are some of the ways in which GCs can respond competitively to the trends that have been identified at the start of this chapter and that are currently arising in the legal services industry. GCs should definitely take advantage of the suggestions that follow, because they allow a diversification of options and shift individual types of work to where they can most efficiently and effectively be undertaken.

Unbundle your work

A trend towards unbundling has recently taken off at both the top and bottom of the legal value chain. A few examples are illustrative, as set out next.[35]

Records management

Historically, companies looked to law firms to handle all records management tasks in a given matter. As those records management tasks became computerised, each law firm would manage the matter-specific litigation and corporate records using their solutions and providers. As a result, companies began to increasingly find that they had large collections of evidentiary records lodged with multiple law firms and on multiple hosting services.

Large companies have begun to strip such non-core services from their law firms, deploying more efficient/consistent solutions across a wider array of matters. This has enabled companies to gain greater control over their legacy data sets and to aggregate their spending in this area with fewer, more sophisticated vendors, thereby driving better pricing and ensuring more consistent handling.[36]

Alternative legal services providers

Alternative legal services providers are increasingly taking components of legal work that used to be exclusively handled by law firms. For example, clients in the M&A arena might retain a traditional law firm to serve as deal counsel, handling the higher-value aspects of the transaction such as purchase agreement negotiation/drafting and advisory work, but use alternative legal services providers to handle much of the routine work, including due diligence, consents/assignments, post-signing/pre-closing follow-up, and post-acquisition integration support.[37]

Higher-level legal advice

Unbundling is no longer limited to commoditised tasks, such as document review and due diligence. There is a trend toward unbundling higher-value services, such as core legal advice (including discovery drafting, routine motion practice and deposition practice) and peeling these components away from any single firm.[38]

This trend is illustrative of how companies increasingly value specific law firms for a narrow band of core expertise, using them less and less as one-stop shops.

Law firm virtual teams

Another unbundling trend is the creation of virtual teams of law firms, with each law firm taking on different parts of a given project. Each piece of work is allocated to the best-suited firm, based on risk and complexity. In some cases, this may involve subcontracting by the lead law firm, while in other cases it may involve the company, acting as the general contractor, employing multiple firms for the same project.

On more complex, multidisciplinary legal projects, large companies may themselves unbundle discrete portions of a project and assign those portions to lower-priced firms, which work in partnership as part of a virtual team with specialist partners at several other law firms.

While the approach described here can demand strong overall project management leadership, it is well worth that investment as the cost savings can be significant. Subcontracting, for example, can reduce the costs of a given project by half.[39]

Classify your workflow

To do this, start by breaking down the types of work that your department handles into categories.

Time tracking

One way to get this started is to track the time spent on legal department work, taking measurements for a limited duration. Regardless of how you go about this, you will want to track time for a sufficiently long period that you get useful data but not so long that you demoralise your people. This should cover enough of a period of time to obtain an accurate representation of projects and workflow.

Avoid unusual periods of the year – eg, the holiday season. And if your business is genuinely seasonal, you will also want to take into account the possibility that certain types of work will skew the results at certain times during the year. In an ideal world, you would have a full year of data so you could understand how such seasonality may affect the demand for legal services.

An argument could be made that permanent time tracking might actually improve performance – the so-called 'Hawthorne effect' suggests that people perform at a higher level when they know they are being monitored.[40] However, permanent time monitoring in an in-house setting is, generally speaking, unrealistic and undesirable from a morale perspective. Lawyers are professionals who very much value their autonomy, and even a temporary exercise of this kind will very likely be deeply unpopular with your in-house team. Many escaped from the drudgery of law firm time tracking and find the absence of that to be one of the most attractive benefits of working in house; so a shorter, temporary period may need to suffice. Emphasise that this is not a permanent state of affairs but, rather, an exercise to determine in broad terms how people are spending their time. See also Part D below for some thoughts on how to manage your team's reaction to change.

You may also want to make the results anonymous in order to avoid the risk that people will fudge their time records so as to skew it in a way that they think you will want to see. No one wants to admit to how inefficient they are.

Time-tracking your implementation options
One option is to roll out a commercially available time-tracking tool that will track how your people are spending their time each day. There are plenty of commercial applications to choose from, which are generally easy to implement and apply. The downside is that they can be costly and somewhat cumbersome, especially if all you want to do is conduct a

sample or pilot to get a sense of how your department's time is spent, rather than track time on a permanent basis. In addition, many of the commercially available tools are designed with law firms in mind and do not necessarily fit comfortably in to the operating environment of an in-house legal department.

A second option is to ask people to track the amounts of time they allocate to different categories of work and to enter their figures into a spreadsheet. The relative merits of this approach may depend on the size of your team: if you have a small group, this works quite well; however, the larger, more complex and more geographically spread out your team is, the harder it may be to effectively use a homemade solution.

Consultants are a third option. You can hire a consultant to run a work analysis in which he will interview your professionals and your business partners to get a sense of how your time is spent. Depending on the project, he may leverage technology to do this as well. This can be a good way of ensuring that you get a decent one-off snapshot of the work situation in your team, but it can be expensive and the methodology may not be entirely transparent or aligned with your needs. Even so, if you are a large organisation, it is definitely the recommended approach. As James Neath, Associate General Counsel, Global Litigation and Environmental at BP notes:[41]

> *This up-front classification exercise is so important that I choose to emphasise the following attributes that consultants bring: (a) independence; (b) expertise; and (c) avoiding unnecessary distraction to the function. A homemade approach is too susceptible of hidden agendas ("What is the company looking for?", "What would make me look good?"). A consultant can do this efficiently; they know what they're looking for and [they] bring valuable independence. And if the firm has an eye on future consultancy use, it is useful for the consultant to deeply understand the legal function, which this exercise facilitates.*

Which option you use ultimately depends on how large and complex the task is in your specific circumstances.

Classification considerations

In classifying or categorising your internal workflow, make sure you consider what your legal department is doing relative to what your external legal service providers (ie, primarily law firms) are currently working on. Neath suggests that you might consider this in three different ways:

- *Tasks that duplicate or overlap with what your law firms are doing:* You should consider here whether your in-house lawyers are just 'along for the ride' or whether they are they adding distinctive value over and above what your externals partners are doing.

- *Time spent on truly strategic work as compared with lower value work:* Consider whether your in-house lawyers are spending time on strategic value-added work, such as owning and designing project strategy. Are they managing/leading projects, or are they mostly just observing and helping to implement?

- *Time devoted to tasks that require inside knowledge:* Consider whether your team is focusing its efforts on work that demands a deep understanding of the business's operation, culture and risk appetite, or whether the work they are doing is of the kind that anyone, either inside or outside of the organisation, could do.[42]

Identifying solutions for different categories of work

Once you have an overview of how people are spending their time, the types of issues they are working on and how long they are spending on such matters, you will be in a position to begin determining which categories of work go where. As you think through your options, consider the role that process improvement and technology can play in both reducing your risks and improving workflow – discussed further in Part C in the chapter entitled "Technology".

Sort each category of work into priority 'buckets' based on high/low value and high/low risk (see Figure 7 and the further description of categorisation below).[43] High-value work is tied to your company's core strategic objectives and will promote those objectives, whereas low-value work is marginally useful in that respect. High and low risk can relate back to the risk analysis discussed earlier in this book.

Some of the buckets will go either to outside counsel or to alternative legal service providers, while some will remain in-house, to be handled either by your team or directly by your business partners, via 'self–service' solutions.

High-value/low-risk items Work that is categorised as high value but low risk is an opportunity. This category often contains work that generates significant returns but can be handled with little or no lawyer involvement.

An example from a sales-driven consumer products context might include standard-form customer contracts for consumer or small-retailer customers. These contracts are clearly value generative to the business; but assuming none of the terms in the agreements are alterable, they are also low risk. The less lawyer involvement that can be constructed the better.

This is a common area where it is worth considering alternative legal service providers or self-service tools. With regard to the latter, alternative legal service providers may be able to assist with cost-effective self-service automation technology because they are leveraging such investments across multiple clients.[44] Self-service options can include e-signature solutions that speed up execution, as well automated filing in a repository for the storage of execution copies.[45]

Innovations, such as 'smart' legal contracts, have long-term potential to provide additional solutions for such high-value/low-risk situations. 'Smart' contracts leverage so-called 'blockchain' technology (ie, data structures that allow digital transaction ledgers to be created, shared and securely manipulated among a network, without the need for any central authority) to replace or complement existing legal contracts by articulating, verifying or enforcing legal agreements in code.[46] Such technologies might in the future simplify and automate routine contracts, including certain financial instruments such as shares, bonds or derivatives contracts.[47] As Josh Stark has observed: "Articulating these contracts in code could allow financial markets to become more automated and simplify many process-intensive systems related to trading and servicing of financial instruments."[48] As this concept is still in its formative stages, there are questions surrounding its legal enforceability, and only a limited range of contracts would appear to be obvious candidates.[49]

Even so, as technology moves forward in coming years, this could open new vistas for the efficient processing of some high-value/low-risk legal work.

Low-value/low-risk items Low-value and low-risk work is either commoditised work or work that should not be done at all. Commodity work that should be done might include routine document processing, such as immigration forms that are essential to personnel management but that may not be core to the company's competitive advantage. This work is a commodity and should be given to the lowest-cost provider that can maintain basic quality.

Work that should be stopped might include work that should actually be done by some other function, such as sales, HR or government relations. But be careful: some categories of work may at first appear to be low risk from a purely legal perspective but could entail significant reputation risk if done incorrectly. The decision by 'sharing economy' companies, such as Uber and Lyft, to treat many of the people who work for them as independent contractors and not employees may seem at first glance to be mainly an HR question. However, lawsuits against Uber by some of its drivers, arguing that they should be classified as employees, have drawn unwanted national media attention to the issue.[50] If all of its 400,000 drivers across the United States had to be treated as employees, the aggregate costs could threaten Uber's business model.[51]

High-value/high-risk items These comprise the core work of the legal department. Work in this category is either tied to the core legal risk areas that were discussed earlier in this book or is closely associated with the company's strategic objectives. It should be handled and given personalised attention by the best-placed internal experts, so that risks can be minimised preventatively and solutions arrived at pragmatically. Leverage outside legal counsel as appropriate to supplement your internal team.

Low-value/high-risk items This work presents little value to the direction the business wants to take but could pose significant risks nevertheless. Examples include large, complex legacy litigation in business areas that the company has long since divested. Litigation is not core to the business, but getting it wrong could be very costly or disruptive.

The work therefore requires expert attention and handling and may cost a great deal to execute, but maintaining the entire internal infrastructure necessary to keep it all in-house may make little sense. There is often significant money or reputation at stake, and active and strategic input and leadership from both the in-house attorneys and outside counsel are critical to getting it right.

This work is therefore often best done by a hybrid mix of not only outside experts who can scale their expertise across multiple matters in different companies but also your specialists or generalists who need to stay close to and manage the matter together with the outside experts.

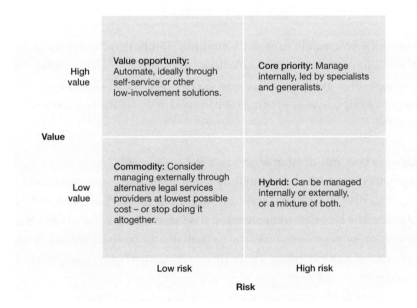

Figure 7: Categorising legal work according to value and risk

Aiming for the best solution

As you determine the value dimension, you may find that some of the low-value work does not belong in the legal function at all and should instead be done by other functions. For instance, you might discover that someone in your team who is overstretched is spending 70% of their time reviewing and commenting on draft legislation, which you may not consider to be a task that should be done by the legal department. You might therefore offload that work to another function (eg, government relations) and redirect the lawyer who was working on those matters towards core legal work.

You should be focusing the bulk of your effort on plugging your company's core risks and providing strategic legal advice to your business partners. Other work should be considered commodity work that is evaluated based on what solution can handle it most cost effectively and efficiently. The optimal solution will, however, vary from situation to situation. You need to evaluate each category of work in light of the options you have available and then determine what solution is going to be best for you.

One option you should consider is running pilot projects where possible, to test alternative or novel solutions. This gives you the ability to determine on a smaller scale what works best. It will also allow you to run the pilot alongside your existing solution and compare the two on various metrics.

Optimise your mix of internal and external resources

As you focus your efforts on building a solid and capable internal team to plug your risks and efficiently allocate the rest of the work across different solutions, the question will inevitably arise as to whether there is an ideal proportion of your overall resources that should be spent internally in comparison with externally. There are several factors that you will want to consider, as set out next.

Size of the internal team

The size of your department and company will influence the ratio of internal to external resources.

If your business is in start-up mode and quite small, the company might not be able to afford a full-time in-house lawyer, and 100% of legal spend is external. In start-up and other smaller companies, both solo firms and individual lawyers in medium-sized firms may act as outside general counsel.

As the business grows, it becomes necessary to hire a lawyer to manage the growing legal workflow. At first, the overhead for the new in-house lawyer means that there is no room for any external legal advice. At this point, the internal-to-external spend ratio shifts from 100% external to 100% internal.

As the business grows further and begins maturing, legal needs and budget grow somewhat and a single in-house lawyer becomes insufficient. At this stage, things get more interesting as the optimal split between hiring more internal lawyers and external personnel shifts. We will look at the question of how to arrive at the best ratio for mid-range to large-sized companies below.

What is clear is that the specific circumstances of each business, including size and available resources, will influence the ratio.

Fluctuation of workflow

Another aspect that will impact the size of the internal or external team is the stability of the workflow. An environment that generates a relatively constant level of work will dictate a different solution from one in which the workflow is seasonal or erratic in volume.

If the workflow fluctuates greatly, it may be wise to maintain a relatively small core of fixed headcount internally and leverage either outside law firms or legal-temp services to supplement that smaller core in times of greater flow. Whether the 'surge capacity' consists of outside counsel or legal temps will depend in turn on the nature of the work at issue.

By contrast, a stable flow of work will allow for a more stable return on investment for fixed headcount that is brought in, suggesting that a higher level of internal core and a lower level of external surge workers may be more optimal.

Amount of litigation or deal activity

The nature of the work is also relevant. If a large part of the work involves intensive and complex matters such as high-stakes class action litigation or large-scale acquisitions, it may be more appropriate to have a higher external spend component.

If, however, the work is mainly routine corporate and commercial work with occasional small-scale litigation, it may make more sense to have a larger internal base. A third variant might present itself where there is a large contracts component to the workflow, where either a large internal in-sourcing or an external off-shoring solution might be appropriate, depending on the nature of the contracts work, its volume and the variation in complexity that it presents.

The best approach might be to benchmark your own situation against peer organisations in your area of work, in order to determine where the optimal spend ratio sits. The best way to do this is to retain an outside consultant who is more able to obtain, aggregate and assess the data for your specific industry.

The golden 60%-40% split

Outside of extremes of size, fluctuation and litigation/deal flow, in my experience there seems to be a 'sweet spot' where the internal-to-external spend ratio moves towards an approximate 60%–40% split. Total costs typically begin to decline as the ratio of internal spend approaches 60%.

The actual ratio that will work for your particular situation will depend on numerous factors, including those described above. For instance, the ratios may vary depending on whether or not you are in a highly regulated industry, where there are generally far more intensive needs for outside counsel than would be typical in less regulated environments.

Evidence provided by the Morae Legal Corporation of likely internal-v-external spend ratios are shown in Figures 8 and 9.[52] Figure 8 shows the analysis for lower-spend industries such as consumer goods and services, manufacturing and industrial goods, and general service providers. Figure 9 shows the same for higher-spend (and highly regulated) industries such as pharmaceuticals, chemicals, oil and gas, and financial services, as well as companies with significant intellectual property and heavy litigation.

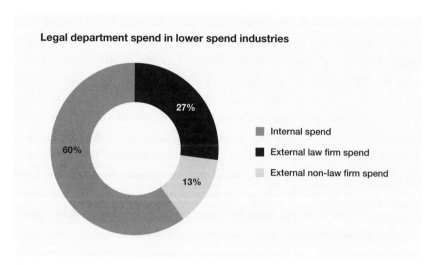

Figure 8: Internal-v-external spend ratios from lower-spend industries
(Source: Morae Legal Corporation. Reproduced with its kind permission.)

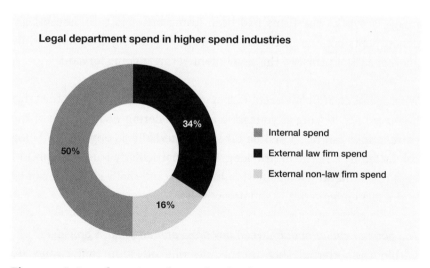

Figure 9: Internal-v-external spend ratios from higher-spend industries
(Source: Morae Legal Corporation. Reproduced with its kind permission.)

At a very generic level, a 60% internal to 40% external mix seems to be a good ratio to aim at for bringing down total costs. That may not be so surprising, considering that the average hourly rate of an external lawyer is typically significantly higher than for a comparable internal counsel.

As will be discussed in the next chapter when looking at alternative legal services providers, it is useful to understand the cost–effectiveness applicable here. In 2016 the average hourly rate of a law firm lawyer in the United States was $500, as compared with an average of $350 an hour for an in-house attorney.[53] Of course, true cost differentials can be much higher than that, depending on what firms are used and where in the world they are located. Average associate rates at major New York City law firms, for instance, can be as high as nearly three times the average rate for partners at law firms in West Virginia.[54] Moreover, New York rates keep rising: a leading Wall Street law firm in 2016 raised first-year associate salaries to $180,000 per annum from $160,000.[55] Several large firms quickly followed suit.[56]

This hourly rate differential is perhaps one reason why there is movement by companies from engaging law firms to using in-house staff. According to one legal management consultant study, in 2016 as many as 67% of law firms had been losing business to in-house legal departments because of the trend toward in-sourcing legal work, while another 24% of firms see this as a potential threat going forward.[57]

What seems clear in any event is that you are leaving money on the table if you are not looking at your ratio and considering what aspects of the current split can or should be taken on internally as opposed to being conducted by a law firm provider. That is particularly true in respect of high-risk work, which ideally should be done internally so that it can be undertaken pragmatically and proactively.

The optimal spend-split between law firms and alternative providers

Within the external slice of the pie, one question that comes up frequently is what the optimal ratio should be between outside law firms and alternative legal services providers.

There is no uniform answer to this. As Figures 8 and 9 illustrate, external spend depends on the structure of your legal organisation and the nature of the work you perform for the company. However, at a general level the typical legal department now devotes 14% of its total legal spend to non-law firms, which is nearly half as much as what it is spending on outside lawyers – see Figure 10.[58]

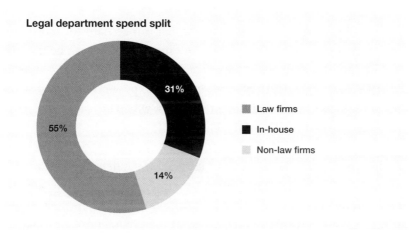

Figure 10: Split of spend for a typical legal department

(Source: Morae Legal Corporation. Reproduced with its kind permission.)

What seems clear is that external spend on non-law firms is growing and is likely to continue to do so. A recent study indicates that alternative legal services providers took business from 17% of law firms in 2015, with another 38% viewing such vendors as a competitive threat.[59] Interestingly, traditional law firms were seen as less of a threat, with only 9% of law firms having lost business to such competitors.[60]

Risk, outcome and quality

In considering how much of your work to outsource and how much to leave in-house, it is important to keep in mind a core principle: in-house and outside lawyers are not fungible. There are qualities that each bring to the table, in addition to cost and quality, that need to be carefully considered in arriving at the optimal mix.

In-house lawyers bring with them unique and valuable attributes that external counsel are not in a position to provide. Foremost among these is the ability to act pragmatically and proactively when addressing core risks. They alone have a deep understanding of the business, its culture, its risk appetite and its senior leaders.

External law firms bring attributes to the table that can be difficult for internal counsel to provide, at least on a sustainable basis. These include a deep and concentrated level of specialised legal expertise, spanning multiple industries and jurisdictions, which can be hard for most legal departments to continually cultivate and maintain. This can be the case even in subjects that the department frequently encounters. Outside counsel also bring a depth of cross-industry experience: they often see similar problems in many different contexts, which brings a perspective to their advice that can be invaluable.

In addition to the above, outside lawyers are independent from the business in a way that differentiates them from in-house lawyers. In-house lawyers are perennially at risk of saying 'yes' when they should really be saying 'no', and this is because of the unique pressures that are placed on them by their business partners. Having an external partner who can back them up with an independent view can be essential.

Put the right policies and procedures in place

A critical step towards determining the optimal internal-to-external mix is to ensure that you have in place the necessary policies and procedures that will govern your interactions with external providers. Three are particularly critical to have in place:

- a 'gatekeeper' policy;
- a billing guidelines policy; and
- having engagement letters in place with the law firms you use.

While these might not be the only controls needed – internal legal department controls will also be required (see below) – they are a start. Let us consider each of these three in turn.

Gatekeeper policy

The legal department must control all decisions about whether work gets undertaken by external resources. As Joy Saphla, Chief Strategy Officer at

Morae Legal Corporation, a premier corporate law department management consulting and services company, notes, "You can't manage your spend if you don't have insight into what work your outside law firm partners are obtaining from your business clients."[61]

This is a common problem in regional and field offices, where the corporate legal team may not have the same budgetary oversight. Spend on these outside law firms might be coming from local business budgets and not from the legal department headquarters budget, but you still need to control this, because managing the spend is not just about cost but also about ensuring that you have a proper handle on external legal advice from a risk perspective. As Saphla further notes, "It's not about command and control but really more about risk and responsibility."[62]

The law firms that these other business clients are picking without your input or control may, for instance, provide legal advice that you disagree with or that is highly inappropriate. Imagine, for example, a local counsel in a foreign country where there is no law against bribery advising your business partners that bribery is legal.

In addition to risk, there is cost. The legal department is the best-placed entity to determine whether a particular piece of work requires external input. There may already be sufficient expertise or capacity in-house to manage the task. Going outside in such instances is wasteful.

To enforce the principle that the legal department is the sole gatekeeper for the procurement of legal services, put in place a gatekeeper policy that establishes the situation across the company.

Billing guidelines policy
You also want to ensure that you have in place a consistent policy on what services and expenses law firms and other external providers are allowed to charge you, how their invoices must be structured, and payment terms.

With the billing policy, depending on the size of your department you may meet some resistance from some of your external partners. Since such policies are increasingly becoming the norm, service providers are fighting them less and less in the United States and the United Kingdom. Elsewhere in the world it can be a bit mixed, but the trend is moving towards acceptance. Your ability to push through restrictions on rates, types of charges, number and level of billers, and intra-office conferences, will depend in part on your bargaining power.

Even if you have the power to do so, do not go overboard on this, demanding extreme rate reductions or other restrictions. Doing this will only frustrate your law firm partners and create a mercenary environment in which there is no sense of partnership or loyalty. The firms will take advantage of you whenever they can, because they resent you and consider your approach to be unfair.

It is far wiser to base your policy on what is customary in your jurisdiction. Ask around, get opinions from other GCs and, if possible, obtain samples of their billing policies to see what is customary (but do not do this with competitors for obvious competition law reasons). It is much harder for a law firm to deny an approach that is customary. Insisting on these as a minimum will give you the moral high ground and establish whether the firm you are planning to deal with is reasonable in its approach – which should be helpful to you if and when you decide to use them.

There are some on-line options that you can use as a starting point when formulating your billing policy. One good source is the Association of Corporate Counsel's model Billing Guidelines, Outside Counsel.[63]

Engagement letters

You also want to ensure that you put a standard engagement letter in place with each of your law firms. Engagement letters establish the basis for the engagement between the firm and the company. It should include, by reference, your Billing Guidelines, which will ensure that your billing rules get enforced. As Rauf notes, this "helps ensure that basic items are covered, such as: required billing frequency, prohibition of block billing, and travel provisions. This is also the vehicle for more novel guidelines, like pegging annual rate increases to an index, fixing rates for the life of a matter, or not paying for intrafirm conferences."[64]

Policy enforcement

All of the above policies, while good to have in place, are useless unless they are monitored and enforced. E-billing technologies, which are discussed later in this book, are a good way to ensure that it is clear from the invoices you receive from firms that they are complying with your policies.

Internal legal department controls

One further consideration in the context of how the company will interact with outside legal advisers is how to regulate such interaction from inside the legal department itself. There is a variety of issues that can come up and be administered by way of internal policies. The need for such policies will depend in large part on the size of your department and its culture. Generally speaking, the larger and more dispersed the department is, the more you may want to consider a tighter approach to management. Indeed, a small, tightly knit and centrally located team may not require any formal policies in this respect.

Here are some thoughts on possible areas in which you may want to consider having some form of internal control:[65]

- *Specialists v generalists:* Some departments put policies in place that specify when generalist lawyers must either involve, or cede decision making authority to, specialists. Such policies will need to strike a balance between the need for subject matter acumen and closeness to the business.
- *Use of outside counsel by internal lawyers:* You may want to consider putting in place rules about when and under what circumstances internal lawyers may retain outside counsel and who can authorise that. This may be essential in order to counter the creeping tendency of internal lawyers to want to cover themselves by means of second opinions. If you have a large problem in this regard, it may indicate a cultural issue that you need to address as part of your culture-hacking efforts (see Part C).
- *Outside counsel selection:* In addition to putting policies in place to regulate when internal lawyers may retain outside counsel, you may want to establish rules around which law firms can be hired for what work. In larger departments with bigger budgets, there is

a risk that internal lawyers hire premium law firms in order to insulate the in-house lawyer from outcome criticism. This can inadvertently lead to inflationary use of such firms. In addition, as noted in the chapter below on "Selecting the right partners", you may want to escalate the decision about what law firms to select for which matters.

- *Procurement involvement:* It can be wise to align your approach with that of your procurement department in relation to when the legal department needs to involve it and when that will not be necessary. Usually, it makes good sense to involve procurement; they are trained in many areas that lawyers are not, such as quantitative analytics, which is used to objectively compare law firms. They can do the work that the in-house lawyer might not want to do, such as conducting pricing negotiations. If you do not have law firm panels in place, you will want to involve procurement in the panel selection process; but you should not have to involve them each and every time you commission work from a panel firm on a particular matter. You will want to collaborate on an ongoing basis with the procurement department, even once the panel has been established, for matters such as invoice audits and regular market and spend reviews.
- *High-value policies:* You might consider putting in place a policy that specifies when you must solicit marketplace competition via bids and when a sole-source engagement is permissible in connection with certain high-value engagements.
- *Billing guidelines exceptions:* You must establish who has the authority to make exceptions to the outside counsel billing guidelines (if anyone other than the GC), who is authorised to negotiate law firm rates, and which firm's terms and conditions are to be negotiated.
- *Outside counsel contracting formalities:* It is crucial to clarify in writing what contracting formalities are required for legal services procurement – eg, what must be signed, by whom, and in what form.

Keep in mind that internal policies can be a two-edged sword, even in large departments. The more policies you impose, the greater the impact may be on morale. Lawyers (like many others in the company) tend to like to work autonomously and dislike being hemmed in by too many rules and regulations. Your responsibility as the general counsel is to ensure that you are running the department in the same way you would run any other business: with efficiency and clarity, particularly in respect of how resources are allocated. Ultimately, you will need to strike the best balance for your particular situation, taking the above into account as suggestions more than mandates.

GCs need to take advantage of the trends that are shaping the legal industry, by unbundling their work, deciding what they will do internally and what they will source externally, and managing external procurement in a strategic and thoughtful manner.

Alternative legal services providers

*Super temps are moving
up the food chain.*
(Julia Shapiro)[1]

As general counsel have begun thinking more strategically about how their work can be handled externally, they are increasingly turning to alternative legal services (ALS) providers. These businesses, which offer competitive rates and typically higher-quality solutions, are here to stay. No one feels this as keenly as their primary competitors – law firms.

A 2015 survey by a legal management consultancy found that 85% of law firm leaders believe that competition from non-traditional providers is a permanent trend.[2] If you are not using such services yet, you should be considering it.

What are ALS providers?

There is no unified definition for ALS providers, but Jordan Furlong, a legal market analyst and consultant, referring to it as 'NewLaw', defines it nicely as "any model, process, or tool that represents a significantly different approach to the creation or provision of legal services than what the legal profession traditionally has employed".[3] Depending on how you define 'legal services', ALS could cover a very broad group of providers, ranging from legal project managers, risk managers, e-discovery firms, consultants and workflow management experts, to legal staffing services.

In considering how to reduce costs and outsource work, you may need to consider a variety of peripheral services that impact the cost and quality of your legal output. Such services might include jury consultants, trial graphics suppliers, transcription/translation services, experts/consultants and the like. These and other areas can be material to the outcome/cost question and they need to be accounted for in planning and budgeting. You would be well advised to consider them for appropriate projects.

Unfortunately, a comprehensive discussion of such tangential services is beyond the scope of this chapter, which focuses only on core legal services. Nonetheless, for the purposes of the chapter we will cover two broad categories of ALS providers: alternative staffing providers and legal process outsourcing providers. Each provides competitive alternatives to the traditional law firm model by offering flexible, business-oriented and tailored services at lower costs that are based on innovative pricing models and technology-driven solutions.

The origins of ALS providers

ALS providers came onto the scene in the early 2000s, driven by a number of key developments,[4] comprising the following (each described further below):

- large law firm consolidation;
- the rise of tech start-ups;
- improved technology; and
- automated problem-solving.

How these changes affected the rise in ALS providers is described further below, and the evolution (actual and anticipated) of the ALS market is shown in diagram form in Figure 11.

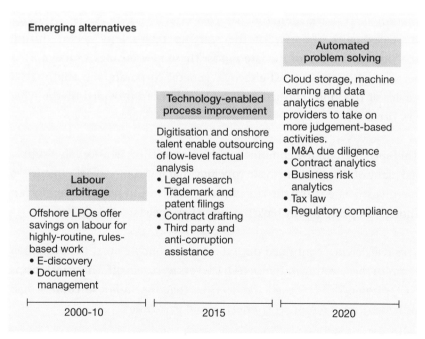

Figure 11: Actual and anticipated evolution of the ALS market

(Source: CEB, The New Legal Operating Model (2016), pp11, 12 and 56. Reproduced with permission.)

Large law firm consolidation

In the mid-1990s, law firm revenues at the largest law firms began to increase significantly, growing at a steady rate until 2009/10.[5] The increased cost of legal services was accompanied by a spike in law firm mergers between 1998 and 2001.[6]

As firms consolidated and focused more closely on the less routine but more profitable work, such as high-stakes litigation and complex mergers and acquisitions, fewer reasonably priced mid-sized firms were available to offer general corporate and commercial advice to smaller companies at a reasonable price. Those that remained could ill afford to provide highly paid associates for general corporate and commercial work in the midst of the boom in more profitable deal work.

The rise of tech start-ups

At the same time as large law firms consolidated and focused on high-margin deal work, demand for cost-effective general legal advice increased with the rise of the start-up technology sector during the 'dotcom bubble' of the late 1990s. These new businesses had a need for sophisticated, yet cost-effective, general corporate and commercial advice of the kind that had previously only been provided by the large law firms.

This spike in demand combined with a contraction in affordable supply led many of these tech firms to conclude that it was more cost-effective to recruit associates from the large firms as full-time in-house counsel, even though they might only have part-time legal needs.

This inefficiency continued until the dotcom bubble burst in 2001, when many of these young in-house tech lawyers were laid off. Those tech firms that survived still needed the services that the in-house counsel had provided, but at a more cost-effective and part-time level.

Improved technology

At the same time that the market was becoming flooded in the early 2000s with unemployed corporate counsel, technology had evolved to the point where it was possible to offer sophisticated legal services on a part-time basis, without the cost of a brick-and-mortar overhead. Firms such as Outside GC and Axiom Global began to provide work for these legions of high-end corporate law refugees.

Many of the unemployed technology lawyers who signed up to this new reality were happy to find fractionalised work with multiple clients. It afforded many of them a better work–life balance than they had experienced previously. Indeed, they were able to secure well-paid jobs that provided intellectual satisfaction, while retaining some control over their hours.

Daniel Pink's book *Free Agent Nation* captured the spirit of the time perfectly. In the wake of the 9/11 atrocities in 2001, many professionals were seeking a more meaningful and better-quality life, and the above trends that spawned the 'super temp' industry – ie, senior legal counsel who work on discrete projects or for limited periods of time inside companies in order to help manage surge periods or help out on discrete projects – afforded them the opportunity to live that lifestyle, evolving into what is now often referred to as the 'gig economy'.

As millennials (ie, people born between the mid-1980s and the early 2000s) increasingly develop deeper skills and experience, there is likely to be an increased flow of talent moving into these organisations.

Automated problem-solving: "The algorithm made me do it"
As technology steadily improved, alternative staffing diversified into multiple niches, ranging from staffing agencies that focus on the human touch to place the right high-end talent in the right assignments at corporate clients, to newer providers that leverage automated staffing technologies allowing customers to select high-end talent directly on the company's platform, thereby reducing both time and cost.

> *Work that is routine, repetitive, not as high risk can be structured,*
> *leveraged with technology, put in a workflow and perhaps put in a*
> *cloud where you can pull it down.*
> (Joy Saphla, Chief Strategy Officer, Morae Legal Corporation)

Other ALS providers have identified savings and process opportunities in the 60% gap between 'untouchable' strategic work, which is the exclusive domain of senior in-house counsel with the support of law firms, and the commoditised end of the work categorisation spectrum, which is typically performed by lower end staffing firms (see Figure 12). These newer firms are increasingly using data and user analytics to create better matches. The rise of these companies reflects the trend toward the 'Uberisation of everything'.[7]

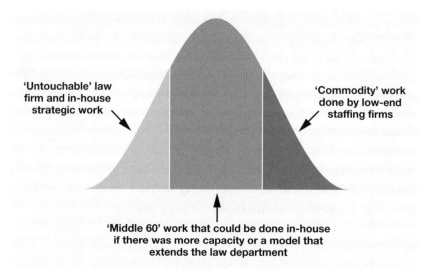

Figure 12: The separation of strategic and commodity legal work

(Source: Morae Legal Corporation. Reproduced with its kind permission.)

The rise of ALS in the United Kingdom

ALS providers have been on the upswing in the United Kingdom. Halebury, Lawyers on Demand and other similar providers emerged in the mid-2000s, shortly after Axiom first launched in the United Kingdom in 2005.[8]

Part of the impetus behind that common wave was a desire to meet a rising in-house demand for better and more flexible temporary staffing. The market for alternative staffing in the United Kingdom at the time consisted mainly of law firm secondees (ie, law firm attorneys transferred temporarily to work in the in-house legal department of clients). This was unsatisfactory for three reasons:

- *Experience:* Law firm secondees were often too junior for the work that needed to be undertaken. If attorneys were needed at a more senior level, the solution was typically to second a partner, which was typically both expensive and only available for short periods of time.
- *Quality:* In-house clients frequently felt the need to repurpose the work product coming from law firm secondees to make it more usable in a corporate environment. There was a clear need for in-house secondees who truly understood what was needed in the in-house context and were able to act accordingly.
- *Cost:* Secondees could be expensive. Some firms would gift them to clients for a limited period of time; however, in most cases they were charged out at either an hourly or fixed rate, which could be well above the average cost of a fixed headcount.

At the same time as demand was on the upswing, there had been increasing movement on the supply side. A growing number of lawyers were disaffected with the work–life balance that law firm employment offered. Many of them were also looking for a broader yet credible career path, in which they would be able to work in a variety of companies, leveraging their knowledge, experience and networks.

The UK market is still evolving. It has taken some time for the ALS market to move from the early-adopter stage to the mainstream, but as of 2016 the number of companies that were embracing ALS providers was growing significantly. So-called 'Magic Circle' firms got in on the act and set up their own ALS businesses. Being a super temp has become a respectable, credible career option.

ALS staffing issues

Recruitment as an add-on
One additional but interesting niche that is developing in the staffing context is 'try before you hire'.

As law department recruitment budgets get tighter, law departments are getting stingier in terms of whom they hire, seeking to ensure better fits up-front. Hiring a super temp for repeated assignments is a good way to ensure that the 'fit' is good before you make a permanent hire.

Alternative staffing providers typically receive a commission or fee on a placement – usually a percentage of the hire's annual compensation in the first year – if the hire is made within a certain timeframe of placement. That aspect has raised the interest of traditional professional recruiters, who are now also in the game, offering temporary staffing solutions with the possibility of a subsequent permanent hire. Global legal recruiters are starting to develop secondment groups that place lawyers ranging from contract negotiators to interim general counsel into companies.[9]

Certainly, this aspect of the legal industry is diversifying, with a multitude of providers servicing many niche staffing areas – from GC level, to specialists in various hot topics such as data privacy, to bread-and-butter corporate work.

The rise of legal process outsourcing

While the ALS industry may have much of its origin rooted in alternative staffing, in recent years it has diversified significantly into a broader range of activities, employing both more junior lawyers and non-lawyers – see Figure 13 for the low-cost range of activities that ALS providers can usually accommodate.

In the early 2000s, Axiom, one of the original alternative legal staffing companies, in response to the explosion of data that became available as a result of improvements in technology and the consequent demand for high-quality data analytics, began providing large customers with a more diversified range of services.[10] Today, this company's portfolio covers managed contract services, contract data analytics, compliance resourcing and response services, and documentary due diligence and search capabilities.[11]

Initially, the demand for labour-intensive work relating to the explosion in data that IT produced went to offshore providers in India and elsewhere, which could process work such as document reviews more

Figure 13: Evolution of the low-cost provider market
(Source: CEB, The New Legal Operating Model (2016), pp11, 12 and 56. Reproduced with permission.)

cost-effectively than law firms or in-house providers. However, the latter types of provider have leveraged increasingly powerful data analytics and IT tools to take market share from offshore players, capturing an ever-greater share of the law department budget.

That move proved to be lucrative. Axiom alone posted revenues of $130 million in 2011, representing a 62% increase over the prior year.[12] From 2002 to 2011, its revenue grew at a compound annual growth rate of 72%. At that rate, it will overtake DLA Piper, the world's third-largest law firm, by 2018.[13]

Numerous other providers have jumped into the fray, each providing their own approaches, including offshore contract management experts such as UnitedLex, and the United Kingdom's Radiant Law, which provides sophisticated contract negotiation and management services via a base of lawyers in South Africa but managed by ex-Magic Circle partners in London.

Law firms have in many cases responded to this challenge by setting up their own internal contract and document management providers. In some cases, these solutions can be both cost-effective and efficient, allowing for a streamlined and seamless approach to not only the substantive legal issue at hand (such as a lawsuit) but also the underlying document review process that is required. However, the need to increasingly invest resources in ever more sophisticated technology solutions, as well as the benefits that scale can have on efficiency, suggests that, in the long term, law firms will struggle to compete on both cost and quality with large ALS providers in this part of the market.

Outsourcing via alternative staffing providers

As you deconstruct your workflow and identify specific and unique strands of work that can and should be outsourced, you will find both alternative staffing providers and legal process outsourcers to be useful. The relative merits of each are considered respectively here and further below.

ALS companies provide super temps. These lawyers are often extremely competent, well trained and highly motivated to perform well.

For corporate clients, alternative staffing services can be a solid opportunity to save on costs, both on an hourly rate basis and in terms of fixed costs and overheads. As Figure 14 indicates, in 2016 outside lawyers cost 43% more on an hourly rate basis than in-house counsel, and 54% more than alternative staffing lawyers.

The actual savings generated by temping lawyers as distinct from their law firm counterparts may be even greater than these numbers would suggest because, depending on the work, the staffing agencies at the higher end of the market may be replacing lawyers from large law firms

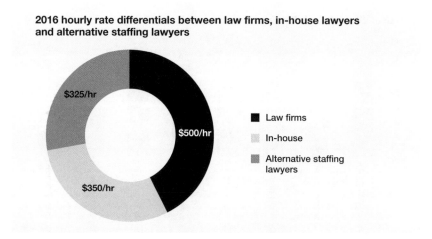

2016 hourly rate differentials between law firms, in-house lawyers and alternative staffing lawyers

$325/hr
$500/hr
$350/hr

■ Law firms
▨ In-house
▨ Alternative staffing lawyers

Figure 14: Comparative 2016 hourly rates for lawyers

(Source: Morae Legal Corporation. Reproduced with its kind permission.)

where hourly rates are significantly in excess of the averages. The staffing process used can also generate additional efficiencies not captured in the raw hourly rates.[14]

Similarly, the average hourly rate of super temps can be well below the law firm average, providing additional savings, especially for attorneys below the GC level of experience.[15] It is also worth noting that alternative staffing lawyers are also less expensive than in-house lawyers – a prospect that is interesting when considering whether to recruit additional personnel on a long-term basis or to fill staffing gaps temporarily.

What types of work should alternative staffing professionals undertake?

Alternative staffing operations work well in respect of relatively commoditised categories of legal work, covering for relatively junior in-house staff who are absent for a prolonged period (eg, sickness, maternity leave, jury service), or supplementing corporate legal departments where there are spikes in routine areas of work (including contract management and drafting, document review, discovery-related work and corporate duties such as entity management). These remain common areas of focus for such providers (see Figure 15).

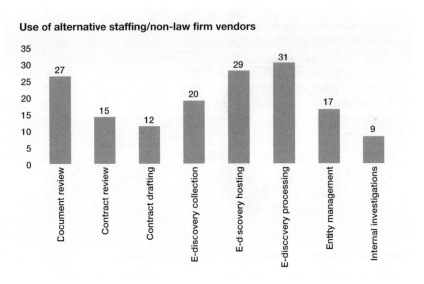

Use of alternative staffing/non-law firm vendors

Figure 15: Range of work undertaken by ALS providers
(Source: Ninth Annual Law Department Operations Survey (2016) published by Blickstein Group Inc in cooperation with Consilio and used with permission. Numbers represent the number of law departments that are utilising non-law firm providers (n= 51).)

But super-temp lawyers are moving steadily further up the value chain. Many now provide assistance in sensitive areas such as compliance investigative work and litigation management, as well as data privacy and other specialisations. ALS providers often provide outstanding candidates for these kinds of fields at very competitive costs.

Such providers will give you a 'surge capacity' that enables you to keep your overheads lean and your headcount to a relatively minimal base, yet with the ability to ramp things up in the event of a sudden increase in work – returning to a smaller headcount and lower cost once your surge need has dissipated.

In recent years, a new service line has been added to the alternative staffing market, consisting of legal project management (whose incumbents can be known as 'legal engineers').[16] These professionals come from a legal operations background and are hired to help generate efficiencies by working on technology, process or other operations projects. In some cases, they provide strategic guidance in this space for in-house teams that have yet to secure their own legal COO or internal operations team.

There has also been a growing demand for lean process expertise, such as six sigma, that ALS providers are increasingly aiming to meet.[17]

Going forward, it is not unreasonable to expect further niche areas to be met by ALS providers, as the business of law continues to diversify and become more complex.

Outsourcing via legal process outsourcers

Legal process outsourcing providers may offer higher levels of technological solutions than your company can. They may reduce costs and improve quality in respect of process-driven tasks, such as contract management, document review and litigation support (see Figure 16).

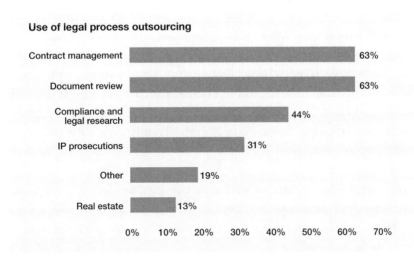

Use of legal process outsourcing

Category	Percentage
Contract management	63%
Document review	63%
Compliance and legal research	44%
IP prosecutions	31%
Other	19%
Real estate	13%

Figure 16: Range of work undertaken by staff from legal process outsourcers

(Source: Ninth Annual Law Department Operations Survey (2016) published by Blickstein Group Inc in cooperation with Consilio and used with permission. Numbers represent the percentage of law departments who are utilising legal process outsourcing (n=16).)

What they are able to support in many cases is a more effective and efficient service in these process areas than is typically available in in-house or law firm environments. These firms invest significantly in process and search technologies and, because they have scale in this kind of work, they can create many more levels of specialisation in their workforce.[18] Unless you have a very significant and consistent volume of documents to review, it will usually pay to use one of these services rather than in-source it.

The cost and complexity of handling document reviews is rising. In 2016, costs in the United States for civil lawsuits were $200–250 billion annually, with 20%–50% of that associated with the discovery process.[19] At the same time, 90% of e-discovery costs are tied to review and analysis.[20] ALS providers supply technology- and process-based efficiencies that drive down review and analysis expenses by limiting the cache of relevant documents that need to be reviewed. The pricing models for these providers are both predictable and rational, based on output rather than input. The models are also often open to new thinking about how such firms charge fees, with a move away from the traditional law firm's hourly model.

Law firms have recently been getting into this business, with many maintaining and offering their clients similar services at heavily discounted rates through internal contract management and document review departments. Some have become competitive with the costs offered by ALS providers.

From a quality perspective, both alternative legal services providers and law firms can offer upsides. On the ALS side, upsides include very sophisticated technology that in many cases is hard for law firms to fully replicate because of the heavy investment that would be required. ALS providers also use efficient process management systems, including service level management arrangements, in which output is defined around the legal department's or company's key performance indicators and measured on a regular basis, with penalties imposed on the ALS provider for underperformance.[21]

Law firms, however, offer well-integrated solutions that fit within the overall legal work that is being undertaken in respect of the matter. If, for example, you are conducting a document review in connection with a lawsuit being handled by the law firm, having the document review undertaken by the same firm and being supervised by the firm's attorneys can be a benefit.

In this area, three broad offerings stick out:

- technology-enabled service providers, who offer contract management solutions that leverage portal, workflow and analytics technologies, staffed by local, regional and globally based attorneys, executed by processes with committed service levels;[22]
- people-based providers that emphasize the use of first-rate process management and qualified attorneys in emerging markets (such as South Africa) as their competitive advantage; and
- providers that extend the law department by providing experienced attorneys backed by data-enabled technology solutions.[23]

These approaches all have a place, depending on the nature of the work undertaken.

Summary

As noted earlier, today's GC has many options, including in-sourcing contract management internally within the legal department. That can be a very attractive solution, depending on your contract needs. If, for instance, you have a relatively erratic contract flow, or you negotiate a large range of styles and types, maintaining an internal team in a cost-effective 'in-shore' environment (eg, Northern Ireland within the UK, or many parts of the Midwest in the United States) can be very effective.

In summary, what alternative legal service providers offer are viable, lower-cost and surprisingly high-quality solutions to parts of your unbundled workflow. They should be considered an essential component to your outsourcing options. It makes good sense to have your own contracts in place with such providers rather than solely working with them through law firms, so that you have complete transparency in terms of cost and service.

Selecting the right partners

Selecting the correct outside partners for your needs is a critical component in optimising your effectiveness. Together with your internal headcount, it is likely to comprise the largest component of your anticipated legal spend. It is important to think carefully about how you tackle this topic.

Leveraging legal procurement professionals

As purchasing power has gradually shifted from law firm providers to legal department purchasers, GCs have become increasingly savvy buyers of legal services. One trend has been for GCs to involve procurement professionals when making their significant purchasing decisions, particularly when it comes to retaining law firms for appointment to company panels or for one-time high-cost work.

This trend largely began in the early to mid-2000s in highly regulated industries such as pharmaceuticals, financial services, energy and utilities, where the volume of legal work can be significant.[2] In recent years, however, the trend has affected the mainstream, with 58% of chief legal officers reporting that the involvement of procurement/purchasing/strategic sourcing professionals is somewhat to very positive.[3]

There are many GCs who continue to resist the involvement of procurement professionals in their buying decisions, because they believe that the selection of law firms is a unique skill that rests on more than mere costs. They worry that a process-driven approach will destroy the relationships they have nurtured with outside counsel and impair the trust each side has developed.[4]

This is highly unlikely, provided the relationship is healthy – ie, when legal and procurement professionals work together to source the right firms and providers. As GCs have become more adept purchasers of legal services, they have increasingly come to appreciate the input of procurement professionals, while more and more procurement professionals have gained deeper knowledge of the legal industry. As Stephen Rauf of Accenture has noted: "Part of being a good lawyer is also being an astute business person, and tapping the best procurement resources and partners is just a smart approach."[5]

Modern procurement theory seeks to elevate the relationship between suppliers and the buyer to a strategic level, thereby securing a more effective relationship overall. That requires transparency and clear communication, as well as professional analytics.

Good legal procurement professionals also recognise the critical role that GCs play in the legal procurement process, and they accept that the legal department is uniquely situated to evaluate and determine who the best provider is for a specific issue. Procurement specialists supplement the GC's judgement with professional analytics and negotiation skills, in order to help clarify and frame ultimate sourcing decisions. But legal procurement cannot be the decision maker as to which firms the company should use; that remains the sole provenance of the GC.

The benefits of involving procurement professionals

There are five key benefits to involving procurement experts that should be kept in mind:

- *Perception by business colleagues:* Accessing large pre-existing business processes to assist the legal function is often viewed favourably by business clients because it demonstrates that the legal department has not walled itself off from the rest of the company and is run just as efficiently as other parts of the business. Working with legal procurement shows top management that you are a good steward of the company's money and a good corporate citizen.

- *Superior expertise:* Lawyers often lack both the skill set and the experience needed to professionally procure services from vendors.[6] Instead of viewing negotiations with providers as a zero-sum game, do what procurement specialists do and appoint providers on a long-term panel basis, giving both sides the incentive to invest in the other.

    Procurement experts will also seek mutual transparency, which ensures a more mature dialogue with partners, enabling the parties to arrive more easily at a solution that takes all needs into account. This too, is worth emulating.

    Procurement professionals best serve the legal department by providing the analytics and data that the legal team needs in order to make critical buying decisions, as well as framing that data in ways that are important to both the department and the company. They can do this by ferreting out and comparing costs, quality and other metrics before purchasing decisions are made. For example, they can help frame true value by looking beyond hourly rates to consider the total offer, including alternative fee arrangements, free advice, ramp-up investments by the outside provider, etc. These can then be compared with the substantive considerations that the legal department brings, such as expertise, reputation and the capabilities of specific partners, and benchmarked in a clear way against alternatives, to arrive at an optimal solution.

- *Independence:* Since procurement professionals are independent of the legal function, they are unburdened by existing loyalties and allegiances and thus able to bring a more dispassionate and businesslike attitude to the selection and negotiation process.
- *Good cop – bad cop:* Procurement professionals will also add enormous value in negotiating actual rates, acting as 'bad cops' to the legal department's 'good cops', thereby sparing relationships that need to be cultivated for the long haul. Once retained, law firm rates and invoices can be monitored and analysed by procurement professionals to ensure compliance with department policies and sourcing agreements. This frees up lawyer and legal professional time to devote to actual legal work, and it provides your legal operations team with helpful allies.
- *Superior analytics:* Procurement professionals are better equipped than lawyers to provide ongoing analytics and market monitoring to ensure that the terms you have negotiated with providers remain competitive.[7] Often, they will be able to subscribe to industry pricing analyses and advise on pricing levels and techniques of which you may be unaware.

Of course, as is the case with business partners in other functions, it is important that the ultimate sourcing decisions are made by the legal department and not by procurement professionals. There are three core reasons for this:

- Sourcing professional services – whether outside lawyers, ad agencies or consultants – is a delicate art that requires balancing risk, quality and cost. Since a firm's legal department is ultimately responsible for managing risk, in-house lawyers need to remain the final decision makers.

- Like all professionals, procurement experts can get caught up in their processes. Detailed procurement policies and nomenclature, most of which does not apply to buying legal services, can complicate the selection process. Procurement professionals may struggle to understand the risk/cost trade-off: hiring the 'wrong' law firm might save some money up front but cost the company material amounts in risk later on. Procurement professionals must understand this and put efficiency savings into a proper perspective. As James Neath has noted, "risk management trumps cost management every day".[8] The risk is not only monetary; reputational risks are equally problematic.

- Any GC who presides over a significant legal budget is failing to do his job if he does not involve procurement experts in his purchasing decisions, taking the above into account. The savings and mutual benefits that flow from this are too great to ignore.

Strategic partnerships

For many years, company strategic procurement experts focused on other areas of company spend – particularly those larger elements of direct spend that were core to their operations, such as raw materials, as well as the largest indirect spend categories, such as IT or finance or HR. If legal spend was considered at all, it was often viewed as too small, too technical or too risky for procurement colleagues to touch.

That situation has begun to change for two reasons. First, legal spend as a percentage of net revenue has continued to increase to a not insignificant 0.38% of US and 0.33% of worldwide company revenues in 2015.[9] Among Fortune 100 companies, it is closer to 1%.[10] That has made the volume of spend in legal more important for procurement experts. Secondly, general counsel are under increasing pressure to contain their costs, leading them to seek ever more innovative and sophisticated ways to control their legal spend. This 'convergence of interests' has led to ever-closer collaboration between procurement experts and legal directors.

This collaboration is likely to lead to procurement engaging with the legal department in ways that go beyond merely streamlining the sourcing process or reducing outside costs. One potential area of future collaboration, for example, might involve procurement assisting with unbundling legal work and matching tasks to the best-positioned service providers; another might include evaluations of law firm information security capabilities.[11] As Silvia Hodges Silverstein, Executive Director of the legal procurement trade organisation Buying Legal Council, has noted:[12]

> How legal procurement will be viewed by its colleagues in the legal department and in the legal industry at large, what it will buy, what influence it will have, and how it will assist the legal department in getting better value and being good stewards of their employer's money, will continue to change.

Legal spend remains a specialised area of procurement. Lawyers need to provide their expert views on whether a particular law firm is the right one to use in a given situation. Fortunately, lawyers are increasingly either borrowing the sophisticated outlook of procurement specialists in evaluating their options and negotiating good terms, or they are co-opting their procurement colleagues into the process. Those who have yet to engage the procurement function in these initiatives are increasingly being put under pressure by their CEOs or CFOs to do so.[13]

> Legal used to be 'off limits' for Procurement. Legal services were deemed too special, too complex, too unique to be sourced by anyone other than the legal department. This view has changed.
> (Silvia Hodges Silverstein)[14]

One way that this has increasingly manifested itself is the way in which legal departments are seeking more strategic relationships with their vendors. Rather than taking an old-style 'mercenary' approach to getting the lowest possible cost from a given law firm on a given matter, general counsel are filtering out law firms and seeking a smaller group of more permanent, strategic partners, to use not just on a given case but on a regular basis going forward. This enables them to negotiate more attractive, volume-based terms from those firms, while giving the firms an incentive to invest in the long-term health of the relationship, learn more about the business and, in general, act as an external extension of the legal department.

What it means to be 'strategic'

You should aim to run your legal department like a business, ensuring that you are delivering optimal service at maximum efficiency and at the lowest reasonable cost. Doing that will require you to be strategic about service delivery, including the source (internal or external?), as well as the vendor category. Which external legal service providers you choose to use is a strategic, not an *ad hoc*, decision, taking the long-term perspective into account rather than applying a short-term, transactional approach.

To be strategic will also require you to make decisions based on rational variables rather than emotional or relational ones, and also require that you are securing the best deal you can for the company. This need not be inconsistent with adopting a partnership approach to your procurement efforts – a good strategy will include both a long-term partnership consideration as well as an arm's length, competitive and rational approach to procurement.

The emphasis you adopt between these two variables will depend on the procurement strategy you select, which can evolve over time. You will want your strategy to take the following elements into account:

- cost *versus* risk – ie, outcome and quality;
- long-term *versus* short-term benefits;
- the role of in-house lawyers; and
- the 'fit' between the provider and the specific need.

Ensuring good choices are made

There are a number of ways in which a GC can ensure, with his procurement professionals, that good partnership choices are made. Relevant methods to help are described next.

Key performance indicators

Your law firm procurement strategy can be aided by putting in place transparent key performance indicators (KPIs). These are metrics used to evaluate key measures of success in the procurement effort.

Here are some possible KPI categories that you may consider when evaluating law firms:

- track record of outcome success;
- degree of expertise/skill consistently deployed;
- problem solving ability;
- strategic thinking;
- diversity;
- quality of people;
- professionalism;
- teamwork;
- responsiveness/availability;
- proactive communication style (ie, progress updates, proactive alerts);
- commerciality;
- understanding of company culture and broader market;
- project planning and execution skills;
- document quality;
- technology;
- office locations;
- cost-effectiveness – ie, budgeting/forecasting accuracy, absolute price, staffing efficiency (weighted average price) and flexibility; and
- relationship management deftness – ie, appropriate aggressiveness with adversaries, general compatibility, credibility with decision makers, responsiveness to the legal function, and knowledge of the business needs.

You need not include all of these. Indeed, a shorter list may be preferable and you might select those above that are most applicable to your situation. Depending on the context, you might replace some KPIs with others that seem more applicable. You can also consider weighting your KPIs, adjusting your weightings to fit the context.

Some legal departments leverage KPIs to align partner law firms with department strategy and track that alignment going forward.[15] Periodic performance feedback can also help with alignment.

Law firm panels

The best way to start down the road of strategic partnership is to establish law firm panels – ie, identify a group of law firms that the legal department selects to act as its primary external provider(s) for given areas of work. Strategic procurement specialists sometimes refer to these as 'preferred supplier lists' (PSLs).[16]

If done correctly, it will give you three main benefits:

- *Cost:* Establishing panels will inevitably yield better terms of engagement, including more favourable hourly rates from your new law-firm partners, as well as other benefits such as free 'ramp-up' time on matters, alternative fee arrangements, better engagement terms, free training, partnership on *pro bono* work, and other initiatives.
- *Quality:* Having panels will ensure that you have thoughtfully allocated the best work to the best firms – ie, those firms that are best positioned to take on the various types of work you are considering. It is, in other words, an extension of the deconstruction task. You will have ensured that premium (ie, complex, high-risk) work goes to the best-positioned premium firms, while less-complex work will go to the best-positioned 'value' firms.

  This approach has both cost and quality advantages. Trying to plough a field with a Ferrari will not only be more expensive than using a tractor, but it will also be vastly less efficient. Similarly, a high-end, sophisticated firm may not only be more expensive to instruct on a matter that is outside its core areas of expertise, but it will likely do it less competently than a less prestigious firm that does that kind of work all the time.
- *Transparency:* When you initiate the selection process to identify potential firms to invite to respond to your RFP (request for proposal), you will likely want to start with current firms, and in particular those that maintain solid, existing relationships with you and have consistently delivered timely, cost-effective and high-quality results. You will also want to include firms that you have learned about from colleagues, as well as firms whose reputations bring them to your attention.

While your KPIs will include many other important factors of equal importance, make sure you include pre-existing institutional knowledge of your business in the mix. Firms with long and solid institutional relationships with your department can be hard to replace. That being said, it is also important that you approach the panel process with an open mind and that your choices of firm are not solely based on close connections involving the managing partners, the CEO, you or others in the company. It is a careful balance of considerations that needs to be made.

By establishing a formal process and weighting the firms in a neutral and objective manner, you will ensure that you are selecting the best firms in a transparent way that is fair and that serves the interests of the company. This can be important later if you are called upon to demonstrate that you have objectively made the best choice in your selection.

You may also find value in considering using the panel concept more broadly than just with respect to outside law firms. This may have particular value in the context of a large department. For example, BP has carried this procurement practice over to alternative legal suppliers, creating panels of preferred suppliers in task categories along the entire discovery value chain, from collection to hosting, search, review and legal holds; and they measure and manage those non-law firm panels the same way that they manage those for law firms.[17]

Small legal departments are unlikely to need panels
Panels are generally going to be more useful to legal departments – and more attractive to law firms – where there is a sufficient amount of external spend to make the effort worthwhile. Very small legal departments, with minimal external legal budgets, will generally not be able to draw firms into the process in a way that will yield significant discounts or other benefits; moreover, firms will be reticent to invest in the process for little or no potential yield.

Of course, even without generating significant discounts or savings, there are still advantages in selecting partner firms to work with through a structured process. Doing due diligence on the best-positioned firms and ensuring that you are doing this in an objective and transparent manner will still yield for you the best quality and expertise for any given matter, because you will have selected the best-positioned firms for the work you potentially have to give them.

You may also find that some law firms are keen to collaborate and incentivise you early on in the life of your company, while your department is still small, because they hope to establish a relationship with you that will serve them well as you grow and expand.

For these reasons, you might still consider running a panel process. However, you might not need to run one in as formal a manner as is outlined below. Instead, I would suggest that you borrow the most interesting and useful points to create your own evaluation process.

The value of law firm panels

Below is a step-by-step guide to establishing law firm panels.

But first a caveat: this is a labour-intensive process and using an internal procurement expert, a project manager or an outside consultant who specialises in the process is a far more efficient way to manage this. Such people will have expertise and experience in this field that you may well lack.

Keep in mind also that many of the larger law firms are well versed in panel selection processes and will have internal experts of their own. Without any experts representing you, you will be at an informational and expertise disadvantage.

Outside procurement consultants will neutralise this law firm advantage, because this is something they do all the time – and perhaps even more than any single firm. They will also bring to the table benchmarking data that will otherwise be difficult for you to get your hands on, which will allow you to ensure that considerations such as the rates being quoted and the terms offered are fair and reasonable relative to the market. This is a huge benefit.

Saving on the cost of consultants for your panel selection process could be 'penny wise and pound foolish', ending up costing you hundreds of thousands or even millions that you might have avoided with professional support. Consider this expense to be an investment rather than a cost.

Another advantage with using outside experts is that it allows them to play the 'bad cop' to your 'good cop' (see earlier in this chapter), which can spare your relationships with outside law firms. Rather than having difficult price, terms and conditions negotiations directly with each law firm, you can leave it to the outside experts to represent you in these negotiations and to come in to help solve tensions rather than be the source of those tensions up front that can permanently strain your working relations. This is actually something with which internal procurement colleagues can also assist.

If you are unable to leverage external experts or internal procurement professionals, make sure you appoint someone on your team to work on this matter full time and to be accountable for the end result. You will, of course, want to do this in any event because this will be a labour-intensive job, even if the project is being supported by outside experts. The objectively best-positioned internal candidates to lead this job may be the COO of your legal operations team (if you have one) or the head of your litigation group. As with all projects, you will have a better sense of your team and who has the personality traits to do this best.

In addition to appointing someone to lead the project, you will want to appoint a broader committee to consider the candidates and determine selection. You will most definitely want to include some of the key lawyers and other professionals who work in the area that the panel addresses, in addition to a broader cross-section of professionals in your team. Don't make the committee too big to be unwieldy, but not so small that it lacks legitimacy in the eyes of the broader team. Somewhere between three and seven people is appropriate, depending on the size of your team.

Make sure that you take the views of the lawyers who are working in the relevant area very seriously. The last thing you want to do is impose a firm on your team that they are uncomfortable working with.

Once you have appointed your internal working group, you will be ready to select the external law firm panel on which you might call to undertake certain aspects of your firm's legal work. The process to go through in order to create such a panel is set out next.

The law firm panel creation process

Select applicable areas of work

The first thing you need to do is decide what work you are going to create panels for. You will most likely not want it to be all of your firm's legal work. In particular, avoid establishing panels for work that you encounter only infrequently, as panels work best for your big areas of expenditure. Indeed, law firms typically have less interest in participating in panels if there is little opportunity to earn back in volume the profits they are giving up on the reduced hourly rates and other discounts they are offering in order to be on the panel.

Do not create panels for 100% of your work as a bundle to one or several law firms, for the reasons just stated. You want to preserve your flexibility to pick the best-positioned firm for a relatively unanticipated area of work at the time that you need them. You will not find a single firm or group of firms that will be perfect for every matter. But you can do this with a discrete subset of matters.

The best way forward is to adopt a Pareto-optimal approach: identify the 20% of your work that comprises about 80% of your total spend. That element of your firm's legal work is what you will most likely want to award to a panel. That will give you the right level of volume and experience in the area to best determine the right firms to be on your panel, and it will ensure that there is sufficient volume for the opportunity to be interesting.

Because a panel selection process is time-consuming and labour-intensive work, you may choose to focus on one market at a time and on one area of work at a time.

Define the intended scope of the panel

Despite the trend toward law firm globalisation, it can be difficult to find sufficient cross-border synergy among law firms to create panels across regions, so a regional (eg, UK, US, Canada, etc) approach might be more effective.[18]

There might be some spill-over in the large acquisitions context, which will inevitably have cross-border implications. If you award M&A work, you may find that the premium firms on your US and UK panels, for example, will have solid capabilities in both markets and thus be able to compete with each other for global deal work.

Many companies establish panels by legal subject matter. This works best when it is necessary to capture deep expertise in critical or strategic legal areas, such as commodity trading regulation, complex environmental regulation or M&A. Such firms tend to be more expensive, and it is hard to get the right calibration between the specialist firms and the general panel firms so that there is no overpaying for legal services.

Decide on the necessary levels of support

You will want to decide how many levels of support you will need for each area of work for which you create a panel. At the very least, create two levels: 'premium' and 'value' firms; consider whether a possible third, 'mid-priced', tier is necessary.

Premium firms

The premium firms are usually large and sophisticated, based in major urban centres, and always much more expensive.[19] These are the firms you will consider using for the largest and most complex work that you source, such as 'bet the company' litigation, unusually large acquisitions, board-level concerns and high-profile regulatory matters.

While these firms are the perfect partners for this kind of work, you don't want to use them for a broad range of work because they are not always best positioned to take on less sophisticated work and because they are much more expensive. You will from time to time be tempted to try one of them for value work because you have a strong relationship and you know that the firm has the resources to get things done on time. But this will usually not work well, both because you will get a shock when you receive the invoice and because the work is often surprisingly poor when you have the firm try to do work it is not used to handling.

Value firms

The value firms can be small or large, but usually focus more on efficiency measures such as project management and process improvement, and are more comfortable managing less high-profile matters. These firms are the ones you might want to consider for the more day-to-day legal work that you outsource, such as routine litigation that cannot be managed in-house and mid-sized acquisitions.

It may be tempting to see if you are able to leverage these more value-conscious firms to do some of the premium work as well. In some ways, this temptation is even more powerful than using premium firms for the value work, because you see cost savings dangling in front you. But be aware that this may not always work out, and you need to accept the risk that you will end up having to instruct a premium firm to pick up the slack, at added cost. As is the case with the premium firms, value firms have their allotted place in your pantheon and you would be well advised to leave them there.

Mid-priced firms

If you have a very large volume of work at differing levels of sophistication, you might also consider a third tier: mid-priced firms. These straddle the divide between the premium and value ends of the spectrum and will be capable of handling mid-level work, such as large (but not overly complex) litigation, mid-sized deals and regulatory work that is either fairly commonplace or very niche, where they happen to have expertise. Unlike their value and premium cousins, mid-sized firms can sometimes migrate up or down the value chain, and it may be useful to give them a try outside their zone of expertise.

Partnerships within each category

In all three categories, you will want to select at least two partner firms because even an important partner firm will from time to time be conflicted from representing you or be unable to assist because they lack the expertise.

You can add more firms to each level, but be careful about adding too many unless you have the work levels to sustain relationships with each one. There must be enough volume at stake for the firms to want to work with you. Too many partner firms can render the entire exercise meaningless.

If you are in a very large department, you may also want to ensure that your lawyers are judicious in the amount of business they are giving to firms in the premium tier by tracking spend volume by tier on a regular basis. You might also consider similarly tracking spend volume on alternative legal service providers, legal process outsourcers and non-traditional firms.

Finally, it can be helpful to determine what work fits within each category before you begin, so that you are better able to evaluate the candidates. You might do this by using a 'box grid' system similar to the one you leveraged when deconstructing your work – ie, on a value–risk axis or, alternatively, on a complexity–risk axis. However you decide to slice it up, it helps to have a clear picture in your mind about what the work you are selling looks like, so that you can adequately match the firm's expertise with the work you are prepared to offer in that category.

Very large law departments at major companies may expand the category concept further. They might add, for example, a specialist tier composed of firms classified by narrow legal subject matter that various business clients require on a sustained basis; or they might create a local counsel tier, comprising very local firms that are required by virtue of very close relationships with local courts or decision makers.[20]

Research and identify candidates; gather market intelligence
One of the most important aspects of the search is drawing up the right list of candidate law firms to consider for your panel. Much as in the same way as when you are seeking candidates for an open position, you can and should throw the net as broadly as absolutely possible to get the right pool of talent.

Set out next are a few thoughts on what you might consider doing.

Use the legal press

One good way to get instant publicity is to announce to the legal press that you are going to launch a panel selection process. Law firms are avid readers of the legal press and will no doubt pick up any panel creation information. There seems to be a similar passionate interest in panels from the press, too.

You can get the attention of the press by issuing a press release or by simply calling up reporters at the key journals in your area. Interviews and articles written about your panel selection process up front will generate an outpouring of interest from law firms, including firms you may not have heard about. In some cases, these unknowns can actually be very interesting and impressive – there are simply too many firms out there for you to know them all up-front, and using the press will draw in firms that you might not otherwise have considered, and certainly those with enough interest and energy to connect with you.

Ask around

Make sure you are leveraging your network to identify potential candidates. Many of your peers will be using firms with whom you are not familiar. Getting an inside look via people you know is a great way to both learn about new firms and assess ones you have not tried.

Ask your contacts if they have used a firm that you have encountered and used. Do not tell them that you use that firm already; just ask them for their opinion. That way, you can gauge their review of the firm you know against your own experience, which will help you to evaluate whether their feedback is accurate for firms you don't know and will help you assess the reliability of their reviews.

If you work with your colleagues in procurement or with external procurement consultants, task them with gathering market intelligence about firms, their respective offerings and their unique features. This exercise falls within their area of expertise.

If you are using a consultant to help you run your search, you might also benefit from asking them which firms they have seen in each of these categories. They have the benefit of having seen and worked on multiple panel selection processes and may have insights you have not considered.

Most importantly, ask your legal department colleagues, especially those who work in the specific fields that you are sourcing for. Many of them will have subject matter expertise in areas that you are considering awarding to the panel.

Undertake documentary due diligence

Finally, check law firm rankings in such sources as *Chambers, American Lawyer*, the *FT Innovative Lawyers* and *The Lawyer Awards*. Also, read press reports and articles and run an internet search to see what other candidates may be out there. Unlike the more qualitative assessments you get through your first-hand sources, this will give you a broad quantitative reach that will catch anything else out there that is worth considering.

You will want to whittle down the broad cache of potential candidates to a more concentrated group of actual candidate firms. These will be the ones that then receive a request for proposal (RFP) from you, inviting them to tender for inclusion on the panel.

Limit the final list of potential candidates to no more than 15 firms. The RFPs will yield a substantial amount of reading material from them; and with more than 15 to read, the details will begin to blur. Again, this is an area you typically want to use legal procurement or consultants to assist you with.

Aim for diversity

Diversity is critical to your success as you build your team, and you should be seeking it in your law firm partners as well. McKinsey has come out with an interesting report that details what should be clear to just about anyone who has ever worked in a highly diverse environment: diverse companies perform better financially than those that are less diverse.[21]

According to the McKinsey research, companies in the top quartile for gender diversity are 15% more likely to financially outperform those in the bottom quartile, while those in the top quartile for ethnic diversity are 35% more likely to outperform those in the bottom quartile. In the United States, McKinsey found a linear relationship between racial and ethnic diversity and financial performance. The same is true for law firms. As you seek out diversity in your team, remember to also do so in your law firm partners. It is both the right thing to do and the smart thing to do.

The National Association of Minority and Women Owned Law Firms (NAMWOLF) is a good place to start when trying to identify diverse law firms to invite to your selection process in the United States. You can find their website at www.namwolf.org.

Generate and issue RFPs

Once you have identified your list of final candidates, you can generate and issue your RFPs. The basic document contains a series of questions that are important to you in evaluating the firms. Break the questions down into two broad sections: questions about the firm's practice in general, and questions about the firm's experience in the specific field at issue for the panel. Limit the total number of questions to no more that 15 – a larger number, when multiplied up by the responses of up to 15 firms, will yield enormous quantities of data that you will not be in a position to meaningfully digest.

Set a deadline for the submission of responses and give yourself adequate time to filter them before announcing the selected candidate firms. At least several months is prudent. Do not underestimate the amount of internal time the review and analysis will take.[22]

Evaluate responses and select finalists

Once you have received all of the RFP submissions from your candidate firms, you will be in a position to evaluate them. Schedule regular meetings among the committee members to evaluate specific firms and decide which ones to take forward.

The best way to break this down is to have the committee put together a deck that compares and contrasts in a visually accessible way each firm's answer for each question. You will want to determine the areas for comparison and the weight you attribute to each factor. This should be put on one page for each question. The deck might also highlight the extreme ends of the spectrum – for instance, in relation to the hourly rate, you might have the least expensive and most expensive firms highlighted in green and red respectively.

In evaluating answers, make sure that there is also some room for qualitative judgement and overall 'feel', but be guided by the numbers and factual answers you get back.

Your committee might make decisions by majority vote, or you as GC might weigh in with a final say, depending on your style of leadership.

This process should result in no more than 5–10 finalist firms, because any more than that becomes unwieldy and difficult to manage.

Establish finalist interviews

Once you have narrowed down your list of finalists, you should establish a process for notifying the firms that were and were not selected.

If you or someone on your team has personal relationships with any of these particular firms, it is a good idea for that person to be the messenger. This is particularly important in respect of the ones that have not been selected – there is no value in burning bridges with any firm. In delivering the message, it might be helpful to be as transparent as you can about what caused your committee to take the decision it did (without, obviously, revealing the confidences of the other firms). You might also, if it is true, hold out the possibility of work in other areas outside the panel's scope of activity. It is also important that you provide the firms with candid feedback on why they lost out (this time), so that they can improve the next time they pitch to you.

For those who have been selected to the final round, you will want to invite each one to a live interview. You could conduct this meeting either at your company or at the firm's offices. Going with the latter gives you an opportunity to assess the firm in its natural state: Where is it located?

Does it seem to have expensive overhead? What is the atmosphere and culture like? The downside with that approach is that you have to coordinate a group from your own firm to travel around to different locations, which is time-consuming and costly. Holding the meetings at your own offices will enable you to conduct multiple meetings in one day. The neutrality of your own office may also help you to evaluate the firms on an 'apples to apples' basis, without being blinded by less relevant variances in the setting.

Set up the finalist interviews

Participants

In setting up the finalist meetings, you will want to identify who from your side will be there and ask each short-listed firm to do the same. Limit the number of people that each firm is permitted to bring, so that you don't have too many people in the room – five or six people from each side is plenty. To discuss financials, you should consider having your procurement people (if any) on the team; the firm being interviewed should bring its pricing director to the meeting.

Materials

You might also ask each candidate firm to submit any materials it intends to bring or use. Ask each one not to prepare PowerPoint presentations. Instead, you want the meetings to be conversational because that will enable you to focus on the people in front of you and the chemistry (or lack thereof) without getting distracted by charts or bullet points.

Agenda

Set up a list of topics that you would like the firms to elaborate on and that you deem to be important to your overall assessment. These might include topics that have already been covered in the RFP submissions, as well as others. There is no perfect list of topics for all meetings and panels, and you will need to identify your requirements based on your own specific circumstances.

However, you will want to skip 'boilerplate' questions and focus on the most relevant topics for your situation as quickly as you can. The quality of your questions will tell your law firm bidders a lot about your sophistication as a buyer. Focus your questions on the key ones that will actually have an impact on your buying decision and skip those that will have little impact on that decision. As Accenture observed in 2016:[23]

> *Consider your audience. Within a few seconds, firms will assess how mature you are from a selection process perspective based on the quality of your questions. Including boilerplate questions, requesting the firm's address, number of FTEs, DnB numbers, etc., will convey to the [candidate] firm a lack of thoughtfulness and rigor ... After managing hundreds of legal selection processes for our clients, the key conclusion is that selection decisions are ultimately made on relatively few pieces of critical information. So why not just start and end there? This streamlines the process, is appreciated by the firms, and allows you to focus on the most important criteria without the distraction of generic sales and marketing material that the firm cringed about providing to you in the first place.*

Here are some topics that you might want to cover:
- what makes the firm unique;
- the firm's 'footprint' (ie, its scope of legal expertise and jurisdictions);
- its experience in the selected area of law;
- its relationships across the industry;
- cultural fit;
- the proposed team, including whether the lawyers and partners present will actually be the ones working with you;
- the firm's client base and whether you will be a large or a small client within it;
- whether the firm is prepared to work with other law firms and with alternative legal services providers;
- the value-added benefits the firm is prepared to offer;
- the level of diversity within the candidate firm; and
- any innovation or novel approaches taken by the firm.

It is helpful to give each firm being interviewed the list of broad topics up front, so that each is able to come prepared to speak on these things.

Conduct an evaluation of the short-listed firms

Evaluation during the interview

There is nothing as valuable as meeting the individuals and hearing them talk you through these topics as opposed to just reading about them on paper. It will help you determine how seriously they care about the things you care deeply about, and whether there seems to be an overall level of alignment that feels right. Just like in a job interview setting, you will get a feel for the personalities and whether there is a fit.

One thing to pay attention to is whether the firms bring along associates or only partners and, if they do indeed bring associates, what role they play in the interview. Some GCs find it very disappointing if no associates are brought along, as they are often the primary interface with the legal department team on actual work. It might lead you to wonder about the quality of their people, and whether they have a dedicated team of associates who will work on your matters or whether it just depends on who is available. Strong associate involvement in the meeting and a sense that the associates and partners are comfortable and connected is key to a successful candidacy.

Equally important is whether the partners who are present seem to be aligned and comfortable with your team and with each other. In terms of your team, are they only addressing you as the GC, or are they paying attention to all of the people present? In terms of their own team, do the lawyers seem to know each other well? Are actual working relationships evident? Are those present the people you will interface with, or have they just brought a 'rainmaker' along whom you are never likely to meet again? Did they bring important members of their firm to the meeting, such as the managing partner, or did they bring only junior partners?

Are people nervous or relaxed? Do they seem keen on the work or are they just going through the motions? How much effort have they put in to preparing for the meeting, learning about your company and your team? Finally, did they bring their pricing professionals to the meeting who are able to 'talk numbers' and discuss how the firm is able to manage quality, innovation and efficiency in your best interests?

Final selection

The final step is to make a final selection on the firms that will be a part of your panel. Have everyone on the committee rank the firms you have met based on the factors you consider to be the most important ones. You might even give separate weightings to these factors to ensure that the score is as accurate as possible. Doing it this way may yield results that surprise you and the team, where firms that you thought were at the top of the list turn out to be in the middle and vice versa.

It is unnecessary to rigidly stick to the weighted scorecard, however. Use it as a tool to spur a more qualitative assessment and discussion about what firms felt right. But also pay some attention to the scores, as they have a way of revealing hidden cognitive biases that may exist.

Final negotiations

Before announcing the winners, you may want to consider first returning to the presumed finalists to negotiate final points that are suboptimal from your perspective. Indicate to them that they are being considered for a place on the panel and discuss with them any sticking points.

This is the perfect moment to negotiate a good final deal for the company. Avoid rushing to make a decision until the details have been hammered out and you have secured the best deal possible. As Stephen Rauf of Accenture has observed:[24]

> *Do not make your decision until the process has run its course. We have seen Legal Departments rush to a decision, inform the firm, and then start discussions with the firm around financials, rates, structures, and value-add services. This is not a recipe for success. A better approach is to shortlist possible contenders to a select few. Entertain advanced discussions with them and then ask for the things that will truly make a difference to your organisation. Is that a deeper discount? Access to senior staff? A "free" helpline? Zero cost of transitioning files and coming up to speed? Whatever it may be, you need to ask for it before the final selection is made.*

Announce the panel members

Announcing the decision to your winners and losers is a delicate task that will require your involvement as general counsel. A personal call from you to the losers will go a long way toward mitigating bad feelings and helping them understand why they were not chosen. As was the case in the first-round cut-offs, you might, if appropriate, emphasize areas that impressed you and that there might be a possibility for them to work with you in the future on other non-panel matters. Again, as in the initial invitation to participate in the RFP process, avoid burning bridges at all costs. That said, you should consider providing them with clear, candid feedback since that is both the right thing to do and can be very helpful in sharpening their competition for work in the future.

As for the winners, your calls will obviously be more pleasant. You may want to invite them out to celebratory dinners or lunches to cement the relationships, especially with the new firms that you are working with for the first time. It is important to get things off on the right foot.

You may also want to circle back to the press and announce your panellists by that means, which will yield some public attention. That will also be helpful to your new partners, who will appreciate the public recognition and free coverage. But make sure you let the firms know in advance that you intend to do this and align with them, so that there is no confusion or misunderstanding.

Are panels for ever?

Once you have established a panel, is it for ever? That is an important question to consider, perhaps even up front. Some legal departments enter into formal contracts with the panel firms for a fixed period of time, while others leave the duration open, preferring to revisit the situation whenever it feels most appropriate. What is best for you may depend on your culture and circumstances.

One suggestion is to revisit the panel every two or three years to make sure that you are capturing changes in the market, including new firm entrants, rotations away from one firm to the next by a partner or group of partners who had skills you valued, and any changes in the cost structures and prices of your partner firms as compared with others in the market. It can also be useful simply as a matter of good governance to clear the air and avoid complacency by the firms on your panel.

However, be careful not to recreate your panel too often, because that will eviscerate the purpose it has from the perspective of the partner law firms. If they feel that they could be bumped off the panel in the not-too-distant future, they will be less likely to consider investing in the relationship for the long term or offering full transparency with you in terms of their price structure, needs and areas of expertise.

Panels for alternative legal services providers

The process described in the preceding section can also be used to create panels for alternative legal services providers or other vendors. As your share of external spend apportioned to these providers climbs, there can be real value in creating panels of these providers as well.

But start with your law firms and gain experience in that area first, as this will likely be your biggest area of expenditure. Only after you are comfortable with having identified the best approach for your organisation should you consider expanding the process outward to alternative providers.

Technology

In the earlier chapter entitled "Law firms", we explored how technology has impacted such firms through a wide range of innovative tools and processes that have reshaped the landscape, including communications- and productivity-enhancing technologies, efficiency and transparency tools, and emerging solutions that leverage artificial intelligence.

In this chapter we will consider how technology can play a role in accelerating your in-house team's performance.

Processes ahead of technology

In order to make intelligent technology decisions, you must first be clear about what problem you are trying to solve. Too many GCs think about technology before analysing and evaluating the problem. As Victoria Lockie, Senior Vice-President and Associate General Counsel, Strategy and Special Initiatives, at Pearson observes, "Technology itself is not the solution; it is only a tool to help you get to the solution."[2]

To understand the underlying problem, you need to focus on analysing your processes and creating a plan to correct any irregularities in them, before you consider acquiring new technology. If you have a highly inefficient contract management process, for example, you must understand and remove the current underlying roadblocks before you purchase expensive new contract management software. If you buy or develop the software first, you are likely to achieve only marginal benefits because the underlying processes that are causing the inefficiencies have not changed.

Technology solutions also require their own inherent process adaptations in order to yield benefits. To get the benefit of contract analytics from a contract management system, for instance, you will have to put in place a process to enter data, create decision trees and escalation clauses into the tool. If you neglect this, that feature will be useless.

Process improvement

To address these process-related challenges, start any planned technology transformation by first undertaking a process improvement project.

These kinds of projects involve identifying and analysing your work processes in order to optimise them.[3]

Process improvement projects often involve the use of one of several systematic approaches or methodologies, such as benchmarking or lean manufacturing, depending on the specific circumstances or needs.[4] Which particular process improvement approach you may need to take in your legal department is fact-specific: there is no universal model that applies in all situations. Problems faced by legal departments vary greatly. You might, for instance, experience problems that stem from how incoming work is being received, handled and allocated. Or you may need to define more clearly what types of work get prioritised, how assignments are properly delegated, or how department work more generally gets done.

Since understanding your specific needs will require an in-depth analysis of your particular situation, the solutions will also be uniquely tailored. For this reason, it is impossible to outline a generic approach to process improvement.

Get help

Legal operations officers can play an important role in process improvement. As noted in the chapter entitled "Designing an integrated team structure", one of the core competencies of legal operations officers is identifying process and efficiency challenges and determining which technologies might help solve them.

If you do not have, or are unable to hire, a Legal COO, you would be well advised to either retain one on a temporary basis through a staffing company, or to hire consultants that specialise in this area, in order to help you tackle process identification and improvement in your department.

Change management

Process optimisation and technology upgrades require changes in behaviour from people in your legal department. Often, there is a gap between the theoretical value of the technology being rolled out and an organisation's ability to effectively leverage it.[5] That gap may exist because the people tasked with using the new tool are resisting it. As Dorothy Leonard-Barton, a Harvard Business School professor, and William Kraus, a technology and systems implementation consultant at General Electric, have pointed out:[6]

> *Tacit resistance does not disappear but ferments, grows into sabotage, or surfaces later when resources are depleted. Because the advocates of change have such a clear view of an innovation's benefits, resistance often catches them by surprise. The worst thing a manager can do is shrug such resistance aside on the dual assumption that it is an irrational clinging to the status quo and that there is nothing to be done about it.*

It is therefore important to recognise the change management aspects of a technology investment and take the necessary steps to incorporate that into your plan.

The same goes for process improvements. As performance-based training company Dale Carnegie Training notes:[7]

> *Change in the workplace can sometimes lead to role confusion and disengaged employees. To prevent this, the change management strategic planning process must be constantly refined to address the needs of every corporation or team.*

Read the chapter in Part D of this book, entitled "Change management", before attempting any technology or process changes. It is important that you take into account the emotional and behavioural challenges that process optimisation is likely to involve.

We will now consider the state of play in technology more broadly before turning to some of the technology options that are available in the legal domain.

The evolving technology landscape
As noted in the first chapter of this book, technological disruption – caused by the information technology revolution – is transforming the

legal profession. Artificial Intelligence, machine learning and networked technologies are increasingly harnessing so-called 'big data' and cloud computing to deliver powerful solutions that are impacting the profession in fundamental ways.

Before looking at the specific applications that may be useful to your legal department, let us briefly survey the landscape and context in which these technologies have emerged.

The Second Machine Age

Professors Erik Brynjolfsson and Andrew McAfee of the Massachusetts Institute of Technology have argued that we have entered a 'Second Machine Age', characterised by "astonishing progress with digital technologies – those that have computer hardware, software, and networks at their core".[8] Bill Teuber, Vice Chairman of EMC Corporation, has described this new age as follows:[9]

> If the first machine age was about the automation of manual labor and horsepower, the second machine age is about the automation of knowledge work, thanks to the proliferation of real time, predictive data analytics, machine learning and the Internet of Things — an estimated 200 billion devices connected to the Internet by 2020, all of them generating unimaginable quantities of data.

The technologies that have emerged during the course of the Second Machine Age have been, and will continue to be, driven by several key forces: Moore's Law, big data and the 'internet of things', cloud computing and artificial intelligence.

Let us will briefly consider each of these below, before turning to specific applications in the legal landscape.

Moore's Law and the second half of the chessboard

The rapid development in technology that has characterised the Second Machine Age has been driven in part by an exponential growth in computing power that is sometimes referred to as Moore's Law.

The term was first coined by Intel co-founder Gordon Moore, who in 1965 observed that the amount of integrated circuit computing power that could be purchased for one dollar had been doubling roughly every year. The time required for digital doubling has fluctuated in the years since then. In 1975, it was revised upward to every two years and then subsequently to every 18 months.[10] Figure 17 gives a generic view of such exponential growth.

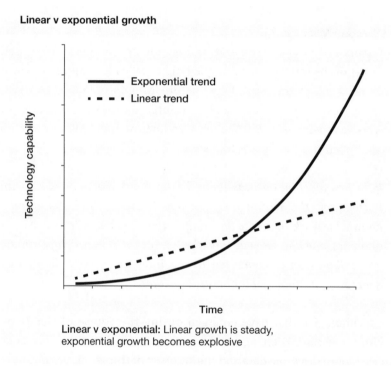

Linear v exponential growth

Exponential trend

Linear trend

Technology capability

Time

Linear v exponential: Linear growth is steady, exponential growth becomes explosive

Figure 17: The power of exponential growth in technological capability

It is difficult to understate the implications that Moore's Law has had on technology growth over the past fifty years or so – and indeed what it might portend for the future. As Professor Emeritus of Physics at the University of Colorado at Boulder, Albert A Bartlett, once famously remarked, the "greatest shortcoming of the human race is our inability to understand the exponential function".[11]

Brynjolfsson and McAfee have illustrated the power of exponential growth as follows: imagine you were to place one grain of rice on the first square of a chessboard, two on the second, four on the third and so forth, through to the 64th and final square. At the halfway point, you would have about 4 billion grains of rice, or roughly one large field's worth.[12] But by the 64th square, you would have more than 18 quintillion (ie, 18×10^{18}) grains of rice – more than has been produced since the dawn of time.[13]

It is this exponential effect that has enabled the explosive growth in modern technology. Moore's Law is the reason why a smartphone today is millions of times more powerful than the combined computing power that NASA used during the Apollo missions to the Moon in 1969: the Apple iPhone 6's clock alone is 32,600 times faster than the best Apollo-era computers and can perform instructions 120 million times faster;[14] and NASA's 1969 Apollo Guidance Computer had less computing power than a modern toaster.[15]

Some observers have argued that by 2016 Moore's Law had finally begun slowing down and that computer chip makers will, in the future, have to work harder to keep this momentum going.[16] Others have argued that, since much of the processing and data storage needed for today's mobile technology is done in the cloud (remote clusters of servers), Moore's Law is less critical.[17]

In any event, what is clear is that this explosive growth in processing power has enabled enormous technological advances and is likely to continue to do so in the future, whether or not it will continue at an exponential rate. Technological development is clearly moving in one direction only and, over time, has the capacity to profoundly transform how the legal profession works.

The internet of things, and big data

The exponential growth in computing power has been happening at a time when more and more things are becoming connected to the internet. Sometimes referred to as the 'internet of things', "computing devices, mechanical and digital machines, objects, animals or people are provided with unique identifiers and the ability to transfer data over a network without requiring human-to-human or human-to-computer interaction."[18]

As objects have become wired into the internet and begun to communicate with each other, network effects have begun to emerge between them, creating new opportunities that were previously inconceivable.[19] The colour and strength of the lights in an office might, for instance, vary in accordance with stock market fluctuations.[20]

All of these developments are together generating masses of data, known as 'big data'. Consider that during every minute of 2014: 204 million email messages were sent; 277,000 tweets were posted on Twitter; 72 hours of new video was uploaded on YouTube; Facebook users shared 2.5 million pieces of content; and more than 4 million search queries were made on Google.[21]

Cloud computing

Cloud computing enables companies to have on-demand access to a shared pool of configurable computer-processing resources that are not owned by the user.[22] It is in some sense analogous to a utility, such as the electricity grid, in that users are sharing a common resource.[23] In the business context, cloud computing can involve multiple solutions, including:

- *Software-as-a-Service (SaaS)*, where a company will subscribe to an application that it accesses over the internet (eg, Salesforce.com);
- *Platform-as-a-Service (PaaS)*, where a company will create its own custom applications for itself and its employees; and
- *Infrastructure-as-a-Service (IaaS)*, where providers such as Amazon, Microsoft, Google and Rackspace provide a 'backbone' (ie, a larger transmission line that carries data gathered from smaller lines that interconnect with it) that is rented out to companies.[24]

Cloud computing provides numerous benefits for businesses, including flexibility (you can scale capacity up or down depending on needs), back-up solutions (the data is offsite), improved collaboration, security and mobility, and reduced capital expenditure on hardware.[25]

Artificial intelligence

Artificial intelligence (AI) involves technologies that are able to perform specific human tasks as efficiently as, or better than, people.[26] AI leverages 'machine learning' technology, in which the machine uses algorithms to sift through and learn from volumes of data in order to make determinations or predictions.[27] Instead of writing specific coded routines and instructions, "the machine is 'trained' using large amounts of data and algorithms that give it the ability to learn how to perform the task".[28] Recent areas of focus have been speech recognition, planning and problem solving.[29]

Developments in AI have evolved rapidly in recent years, particularly since 2015, as a result of ever cheaper processing costs stemming from Moore's Law, the deluge of all kinds of information that has become increasingly available with the advent of big data, and the virtually limitless storage solutions made available through cloud computing.

One particularly interesting type of AI is so-called 'deep learning', in which software is designed to imitate the human brain – more specifically, the large array of neurons found in the neocortex, via an artificial 'neural network'.[30] This design is being combined with "reinforcement learning" technology, which enables the computer to teach itself by learning from its exposure to new data without being explicitly programmed to do so.[31] Deep learning has made remarkable advances in image and speech recognition, by giving machines the ability to self-learn.

Deep learning has also proven to be very adept at pattern recognition. As technology journalist Michael Copeland notes:[32]

> Today, image recognition by machines trained via deep learning in some scenarios is better than [that by] humans, and that ranges from [identifying] cats to identifying indicators for cancer in blood and tumors in MRI scans.

In 2016, a deep-learning-based computer program called AlphaGo beat one of the world's top players of the strategy board game 'Go'.[33] While AI-based computers have beaten some of the best humans at chess for many years, Go is far more complex, and hence difficult to program for success. *Scientific American* has characterised this as follows:[34]

With its breadth of 250 possible moves each turn ... there are about 250[150], or 10[360] possible moves. This is a number beyond imagination and renders any thought of exhaustively evaluating all possible moves utterly and completely unrealistic.

Given this virtually illimitable complexity, go is, much more than chess, about recognising patterns that arise when clutches of stones surround empty spaces. Players perceive, consciously or not, relationships among groups of stones and talk about such seemingly fuzzy concepts as 'light' and 'heavy' shapes of stones, and aji, meaning [in Japanese] latent possibilities. Such concepts, however, are much harder to capture algorithmically than the formal rules of the game.

AlphaGo achieved this victory in part by being able to "split itself into two, playing against itself and continuously improving its overall performance".[35]

This technology has promising applications in the legal document review context. One current focus in the legal area "is on computers looking for patterns in data, carrying out tests to evaluate the data and finding results".[36]

Autonomy and replacement

The above developments in the broader technology landscape have profound implications for society, including how lawyers work. Indeed, as the ABA Journal observed in 2016, AI "is changing the way lawyers think, the way they do business and the way they interact with clients. Artificial intelligence is more than legal technology. It is the next great hope that will revolutionise the legal profession."[37]

One question that arises is whether machines will soon replace lawyers entirely. If Moore's Law continues into the future, it could certainly have profound implications. At the current rate, by 2020 the average desktop computer would be able to process approximately 1,016 calculations per second – ie, the same processing power as the human brain; and by 2050 the average desktop machine would have more processing power than all of humanity combined.[38]

Yet these fears may be exaggerated, or at least premature. As noted above, Moore's Law appears to have been slowing in recent years; and it is therefore at least questionable whether the speed of change will keep going at the same pace.

In the near term at least, the likely focus will be on human–machine partnerships rather than on full machine autonomy. If current experience is anything to go by, the most sophisticated technologies "are not those that stand apart from people, but those that are most deeply embedded in, and responsive to, human and social networks".[39] Unmanned aircraft, autopilot systems and underwater robots, for instance, do not work autonomously – they work best when paired with humans.[40]

While it is impossible to predict where technology will take us, the future may involve more complex interactions between man and machine than the simple replacement fear so often voiced by doomsayers. Every new breakthrough tends to generate ripple effects that create new opportunities (as well as new fears) for people. As Massachusetts Institute of Technology Professor David A Mindell has observed:[41]

> *Human-factors researchers and cognitive scientists find that rarely does automation simply 'mechanise' a human task; rather, it tends to make the task more complex, often increasing the workload (or shifting it around) ... Yes, automation can certainly take on parts of tasks previously accomplished by humans, and machines do act on their own in response to environments for certain periods of time. But the machine that operates entirely independently of human direction is a useless machine.*

This approach seems to be holding up well in the context of the legal profession. Technological developments such as AI will in all likelihood transform the legal profession in coming years; but that does not necessarily mean that lawyers will become redundant. Innovation will no doubt profoundly alter how things are done, perhaps in ways that are not yet imaginable. Certainly, the basic tasks that lawyers currently perform will change.[42]

But whether this is a good or bad thing depends on one's perspective. For lawyers who aspire to partnership in a traditional law firm, this kind of technological change could be negative. But for those who are excited about the possibilities that technological disruption present, including new legal business models, the Second Machine Age could very well be the most exciting time ever in law. New vistas will open up and entirely new career pathways are likely to present themselves.[43]

The good news is that the millennial generation and the one coming behind it (Generation Y) – discussed in the chapter entitled "The generational context and the rise of the millennials" in Part C of this book – have grown up with technological disruption. It is their state of normalcy. As Susskind has observed, "many of the changes brought by technology … should be familiar to younger members of the legal profession, as full fledged members of the Internet generation".[44]

Perhaps, at least for young lawyers, the glass that technology presents to the profession appears half-full rather than half-empty.

In-house technology applications

The pace of technological change is so rapid that it makes little sense to discuss specific applications for your legal department, because whatever specifics are given here will quickly become outdated. Instead, this section will provide you with a broad overview of the categories currently available to help you enhance your team's performance and support the process optimisation efforts that have been discussed above.

Communication and collaboration tools

Sometimes the simplest and most obvious technologies can have the greatest impact. Communications and productivity tools, including videoconferencing systems, e-mail, mobile telephony and cloud-based servers, are not new. Yet they are often overlooked by GCs eager to upgrade their technology.

These tools have had a profound effect on the recruitment and retention of talent, and will continue to do so as millennials increasingly take over the workforce. They have done so by reducing the need for people to be based in centralised locations.

Today, some or all of your team can operate from anywhere. There are three significant benefits that flow from this, as described next.

Telecommuting

Communication and collaboration tools enable people to telecommute, or work remotely from home offices, allowing firms to attract talent that would otherwise be difficult to procure. Single parents or some disabled people, for instance, might not be able to easily commute on a daily basis to a central location. Allowing such professionals to telecommute most of the time will attract top talent that you might not otherwise find; and it may also boost your team's diversity.

A permissive attitude towards working remotely will also attract top millennial talent, many of whom have grown up with the notion of remote collaboration and are seeking that same approach in their professional lives. A 2015 survey from job service company FlexJobs revealed that 85% of millennials want to telecommute 100% of the time.[45] The ability to work remotely will be powerfully attractive to that segment of a workforce.

Allowing people to work from home will require you to establish certain ground rules, including appropriate attire during conference calls, and adequate office facilities and work equipment at the employee's remote location. You may have to pay closer attention to ensure that productivity is maintained, and team members may be required to commute into the office once or twice per week, making themselves available in person for physical meetings. But these are mostly surmountable hurdles that, in large part, are vastly outweighed by the benefits.

There may of course be specific job functions that require people to be physically present in a location, and corporate culture may also discourage telecommuting. But unless you cannot get round such limitations, telecommuting needs to be on your list of options to attract top talent in the 21st century.

Remote domestic teams

Communication and collaboration tools also enable GCs to establish parts of their team in lower-cost domestic jurisdictions. In the United Kingdom, for instance, GCs might establish a team in Northern Ireland; in the United States, many parts of the Midwest or the South might be cost-effective locations. Setting up such a team can save you significant costs while ensuring continued quality.

Your ability to do this may depend on whether the company you work for has made such a move. If it has, take advantage of the facilities it has already established and hire some lawyers to work from there.

Global collaboration

Collaboration technologies will allow you to better manage teams remotely across the globe. If you have an international team, communication and collaboration tools will enable you to virtually bring the team closer together, breaking down silos to leverage your global strength, as will be discussed later in the chapter entitled "Strategic direction" in Part D.

You might, for instance, establish global practice groups, made up of your specialists who educate your field lawyers and formed into a group, thereby enabling them to supplement the deep-knowledge experts with triage and local training. You might also consider establishing project groups consisting of lawyers located in different time zones to enable your team to work on a matter 24 hours per day.

Self-help tools

Numerous cloud-based solutions exist that enable legal departments to conduct work that previously could only be done by law firms. These solutions include legal know-how, best practice and legal research, each of which is described further below.

Know-how

Know-how sites enable legal departments to access the information they need in order to help themselves. Firms such as Practical Law Company provide legal departments with various types of information, including:[46]

- *practice notes* on key legal topics, ranging from antitrust law to taxation, which are kept up to date by law firm partners and which thereby empower in-house lawyers to put together briefing memos for clients or educate themselves in areas in which they are not experts;

- *standard templates and clauses* on a similarly broad range of topics, which can be used to develop new agreements or clauses for contracts under negotiation; and
- *checklists and toolkits*, including charts, tables, timelines and flowcharts, as well as bundled resources in specific subject areas, which allow lawyers to access a multitude of best-practice guidelines when working in a new area.

Rather than paying law firms significant sums for generating such material, for a fixed subscription fee legal departments can have limitless access to such information in formats that enable them to be easily digested and/or customised.

Some law firms have realised this and now provide their clients with similar tools on a client portal on the law firm intranet, enabling clients to configure and download basic memoranda, templates or checklists.

Best practice
Best-practice sites provide legal departments with management insights that assist GCs and senior legal leaders to develop their people and run their department more effectively. These include:[47]

- *people solutions* to improve GCs' ability to recruit, assess, develop and engage staff;
- *practice management insights* that raise the bar on efficiency, process, performance, strategy and other aspects relating to running a legal department; and
- *technologies* that improve analytics, cost, engagement and other performance aspects of the function.

In the same way that self-help tools have chipped away at the margins of what law firms used to provide, best-practice tools are replacing some of the need to seek tailor-made advice from legal consultants for all best-practice advice. Much of that can now be obtained online (albeit usually behind a pay wall). These firms will sometimes supplement their online offerings with in-person briefings and analyses that are more specifically tailored to your department's needs.

Legal research

Legal research tools offered by companies such as LexisNexis and Westlaw provide content-enabled workflow solutions and online legal research that allow in-house attorneys to conduct their own legal research without the need to resort to external counsel. Some of the information available includes:

- *primary law tools* that help in-house teams find and verify primary legal sources, including case law and summaries, statutes, citations, head notes, case summaries, and law publications;
- *drafting and strategy solutions* that help organise and manage search results and research; and
- *databases* – including public records, background profiles, dossiers, and verdict and settlement analysis tools – that can be used to identify facts and build connections.

When taken together, these technologies provide in-house teams with powerful capabilities that provide greater transparency into what law firms and other providers should and should not be doing, allowing departments to more effectively focus their external legal expenditure on work that is truly value-additive.

Efficiency tools

Efficiency tools give legal departments powerful, innovative technologies that boost legal department effectiveness, productivity and speed. Many of these tools are cloud-based, eliminating the need for large up-front investment costs. Examples include contract management and matter management systems:

- *Contract management tools* enable a legal department to more effectively create, store and manage contracts, generating efficiencies across the entire contract lifecycle. At the creation stage, contracts can be more efficiently created and negotiated, using secure environments that facilitate draft mark-ups and sharing. Professionals can route contract related tasks to the appropriate parties, and track and record interactions and cycle times. When finally negotiated, agreements can be signed electronically and stored automatically. Renewal and other key milestones can be monitored and reported, facilitating document management.[48]

- *Matter management systems* allow legal departments to track cases and transactions, including current status, workflows and time spent. Contact systems can track, log and store details about telephone calls, e-mails and other communications involving the matter, while calendaring and docking solutions organise deadlines, tasks, appointments and meetings.[49]

Transparency tools

Transparency technologies help legal departments clearly determine how much they are paying their external providers and what they are paying for. Examples include e-billing software and online bidding platforms.

E-billing software

E-billing solutions analyse and enforce law firm invoices against billing policies, provide over-budget spending alerts, automate currency conversions, track taxes and customise fields and outputs to facilitate invoice analytics. The information generated by these systems provides GCs with enormous volumes of data about how department funds are being spent.[50]

Information such as this enables GCs to manage and track expenditure and negotiate better rates from providers. For any large department, this kind of technology is essential. As Accenture has observed:[51]

> We continue to be surprised when we discover that the legal department of a major company is still reviewing its legal bills on paper, or using an outdated, home grown solution. GCs no longer have the time to review bills to confirm the company is not being overcharged or that their Outside Counsel Billing Guidelines are being adhered to. This process should be automated—it saves time, is more accurate, and can produce insights that get lost in the minutiae of manual review.

As the saying goes, if you cannot measure it, you cannot improve it.

E-bidding platforms

E-bidding platforms enable large departments to secure the best deal among competing firms at any given moment for any given matter, by requiring providers to bid for the work. If your company generates a large volume of similarly situated transactions, you might consider putting each transaction up for tender with a preselected group of law firms on a panel (see the chapter entitled "Selecting the right partners" above in order to learn more about establishing law firm panels). Each firm will place a bid within a given time frame, with the lowest bidder being awarded the work.

This kind of solution can yield significant savings, since the firm that has the greatest capacity at any given time is likely to bid more aggressively. If the firms are preselected and similarly situated in terms of quality, there should not be significant deviations in that respect. The downside with this sort of approach can be that it may be perceived as somewhat mercenary by law firm partners, which in turn might discourage those firms from investing in a relationship because it seems to be primarily driven by cost.

Contract management systems also typically contain transparency components in the sense that they can track contractual terms, in addition to facilitating the creation of contracts. Renewal dates, payment deadlines and other critical timelines are tracked and highlighted. These, as well as the contract data points that can be gathered during the contract creation process, can yield information to help drive revenue or reduce costs. This benefit is, of course, reliant on having a solid process in place to provide the necessary inputs.

Artificial intelligence and machine learning

As noted above and in the first chapter of this book, AI technologies are performing ever more high-value work, including cross-disciplinary legal thinking and sophisticated document search-and-review solutions.

According to IBM, an astounding 2.5 quintillion (2.5×10^{18}) bytes of data are created every day, with 90% of all data ever created having been generated within the past two years.[52] This explosive growth in data has had a profound impact on lawyers in the document review context. Whether you are managing a document discovery process in connection with a lawsuit or conducting an internal investigation, the sheer volume of information can be overwhelming. As the *ABA Journal* has noted: *"Instead of wading through piles of paper, lawyers now deal with terabytes of data and hundreds of thousands of documents."*[53]

Rather than relying on outmoded Boolean search technologies (ie, where keywords are combined with connectors, such as 'and', 'not' or 'or', to produce relevant results), newer solutions are employing AI and machine-learning technologies to conduct more sophisticated searches that include visually identifying and understanding key topics or individuals, and employing pattern detection tools to find key events and anomalies.[54] This significantly reduces the time required to conduct e-discovery and document review because the sample data allows the program to search for concepts as opposed to simple keywords.[55] Instead of the lawyer being required to look at 10,000 contracts, she may only need to look at 100, saving time, money and drudgery.

Preventive technologies have also emerged that employ predictive coding that helps detect litigation or risk in real time. For example, a software program might monitor and overlay communications between traders with stock price movements, comparing these with other data points to detect patterns that might indicate fraud.[56] Such programs "can read through unstructured data and summarise conversations, including the ideas discussed, the frequency of the communication and the mood of the speakers."[57]

AI is also transforming legal research. Ross Intelligence, which leverages IBM's Watson technology, "responds to lawyers' questions in natural language by reading through the law, gathering evidence and drawing inferences. The program learns from the lawyers who use it to refine its search results. It also monitors the law and notifies users of new, relevant court decisions."[58] While the first customers in this area seem to be law firms,[59] this technology has promising applications in the in-house context as well.

Stay ahead of the curve

All of these technology categories, which are only a sample of what is available in the market today, are already impacting the way law is practised in-house. In the future, they will have increasingly profound implications for both legal departments and law firms, including the type of work undertaken by lawyers and legal professionals and how GCs will source work.

You would do well to stay ahead of these developments by keeping up with the legal-trade press and applying new technologies as and where appropriate, taking into account the limitations inherent in any technology solution and recognising the implications in relation to processes, behaviour and change management.

The procurement of technology

Once you have optimised your processes and determined what technology you need, you will have to decide whether to build it yourself or buy it from a provider in the market.

Build or buy?

Building your own solution has the advantage of being tailor-made to address your specific problem. Moreover, custom solutions will be designed to configure perfectly within your technology environment, ensuring there is less of a likelihood of technology interface issues in implementing and operating the tool within your broader environment.

The size and complexity of the department you run and the problems you are dealing with will probably determine whether this makes sense. In some cases, if the problems are small and simple, your technology team might be able to develop a simple and cost-effective fix; in such cases, a tailor-made solution would obviously make sense. Alternatively, if you are wrestling with a highly complex and very specific problem in a large department, there may be no alternative to commissioning a custom-built tool.

As a general rule you should opt for a ready-made solution rather than create something entirely from scratch. Custom-built solutions can be expensive and complex to construct, and cost overruns and delays might hamper your ability to operate or manage costs. There will also be the inevitable kinks and bugs to sort out once the system is up and running. Further, the system will require regular upgrades.

By contrast, cloud-based solutions that are sold in the market are generally of high quality, often have solid track records with other users, and contain most of what you need to address a large swathe of problems that you are likely to confront. Moreover, it may be easier to shift from one commercial tool to the next if you are unhappy with it than it will be to depart from a home-made solution that you have invested significant time and money into. This becomes increasingly attractive as available external technologies grow ever more advanced.

Off-the-shelf or customised?

If in the end you decide to buy in the market, you will also need to decide whether to buy a product off the shelf or configure it to your precise needs.

The same analysis will apply here as to the question of build versus buy. The optimal approach will depend on the specific needs you have and the problem you are trying to address. One common mistake that GCs make is to assume they need more configurations and options than they really do. It is important to keep in mind that each addition of functionality comes with an additional process or behavioural step that needs to be embedded into your workflow.

Before proceeding with an add-on, always ask yourself why you are looking at adding a particular configuration. What is the purpose? Why is it important to know a particular piece of information or have the ability to do something specific? What behavioural change needs to be driven in order to accomplish that additional task? Consider the change management implications that you will face, as outlined in the chapter below of that title.

The best tools are usually the simplest. Often, GCs build something only to subsequently discover that they do not really need or use the 'bells and whistles' they have added. So think long and hard about data you intend to collect or the functionality you are seeking, and then ask yourself whether it is worth the turbulence and cost. Run a cost–benefit analysis before you proceed. Simply put, if you do not currently need particular types of customised reports or data, having access to it may not be worth the cost.

Process, technology and risk reduction

Process improvement and accompanying technology solutions will not only help you to improve effectiveness; they can also help reduce overall legal risk by providing transparency and standardisation.

In terms of transparency, a solid process, supported by the right technologies, can make it less likely that you lose sight of important legal developments. For instance, contract management technology can be configured to alert your team in advance of upcoming contract renewal dates, payment events and other important moments in the contract life cycle.[60] Of course, such technology solutions ultimately depend on proper data input, which in turn is reliant on a good process.

Standardisation also can reduce legal risk, because by improving your effectiveness through standardisation, you will both minimise errors caused by deviations from correct procedure and free up resources to focus on more value-added and high-risk work.

The right process, supported by good technology will enable you to decide what work you need to focus your best people on, and what gets handled in a more routine manner. Instead of having a host of lawyers each doing their own variants of non-disclosure agreements, for instance, you might automate and self-service that need by using an intake process and the right technology, escalating to a lawyer only those cases that require departures from the norm.

Part C: The software

Culture

Culture is more like software than hardware because it needs to be constantly updated.
(Dharmesh Shah)[1]

Culture is the medium that makes or breaks your talent. It must therefore be the first stop on the 'software' side of your transformation. Culture is both the glue that holds a team together and the fuel that propels it toward high performance. A negative culture will destroy and repel good people, and a good culture will raise the performance of even the weakest performers.

This chapter will look at what culture is, why it is important, how you can influence it to move it in the right direction, and then what you can do to internalise it and make it meaningful for your people.

The company's broader culture is created at the corporate level and flows from there into all parts of the company. It is the company's board and senior leadership that set the tone and tenor of the company's culture, and the legal department and other enabling functions ultimately exist to support that effort. The legal department, as the legal guardian of the company's assets and reputation, has a vital role to play in shaping the company's broader culture by reinforcing governance and compliance. It is the GC's job to ensure that the board and senior leadership focus on these aspects of the company's broader culture.

With that in mind, and while the legal department must never seek to create its own separate culture that is independent of or in contradiction with the broader company culture, it is both possible and indeed desirable for the department to foster a subculture that enhances its ability to support the company's objectives by accelerating performance.

Culture has a critical role to play in how people are viewed, hired and managed. A healthy culture, one that moves the organisation's goals forward, is crucial to success. It is in this respect that we consider the role that culture has to play on the software side. This chapter is about how you can shape your department subculture so that it is better positioned to achieve excellence, without going against the company's broader culture.

What is culture?
Culture can be viewed and understood from two levels: behaviour and beliefs.

Culture as behaviour

At a surface level, culture can be defined as a way of behaving or working – ie, how people are encouraged to interact with each other, how they dress and speak, or what the workspace looks like. In this sense, culture might be manifested in how people talk to customers, how they interface with each other, or the humour they share at the water cooler.[2]

Culture as values and beliefs

At a deeper level, culture embodies the core values and beliefs that a group shares. An example of a value or belief is grit – ie, motivation and determination to succeed over long periods of time, despite setbacks and hardship. This belief may explain why a football team performs so highly and scores so many goals.[3] In her book *Grit*,[4] Angela Duckworth describes the culture of the Seattle Seahawks, an American football team that is famous for being gritty. She notes how coach Pete Carroll has created a program that reinforces that culture of grit through innumerable competitive opportunities, moments and illustrations, all feeding the sense of passion and determination that defines the team's values and beliefs. Coach Carroll notes how he looks for players who "really have grit. The *mindset that they're always going to succeed*, that they're resilient, they're not going to let setbacks hold them back ... It's that attitude – we really refer to it as grit"[5] (my emphasis).

Values and beliefs cause outcomes.

Culture as a synthesis of the two

The best way to understand culture for our purposes is to bring these two viewpoints together. Culture can be deemed the shared values and beliefs that influence the way people behave or work in a given group.

Cultures and subcultures

As you think about how to approach culture, take stock of the differences in your company's culture and its subcultures, so that you can improve effectiveness through alignment.

All companies have multiple subcultures, usually emanating from the different functional or geographic groupings that exist in the company.[6]

While distinct from the broader and overarching culture, these subcultures share most of the broader culture's values and beliefs.

The legal department may, in its turn, have multiple subcultures that are distinct from the broader subculture of the legal department as a whole. For instance, a legal team in Iowa and a legal team in India may display subcultures that are very distinct from each other and from the subculture of the headquarters legal department, even as they share the broader values and beliefs of that department – just as the legal department itself will be distinct from, but share the broader values and beliefs of, the corporation.

Usually, there is relatively little you can do to meaningfully shape the corporation's broader culture. It is what it is, and you are likely to have to work within it, for better or for worse. There are some changes, however, that can be made to the legal department's subculture, as well as any subcultures that exist within it.

Subcultures must be aligned with the company's culture
Subcultures can be constructive. Cultures are what tie people together through shared values and beliefs – and local ties are often the strongest. But in order to be productive, subcultures must be aligned and consistent with the broader culture's pivotal values.[7]

'Pivotal' values are those values that the company has identified as central to its identity and functioning.[8] Individuals who fail to conform to these values are typically terminated for good reason, because they threaten to disrupt the company's core values and beliefs. Subcultures that are inconsistent with these values will similarly have a detrimental effect on the broader culture.[9] Subcultures can, however, differ from the broader company's peripheral values – ie, those values that are non-essential to the broader company's functioning, without negatively impacting the broader company culture; indeed, in some cases this can be very positive.[10]

An analogy might relate to the US military: the broader culture is that of the United States as a nation. Below that are subcultures such as the Army,

Navy, Air Force and Marine Corps. Below these are additional subcultures, such as those expressed by the divisions, brigades, battalions, companies, platoons and squads that make up the US Army. These subcultures hold the smaller units together, maintaining peoples' pride in their uniqueness. This is positive, *provided* the subcultures are aligned with the pivotal values of the Army, Navy, Air Force and Marine Corps and, ultimately, the United States of America.

In order to ensure that a support function such as the legal department is able to provide optimal client service, it is critical that the subculture be aligned with that of the broader culture, such that the department's subculture promotes rather than detracts from the company's culture. For example, the legal department might have an exceptionally pronounced customer service culture that goes above and beyond that of the company as a whole. Such a deviation would in no way detract from the company's broader culture. By contrast, if the legal department were to adopt a radically hierarchical culture within a broader company culture that was radically non-hierarchical, it would then detract from the company's pivotal values.

Actual culture in comparison with stated values and beliefs

Consider the interplay between actual and stated culture. A culture may consist of shared values and beliefs but it does not necessarily follow that these are the same as the company's stated values and beliefs. In an ideal world they would be the same; but words on a page do not a culture make, even if well written and obvious.

While merely having a defined set of prominent corporate values has been shown to have no impact on a company's short or long-term financial performance, the actual behaviour of the company's senior managers (and the values they embody) can make an enormous difference.[11] Having stated values that are misaligned with your real culture can be worse than meaningless, because it can create cynical and dispirited employees and can alienate customers, undermining credibility in the leadership.[12] Furthermore, the values stated may have been created by a public relations function or a marketing team having nothing to do with the real views of the company's leadership.

Rubberstamping a list of nice-sounding words does not change the culture into something new.

Enron Corporation's Code of Ethics is a case in point. It is clear and well written, and everyone can agree with it. But Enron filed for bankruptcy in 2001 after it transpired that it had engaged in institutionalised, systematic and creatively planned accounting fraud and corruption.[13] The company's stated values were clearly at odds with its actual culture. The dichotomy between Enron's stated values and its actual culture came back to haunt its leaders when its Code of Ethics was held up by journalists and commentators as evidence of Enron CEO Jeffrey Skilling's guilt.[14]

That's not to say that Kenneth Lay, Enron's chairman, and Skilling intended to end up where they did (Skilling was convicted of federal felony charges in connection with Enron's collapse and was sentenced to more than 24 years in prison, while Lay was found guilty of 10 counts of securities fraud but died shortly before sentencing).[15] As Professor Clayton Christensen of Harvard Business School (who attended business school with Skilling) noted, the "Jeffrey Skilling I knew from our years at HBS was a good man. He was smart, he worked hard, he loved his family."[16] Skilling himself may even have believed that he was doing the right thing. He noted in a 2001 interview just months before the collapse of the company, "[w]e are the good guys. We are on the side of angels."[17] It is unlikely that either of them woke up one morning and decided to begin a life of crime; people have a tendency to overemphasise character and underemphasise situational circumstances in the ethical decision-making context.[18]

The main story of Enron is less about evil leaders than it is about what Harvard Business School professor and corporate governance specialist Malcolm Salter calls 'a case of ethical drift'.[19] In his opinion, "Enron is a case about how a team of executives, led by Ken Lay, created an extreme performance-oriented culture that both institutionalised and tolerated deviant behaviour."[20] That culture stood in stark contrast to the values the company espoused.

As David Burkus has pointed out:[21]

Instead of reinforcing the code of ethics and the list of virtuous core values, the actions of leadership established a culture with values of greed and pride. While the printed code of ethics described the company's commitment to "conducting the business affairs of the companies in accordance with all applicable laws and in a moral and honest manner" ... and espoused the virtues of integrity and respect as core values, the behaviours and attitudes of its people often stood on the opposing pole.

Words have consequences, especially when they are at odds with actual behaviour.[22] So stated values should not be aspirational; instead, they should reflect the culture you actually have, reinforcing the best of that culture. People within your organisation should intuitively nod their head and agree that they reflect who you are.

If you already have stated values and are unsure whether they are authentic, a quick test devised by Levi Nieminen[23] will help you to determine whether that is the case:

- Think of the three most challenging situations your team has faced in the past couple of years, and then ask yourself whether your values helped to make sense of what was done and why.
- Recall the last three times when your team had to make a decision based on insufficient information. In each case, think about how the decision was reached and whether your values helped to explain or justify what was decided and why.

If your answers are that your decision-making in these situations was divorced from your values, there may be a disconnect between your culture (how you actually dealt with these situations) and your values (how you stated you would act).

There may be certain limited times and places to set out aspirational values, but that is a dangerous game to play as you are building your team. There is little upside in most cases, and a lot of downside.

Why is culture important?

Culture as a baseline

Your legal department's culture is the essential medium in which your team works. If the culture is polluted or suboptimal, your team will be unable to perform at their best. You will fail to keep your top talent if they find themselves stuck in a mediocre or counterproductive culture that neither values their efforts nor allows them to feel self-fulfilled.

Money alone will not keep good people engaged and loyal. According to Leigh Branham, while 89% of managers believe their employees leave for money, in fact 80%–90% of employees leave for reasons other than money.[24]

Poor or negative culture can also be an indicator for actual destruction. The behaviour patterns that reflect organisational culture are a powerful tool for getting people to follow encouraged norms. A culture that tolerates loose ethics or corruption, or that values winning over all other values, may give people a sense that they have a licence to commit crimes or violate ethical norms. An ethically weak but strongly reinforced culture can, as Kotter and Heskett have noted, lead to lots of bright people walking together off a cliff.[25] The best way to kill an organisation is to instil a negative culture and leave it to fester.

Culture as an attractant

A good culture is a predominant factor in the hiring and retaining of talent.[26] That dynamic will only grow as millennials increasingly take over the workplace. Millennials often value good culture and seek out organisations that have it. A recent study, for instance, found that millennials searching for a new job were willing to take an average pay cut of $7,600 for an improved quality of work life, such as career development, purposeful work, work–life balance and/or company culture.[27]

The ultimate purpose of having a great culture is therefore to attract the best people and enable them to do their best work, which in turn significantly impacts an organisation's long-term performance.

In one study, companies with cultures that emphasised customers, stockholders, employees and leadership outperformed those that did not over an 11-year period.[28] The same study showed that companies with strong performance-enhancing cultures achieved revenue growth that was four times that of companies without strong cultures; in similar fashion, employment growth was almost eight times as good, stock prices were more than 12 times as good, and profit growth was more 750 times as good.[29]

Building a culture

Building a legal department culture can be difficult because it reflects the collective values and beliefs of a group of individuals, heavily influenced by senior management. Culture grows from deep within the base of those who come together to lead the team.

The extent to which you can build a culture from scratch depends greatly on whether the culture you want to influence is a 'legacy culture' – ie, a culture that already exists in an organisation – or a completely new culture.

It is virtually impossible to rebuild a legacy culture from scratch. The culture is already there, is probably very well-rooted, and any attempt to tear it down and rebuild something in a different (ie, your own) image will undoubtedly end in failure. You can, however, change the shape of a legacy culture. Indeed, one of the core responsibilities you have as a new leader is to shift your team's culture in the right direction. But you will be unable to single-handedly impose your version of a culture on people who already exist in the context of a legacy culture – it must be a collective effort.

By contrast, building a culture from the ground up is possible in a new culture that does not yet fully exist. However, to do so demands that you be disciplined about who you hire and how you reinforce the cultural norms to ensure that it grows in the direction you want to grow it. Even then, it is easier said than done to fully build a culture from scratch.

Two scenarios are worth considering, as set out next.

Legacy cultures – evolution not revolution

In legacy organisations, there is already a culture present. The reason you cannot readily establish a new culture in a legacy organisation is because it requires a collective effort of everyone involved, and you are likely never to be able to move everyone, especially long-serving employees, over to your view. But you can *shift* the existing culture in the direction you want to take it, which will free you up to focus on accelerating performance.

This is a very delicate operation. If you push too far too fast, you will damage the foundations of the existing culture, which can have disastrous consequences.[30] It is far easier to destroy a culture than it is build one up. Robert Richman, former culture strategist at Zappos and author of *The Culture Blueprint*, likens culture to a skyscraper: it can take years to build, but moments to destroy.[31] Once you have destroyed it without replacing it with something else, you will lose most of your talent and find yourself adrift – or, more likely, you will be so disliked that you will find yourself out of a job.

Think of it as you would the pruning of a bonsai tree. You need to be very careful not to damage the trunk or kill the tree, which takes a long time to grow. But you can prune the branches and gradually tilt the tree's direction, so that its shape changes over time. Yet all the while, the trunk remains firmly in place. In the same way, within a legacy organisation you will want to identify the core elements of its culture and the subculture of the legal department, so as to determine which aspects you want to influence. Which branches do you want to develop and which will you prune?

The changes you are seeking to instil are more iterative than revolutionary. You are seeking to improve those parts that are suboptimal, keeping the base intact. To do that, you need to find an opening and build on your credibility.

Find an opening

You need to find a legitimate reason to convince people in a legacy culture to change. All change is hard, but culture change is even more difficult because it requires people to change their practices in ways that impact their beliefs. In order to institute meaningful change, you have to find an opening – a reason why the change is needed. Cultures tend to be stable, but they are never static; changes, ruptures and events continually shape them.[32] In the legacy culture context, such changes provide the openings that you need to create that "why".

Openings can occur when the company enters a new market, or experiences a financial crisis or other setback. Be alert to such changes and take advantage of them, as they can meaningfully accelerate the influence you want to impose on the culture.

If you are beginning your tenure as a new GC, be careful about considering your arrival to be such an opening, at least in the near-term. It can be an event that focuses the minds of everyone and could give you an opportunity to voice your opinion. But you will have very little credibility in the first 100 days in a new job. If you are coming from outside the company, you may not be able to fully understand the culture or the business. And even if you rose up through the ranks, you have yet to gain any meaningful credibility in your new job.

Build on your credibility

People are unlikely to listen to you unless you have established credibility. That is one big reason why you should work on the hardware before you touch the software. Improving the hardware gives you the credibility you will need to shape the software.

It is, of course, possible to start the other way round. Indeed, there may be occasions where it could be sensible to start with the software, depending on the political, transitional or other circumstances your team finds itself in. But generally speaking, if you attempt to change the firm's culture without having changed any of the tangible aspects of the organisation, people will be reluctant to take a risk and follow you. Why should they? Your ability to successfully drive change is untested.

Culture change is hard work and can be risky for people. They will not follow you if all you can point to are mere words. They want to see *action* – proof that you can deliver – before they even take one step along your pathway.

But if you have successfully defined your core risks, shifted your organisation structure in alignment with that definition, introduced a new strategic framework, appointed a new leadership team, rolled out new technologies, recalibrated your outside counsel relationships and brought department costs under control, you will have demonstrated your staying power and your ability to deliver on the message of change.

In addition, changing the hardware before the software helps you to identify more specifically what aspects of your culture need to be changed and gives you the narrative underpinning that you need in order to advocate for those changes. For example, if you have introduced new productivity tools and data analytics, it will be much easier to advocate for a cultural shift on how people are prioritising their time.

Influencing within a new culture

If you are involved in a start-up or some other very new organisation, you will be in a different place from a GC operating within the confines of a legacy culture. The same applies if you are the founding lawyer in a legal department and you have the opportunity to hire every member of your team from scratch. In both of these cases, you will be in a position to shape the culture or subculture in profound, foundational ways from the start. Unfortunately, many people in this position consider themselves to be too busy building the business or department to be conscious about how they are building their cultures.[33]

That is a big mistake. Poor culture will kill your organisation as quickly and efficiently as poor products, lousy service or a maladapted strategy. If you allow a poor culture to grow and flourish, you will repel the talent you need to deliver excellence. Establishing the culture you want to see is truly foundational and comprises a number of steps as set out next.

Write your cultural basis down

You need to ensure that you take the time to decide up-front what kind of culture you want your organisation to have. Write down the key elements, actions you need and results you expect; and then validate it. Design what you want as you would any other aspect of your organisation. It is crucial to do this early on, because the faster your growth trajectory, the less time you will have and the harder it will be to change.

Dharmesh Shah, Founder and CTO of HubSpot, has noted that writing down the things that are important in your culture puts you in a position to consciously recruit talent that reflects your cultural norms (see Figure 18). Lawyers can be particularly skilled at this sort of exercise. For online retailer Zappos, the legal department was the entity that actually took the initiative at the very beginning to map out the company's desired culture to a set of criteria, refining its values from 30 down to a set of 10.[34] Each department was then told to apply those criteria to their approaches to recruiting, training and termination.[35]

If you fail to write your culture down, you run the risk that you will only hire people who are like you, because you have no loadstar to guide your decision-making and ensure diversity. You need to be vigilant and weed out those who don't fit your cultural criteria.[36]

While writing down the cornerstones of your culture is important at any time in the life of your organisation, it is particularly critical in the beginning, when your culture has yet to take firm root. The cost of hiring a few maladjusted people early on is much higher than the cost of hiring those same people later, because the tender shoots of your culture are more fragile in the beginning and easily prone to destruction. Later on, when the trunk is firm, it takes more strain to tear things apart.

Writing down the key elements of your culture will also give you the opportunity to measure your culture against an ideal, track where it is veering away from that ideal, and design your reward and reinforcement mechanisms with the ideal in mind. Not having it written down means you do not really know what your culture is. That in turn is leaving the development of your culture to chance.

Beware of the unwritten rules
Every culture has unwritten rules and assumptions upon which it rests. These typically have more influence over culture than the written ones. One big aspect of writing down your culture is ferreting out its unwritten

components and spelling them out. In order to understand your culture, you must understand its unwritten components as well as you do its written ones.

It can be useful to test how accurate your stated cultural cornerstones are by identifying and spelling out the unstated rules that actually govern your culture in day-to-day situations. For example, if one of your stated rules is that people look out for each other, you might consider carefully how the department actually is expected to act when someone has a birthday or has secured a big win. Do the unwritten rules mandate flowers or recognition in such cases? Or not? How people are actually expected to behave in such cases will tell you a lot about the authenticity of your stated rules.

The HubSpot Culture Code

1. We commit maniacally to both our **mission** and our **metrics**.
2. We look to the long term and **Solve for the Customer**.
3. We **share openly** and are **remarkably transparent**.
4. We favour **autonomy** and take **ownership**.
5. We believe our best perk is **amazing people**.
6. We dare to be **different** and question the status quo.
7. We recognise that **life is short**.

Figure 18: The HubSpot Culture Code
(Source: HubSpot – see www.slideshare.net/HubSpot/the-hubspot-culture-code-creating-a-company-we-love/)

Consider also benchmarking your existing employees against your cultural criteria, for example when conducting regular performance reviews, as this will help to reinforce cultural norms with your existing team.[37]

Culture hacking

Culture can change and evolve over time as people come and go and as the organisation shifts. Your job is to ensure that you help to guide the evolution of your culture. You do not want to leave it to chance, because too much is riding on having a thriving and constructive culture. As GC, you need to continually focus on your department's culture, influencing it and ensuring that it is growing in the right direction.

That is not to say that developing and nourishing a culture is only a top-down activity. As noted earlier, while senior management is the primary influencer, an organisation's culture is ultimately created by everybody and is the product of collective principles and practices, much like a garden is the sum of all of the trees, plants, insects and animals that live within it. But like a garden, you can either let your culture grow wild or you can prune it, manage it and ensure that it has a particular look and feel. The best gardens tend to be those that strike a balance between the organic and the designed. As a general counsel, you must be a constant gardener – removing weeds, planting flowers, watering and nourishing, and adapting to the needs of the season. Yet you can't be overbearing or the end result will be artificial and contrived; nothing will flourish.

'Culture hacking' is another way to think of how this constant process of culture improvement works. In the IT context, a hacker is someone who is constantly probing software systems, looking for vulnerabilities and a way into the system. Sometimes the hacker will be iterative, employing frequent but small efforts to identify opportunities; at other times, he may apply a more concentrated burst of organised effort. Similarly, as GC you can borrow this concept to 'hack' your legal department culture.

'Culture hacking' can be defined as taking intentional actions to affect positive change in the organisational culture.[38] Unlike real-world hackers, however, the purpose is uniformly positive. You are seeking to strengthen and improve the culture rather than break in and destroy it.

Culture hacking is a concept that emanated from, and is typically associated with, entrepreneurial companies, particularly those in Silicon Valley. Zappos typifies this approach. As Richman sees it:[39]

> *Hacking goes beyond programming when people realise that, like a computer network, all of life is made up of complex systems. And if we know the vulnerable points where a small action can have a big impact, then we can "hack" those systems. ...*

What hackers do is look at a whole system and find the weak point to exploit. It's a vulnerable place within the system. Then once they find it, they experiment until they find something that makes a big impact.

Richman and many of his Silicon Valley compatriots see culture hacking as confined to small, iterative acts. However, culture hacking can also involve large-scale efforts. What follows below are some approaches on how you might hack your culture in both large and small ways.

Large-scale hacks

Every now and then you need to step back and consider the state of your culture in a coordinated and organised fashion. This should be done using a structured format as outlined below.

Make time together with a select group of members of your team, in an off-site location, for three to five days of concerted thinking about your legal department's culture. Your aim is to probe it to identify and disrupt unwritten assumptions that are no longer relevant or are actively blocking the department's progress. It is also an opportunity to think in new ways about the team's purpose and how its culture can best serve that purpose.

The process of a large-scale hack is time-consuming and labour-intensive, but it is well worth the effort, as it will tell you a lot about your culture, what ails it and what gives it strength. Best of all, it will start a dialogue within the department about how to improve it so you can accelerate your team towards top performance.

Form a culture-hacking team

The first step in this process is to form the right team. As culture comes from everyone in your team, a large-scale hack must be done collectively. Pull together a diverse group from across the department. The group should ideally consist of no more than five people.

In order for the hack to have legitimacy, it is critical that the team remain connected and engaged with others as an ongoing process across the organisation, taking ideas from the broader organisation back in to the working group and vice versa. The group should act as a catalyst for broader alignment rather than as an elite group that comes back with all of the answers.

To ensure that the team has cultural legitimacy, the selection process must be perceived as fair and transparent. You might invite people to submit a statement of interest, explaining why they can best contribute to the team's effort. You could then select the team based on a combination of best fit between their statements and the team's objectives, and the need to appoint the most diverse team possible.

To be truly diverse, the team must consist of more than just senior attorneys, leadership team members, or people from headquarters or the largest market; it should consist of people from all levels and all parts of the department.

Once you have formed your team, invest in time away for several days to brainstorm. This may not be the only time the team will be working together; the project could go on for several months.

But it is critical that you get everyone in one physical location on at least one occasion during the hack. Brainstorming is a creative process that requires trust and sustained interaction. Failure to bring your group together in the same place for a period of time will make it hard to build that trust and the sustained intensity needed to light a creative spark. To this end, it may be appropriate to bring in an outside facilitator who ensures properly directed brainstorming and knows when and how to put ideas and concepts into a "parking lot" when not central to the topic under discussion yet crucial to the entire process.

Clarify your roadmap

Before you attempt to hack your culture, be clear on what your vision, mission and strategic priorities are. If you don't yet have these in place, make sure you establish them before you go any further (see Part D of this book on how to do that). Your vision acts as your destination; your mission is about what you will do to help achieve the vision; and your strategic priorities are the how that will help you achieve your mission.

This strategic framework serves as both your destination and your compass. Your culture serves as the fuel for the journey.

Identify your unwritten cultural assumptions

Once you have clarified your roadmap, you can begin to assess the underlying assumptions on which your culture rests, so that you can compare these with where you want to head and decide which of them will help and which will hinder you in getting there.

Every culture operates based on certain assumptions. Some of these might be openly and clearly stated, such as your core values. Others, however, will be unwritten and perhaps even subconscious. For purposes of your hack, these are the assumptions that you want to identify, so that you can determine whether they are ripe for disruption in order to strengthen your culture.

The Ryanair example is worth noting. Michael O'Leary, CEO of Ryanair, became famous for disrupting the airline industry.[40] He identified the basic unwritten assumptions that the airline industry had come to rely on, such as bundled ticket prices for seats, luggage and meals, and the use of different aircraft models. He then questioned the validity of each of them in order to decide which ones were ripe for disruption. This in turn led him to arrive at a new model for how an airline should be operated.[41] O'Leary effectively hacked the airline model by identifying the unwritten assumptions that the industry rested on, decided which ones were ripe for disruption and then disrupted them.

Like unwritten industry assumptions, organisational culture rests on a score of unwritten assumptions that form the basis for day-to-day interactions within the organisation. Identifying and examining these, and then asking in a structured manner which ones are helpful and which ones are not in terms of moving you toward your vision, can be a powerful way to hack your culture.

Tease out your assumptions through creative thinking

The foregoing process can be more difficult than it sounds. You will need to get the team to think loosely and freely in order to come up with the list of assumptions that underpin your culture. These could be correct or incorrect assumptions. The point is to get them out in the open so that you can understand them and evaluate them in light of your strategy.

One way to tackle this is to categorise your organisational assumptions in broad themes based on how you and others see your culture. For instance, you might conduct separate brainstorming sessions on work prioritisation, responsiveness, cost effectiveness and collaboration. You might tease out the unwritten assumptions in each category via hypotheticals. Some examples, inspired by or based on the work of Alan Iny and Luc de Brabandere, both of the Boston Consulting Group, are presented below.[42]

- *Imagine your legal department was shut down by the CEO.* The legal department is eliminated five years from now. Why did that happen? Who is doing the legal work now? What was the competitive edge that the latter had?

- *Imagine you have 10 minutes to decide how to cut the department in half.* What if you had to do this? How could that be done? What would be the rationale for it? What would the benefits and disadvantages be?

- *Imagine you have 10 minutes to decide how to double the department's size.* What implications would this have on the way you provide services? Would it be good or bad? How would the relationship with external providers change? What would the cost implications be?

- *Imagine a forced merger of the legal department.* If the legal department were forced to merge its activities with another support function – either one it has some synergies with or one that it has no synergies with – what would that look like? How would it impact, for better and for worse, such things as the department's service delivery or work prioritisation? What new models might arise from it?

- *Describe the department from a different angle.* Try to imagine describing what the legal department does to non-experts of all stripes. Describe the department to different people, such as a small child, a sanitation worker or a teacher.

- *View the department from the perspective of a third party.* What are the things you, as a supplier, love about the department? What would an internal client or business partner love and hate about the department's culture? Consider validating your conclusions by asking your actual suppliers and business partners, before bringing it all back together in one list.

Identify those assumptions that are ripe for disruption

These exercises will generate a list of ideas, thoughts and assumptions about how the department is working. Once you have a comprehensive list, examine each assumption sceptically, asking which of these assumptions are true and which are those that you think truly create barriers to achieving your strategic objectives. You will want to identify what Iny and de Brabandere characterise as "those 'ways we've always thought about things' that could most benefit from reconsideration and/or reinvention".[43]

You might, for example, conclude that your department culture rests on the following assumptions:

- All issues are unique and require a tailor-made solution.
- Trust is essential to legal department credibility.
- Communication among department personnel is vital to success.
- All work is of equal importance.
- All important work needs to be validated by outside counsel.

Your next task is to decide which of these assumptions should be left intact and which should be disrupted. Do this by asking which ones help to achieve your mission and strategic priorities and which ones are hindering you from doing so. Some will be obvious. In the above example, the second and third assumptions are likely to be left intact, whereas the first, fourth and fifth assumptions may require further investigation.

Test the list of questionable assumptions

Once you have identified your list of possibly questionable assumptions, probe them further. Explore what the department might look like without these assumptions in place.

Roll out timescales for disrupting the finalists

Once you have identified which assumptions need to be laid to rest, you will need to think through which of these can be disrupted now, which you may need to wait to disrupt until next year and which are longer-term disruptors – eg, in five years.

Ensure you circulate the ideas before reaching conclusions

As noted earlier, it is important that, during the entire process, those who are not on the hacking team are kept informed and involved, because the effort needs to be a collective one. Each team member should take back the conclusions reached during the brainstorming sessions for feedback and calibration before the final list of disruptions is settled on. There should also be a discussion before the timescales are determined.

You may consider airing your conclusions with business partners before moving forward, both to validate this process and to ensure there is broader organisational alignment behind your activities.

Finally, as noted earlier, make sure that any changes you are making to the legal department culture are aligned with the company's broader culture. This is absolutely critical.

Small, iterative hacks

In addition to, and perhaps more importantly than, the occasional large-scale hacks of the kind noted above, you should be focused on conducting small, iterative hacks because "culture is living and breathing, not something that you work on once a year, after your annual employee engagement survey".[44]

You must nourish your culture because it is the environment you live in. Like the global environment, pollution is something that is combated every day, not once a year. These are not hacks that are conceived at an offsite meeting. Rather, they are small, incremental improvements that people discover and attempt to instil during their daily work.

Small-scale culture hacking is therefore about constantly seeking and probing to find new, small ways to adjust your culture so that it is moving towards the values you have identified and, ultimately, the mission and strategic priorities that are critical to accelerating your department's performance.

How and when iterative hacks are done will depend on the needs of the individual organisation. However, the steps that should be taken should be similar, regardless of the nature of the hack. Here is a five-step approach.

Step 1: Be clear about the strategic and cultural framework

The first step is to ensure that everyone in the department is very clear on what the cultural values and strategic framework are. If your company or department has written down its culture in a culture code, this is clearly a critical part of that effort. Make sure everyone knows where you want to head, because culture hacking is ultimately aimed at improving the department's ability to get there.

Step 2: Identify problems and shortcomings

Be constantly on the lookout for issues and situations that frustrate the department's ability to achieve its values and strategic framework.

One thing that is essential to getting this right is that it cannot be a top-down process. Everyone needs to be observant and able to raise concerns. As Zappos's Richman has noted, culture is co-created:[45]

> *If you think culture is a one-person job or you think you can have a Chief Culture Officer; if you think you can delegate culture, or just 'get it done' like a project or a task on your to-do list, think again. Culture can never be created. It can only be co-created.*

The key to securing collective buy-in in this respect is communication. There are several approaches here that can work:

- *Iterative communication:* You need to ensure that there is a mechanism for people to alert you to problems that are frustrating the culture at any time, so that they don't have to either wait for a formal survey, or figure out where to go if they have concerns or ideas.

  If you are in a large organisation, you need to devise some means to ensure that people are able to notify the broader team about the frustrations they see. You might therefore appoint a person or group to be the collectors of information, or have a website where people can post their ideas. Or you might make each manager responsible for picking up the ideas that are generated by their teams.

In a smaller organisation, people might address problems themselves, without any formal mechanism, alerting the others informally.

- *Regular surveys:* In addition to an iterative process, you can conduct regular department-wide surveys outside the formal human resource process, to capture what people are thinking and feeling. This could be a simple 10-question process that tracks key metrics over time, with room for people to add comments or open thoughts. Make sure you communicate the results of these surveys to the entire department, so that everyone is involved.

- *Unplugged sessions:* Hold regular, informal, off-the record sessions with small groups of people, led by yourself and senior leaders in your department at regular intervals across the organisation. Use these sessions to capture good ideas and bring them back for handling, or allow them to go forward with your encouragement if they are local.

- *Town hall meetings:* Conduct regular department-wide meetings, where you provide feedback on how you are handling culture issues that have come up and take questions and comments.

Step 3: Identify the source of the problem

Once you have identified a problem, you need to find its source so that you can address it. For example, if someone has identified a process that is cumbersome and contrary to your stated goal of efficiency, consider the process in detail and determine whether and how the current configuration could be improved. Where is the pain point? Is each step in the process truly necessary?

Step 4: Fix the problem

Identify a simple way to improve the problem that has maximum impact. You may need to try to solve the issue through several fixes before it gets solved.[46] Once it gets solved, make sure that the solution, and the person or people who identified both the problem and the solution, are publicly celebrated in some way.

Step 5: Democratise the process

It is critical that the process for iterative culture hacking be as flat as possible. Most fixes will not require your involvement at all; they can be developed and implemented directly by the teams involved, perhaps with the input or awareness of one or two of your senior leaders.

You want to ensure that these issues get communicated up the chain so that you can track and announce problems and improvements, holding up solutions as examples for the rest of the team. There is a valid control aspect in ensuring that you consider large-scale problems or solutions that may have far-reaching consequences before they are implemented, but this will be the exception rather than the rule. As a general rule, though, you do not want to let processes and procedures, which can serve a useful purpose, mire you down or prevent people from improving and drawing upon their own insights to strengthen the culture on a daily basis.

The saying that "you can't teach an old dog new tricks" is incorrect; you can actually teach old dogs tricks. But you can't teach a scared dog new tricks. You must ensure that the process you put around your approach to culture hacking encourages people to try to improve things, rather than frightens them away. Celebrate small improvements by publicly praising the person who uncovered the hack.

The more people are able to identify and solve their own issues within the framework of the roadmap you have laid out together, the more they will improve the culture independently of anything you are doing. As Barbara Gago notes:[47]

> *Small changes are going to be unique to every organisation because what matters to the culture will be different. Having the understanding and knowing where you are currently is half the battle ... having data on a regular basis will better support a culture that's living and breathing and increasing engagement regularly, not just 'revived' once every three years.*

Whether large-scale or small-scale, iterative culture hacking is not a one-time event. To reap its full benefits, it must become a constant probe that is built into your environment so that you are continually improving your culture and adapting it to changes taking place in your environment.

One way to keep this spirit alive is to conduct regular discussions about the importance of culture hacking and its centrality to the culture you are fostering. You might consider having regular culture 'hackathons' where people gather for a time to reflect on the culture and what needs to be improved. You can also consider stating the principle in writing and setting up an organised way of rewarding those who successfully identify ways to improve the culture.

Mars Corporation, which is well known for its strong and successful culture,[48] has listed as one of its Five Principles – which are the central tenants of its culture – the principle of responsibility, stating on its website:[49]

> *Our company is complex, with brands, businesses, and operations around the world. How could we continue to thrive if every decision were made centrally? For this reason, we give all Associates freedom to act with full responsibility for doing their assigned jobs. In return for accepting responsibility and delivering superior results, Associates receive respect and support, and are appropriately rewarded in line with their performance. We celebrate success and recognise the many Associates who make an extra effort.*

Mars follows through on this, publicly awarding employees who discover novel ways to improve their work, whether large or small.[50] This approach is a good example of how a large company with global operations has effectively embedded a hacking mentality into its culture in a very direct and public way. Culture hacking is not just the preserve of Silicon Valley start-ups.

Making cultural beliefs stick

The core beliefs that underpin a strong culture are invariably 'sticky', meaning that they are memorable and meaningful to the group. They tend to endure, even when old members leave the group and new ones join.[51]

It is important to do whatever you can to ensure that the culture you have worked so hard to develop and improve upon becomes resilient and meaningful to the people in your organisation. Otherwise, so much of what you have worked for will be lost.

There is no single way to ensure that your culture becomes 'sticky'. However, there are several principles that are often impactful and that are worth following. You might consider using some of the following concepts, used by leading companies, in your own culture, in order to nurture and protect it or reinforce new elements that you want to strengthen.

Screening

High-performing cultures screen all new employees against cultural norms. They take this very seriously at the hiring phase.[52] Amazon, for instance, has a group of employees it calls 'bar raisers', who sign off on potential hires to ensure they will be a good cultural fit.[53] Bar raisers can veto any candidate, even if they themselves are not proficient in the prospective employee's area of expertise. Amazon believes the programme, created by founder and chief executive Jeff Bezos, screens out those who won't fit in culturally.[54] Of course, adopting such an approach requires that an enormous amount of trust be placed in the bar raisers and there may be value in considering how to instil checks and balances into the process to ensure that they are not just bringing their own biases and prejudices into the analysis. One alternative might be to leverage such a system but have the decisions made by a group of bar raisers collectively, rather than by any one of them alone.

HubSpot also makes a point of ensuring that new hires will fit in culturally. The sales and marketing company has established 'culture parameters', which it uses when hiring new employees: candidates are asked questions on these parameters and their answers are rated.[55] A similar process is undertaken with existing employees as part of their performance evaluations.[56]

This kind of pre-employment screening is essential to ensure that you do not bring in people who are going to poison your legal department culture with antithetical values and beliefs. Consider imposing a similar policy, making sure to measure all newcomers against the cultural norms you are seeking to reinforce and weeding out all candidates who don't fit in with them.

Induction

Screening can be followed by an organised induction of all new employees. This is usually achieved through courses, seminars or shared experiences that indoctrinate newcomers into the culture's common beliefs. Facebook exemplifies this, organising a six-week induction programme called Bootcamp, which all new engineers, regardless of age or experience, must participate in.

During Bootcamp, new employees are immersed into the culture through shared experiences and indoctrination. It has been described as "one part employee orientation, one part software training program and one part fraternity/sorority rush."[57] David Kirkpatrick, author of *The Facebook Effect*, goes further, characterising it as "a quasi-religious iconoclasm"; "Facebook", he says, "takes its culture deadly seriously."[58]

Never turn your induction period into a "quasi-religious iconoclasm". Nevertheless, there can be significant value in doing more than just allowing HR to walk inductees through the pension plan and vacation schedule. Induction is a valuable opportunity to leave a first impression on newcomers about the role and importance of culture. Consider having a session on it, describing it and allowing others to do the same. Be structured about what you want people to take away as important; what you celebrate and what you enforce.

Rituals and reinforcement ceremonies

Once employees have been on-boarded, outstanding companies expose them to ongoing rituals and ceremonies that further reinforce their culture's shared beliefs and values.

David Novak, former CEO of Yum!, which owns fast-food giant KFC, is famous for having handed out funny awards to reinforce the company's quirky and expressive recognition culture, such as floppy rubber chickens that he personally gave employees at their desks in surprise ceremonies, replete with a roving brass band that played in the background.[59] As Novak noted: "when I first started giving out recognition awards, I decided I wanted them to be much more memorable than your typical plaque or a pen".[60]

This gets to the heart of what culture ultimately is all about. At its deepest level, culture is a feeling.[61] Just as the behaviours and cultural norms reflect commonly held beliefs, those beliefs in turn reflect feelings and emotions that make them come alive. However, be judicious in your process. The line between clever and embarrassingly silly is easy to cross and can then alienate a new employee and do more harm than good.

Memories and shared experiences are what create feelings. Consider how you might do the same in your culture. Awards and recognition ceremonies, even if different from the ones conducted at Yum!, can be vital reinforcement mechanisms.

Stories

Feelings about a culture are often further reinforced though stories and the examples of company legends and heroes who exemplify its values.[62] Employees are told and retold stories of great leaders who, in the past, have exemplified the culture, lived it and spoken its language. Videos of the speeches of such leaders are shown, explaining and reinforcing aspects of the culture.

At The Coca-Cola Company's headquarters, a quote from Robert W Woodruff, one of the iconic early presidents of the company, is etched in stone on the wall in the entrance foyer; furthermore, new employees tour Woodruff's office, which is preserved exactly in the same state it was in on the day he died in 1985, creating a shared bond of experience that transcends any single employee generation. Similar in many ways to the founding myths used by nation-states to align its citizens, stories about the company's founding fathers and successive later heroes who lived and sacrificed over generations give today's Coca-Cola employees a sense of pride and pedigree that goes back generations. As Richman notes, "ultimately it's stories and language that are powering culture. The more you develop the language and the stories in your organisation, the more you strengthen the culture."[63]

You might consider reinforcing your own culture with stories about colleagues who helped to shape your department culture. Whether you knew them or not, founding figures can help to put context to the legacy culture you are articulating – assuming their contributions were helpful, of course.

Influencers

Culture can be powerfully supported and reinforced by influencers from within your population.

Certain people have a disproportionate influence over others by virtue of their personal power – ie, their ability to connect and inspire people, ask the right questions, listen, provide support and encouragement, and create a safe environment.[64]

In his book, *The Tipping Point*, Malcolm Gladwell explores how ideas, trends and behaviours 'tip' and become social epidemics that spread like viruses.[65] Citing the 80/20 Principle, Gladwell notes that when it comes to social epidemics, a small number of people have an outsized influence over others and that "by finding and reaching those few special people who hold so much social power, we can shape the course of social epidemics".[66]

You need to identify those people within your culture who wield social influence over others. Identify them early on and co-opt them into your efforts. Lavish extra attention on them and spend time convincing them that your efforts on culture are critical. Ensure that they get leading roles in shaping your initiatives, and have them spearhead your communications efforts. Encourage them to write blogs, work on communications plans to roll out your effort, and outline elements of the cultural work they find appealing.

You will have an outsized impact if you are able to encourage your influencers to advertise and market your initiatives to the broader organisation.

Sanctions

Finally, great cultures recognise the importance of punishing those who transgress its norms. If people are allowed to defile a culture's shared beliefs, the 'sacredness' of the culture will lose its potency.

David Novak strongly believes that you need to get rid of cynics who don't buy into a company's culture, regardless of how good they might otherwise be. In his book, *Taking People with You*, he recounts an experience that illustrates this:[67]

> *There was this guy in our legal department at Yum! who was brilliant, but he didn't buy into our recognition culture; he wouldn't even pretend to participate. One time, when our roving recognition band started playing to honor someone receiving an award, he came out of his office and yelled at everyone to pipe down because he was trying to work. I couldn't imagine anything that would undermine the spirit of giving and receiving recognition more than that. He had to go ... I just couldn't have someone around who was actively working against that.*

While Novak's approach may seem harsh, it hits at a critical point: those who challenge the culture's norms and values must be removed or they will poison the well. You should consider instilling a similar policy.

Culture is a never-ending effort that, if approached correctly, will give you the medium within which your talent will thrive. It is to developing that talent that we next turn our attention.

The generational context and the rise of the millennials[1]

There is nothing more sad or glorious than generations changing hands.
(John Mellencamp)[2]

Millennials, gen-Xers and baby boomers

'Millennials', 'gen-Xers' and 'baby boomers' are terms used to characterise the three most recent demographic groups in the workforce. 'Millennials' are defined here as people born between the mid-1980s and the early 2000s; 'gen-Xers' (those in what's known as 'generation X') will have been born between the mid-1960s and the mid-1980s; and 'baby boomers' (the post-WW2 generation) are people born between 1946 and the mid-1960s.[3] Immediately following the millennials is 'Generation Z', born after the early 2000s and entering the workforce over the next 10 years or so;[4] they comprise an even larger generation whose traits and characteristics are just starting to be defined.[5]

One of the biggest people challenges facing general counsel is how to successfully manage the changeover between these generations. A particular challenge will be how to assimilate millennials with the earlier generations. The next generation of GCs will face similar issues with integrating Generation Z into their workforce, but at the moment the contours of that generation are still being shaped.

As baby boomers, who comprised nearly 70% of law firm partners in 2010,[6] retire in increasing numbers, millennials will take over around the globe. At an estimated 75 million people, millennials are already the largest living generation in the United States,[7] outnumbering gen-Xers by nearly three times.[8] By 2020 more than half of the world's workforce will consist of millennials;[9] and by 2025 they are expected to comprise three-quarters.[10]

The rise of the millennial generation is beginning to impact both the way in which professionals interact with each other as colleagues, clients, customers and suppliers, and how the work environment is structured. If GCs do not successfully manage this transition between workforce generations, they will find themselves unable to recruit, retain and motivate top talent, or to successfully integrate that talent into their cultures.

Before considering the rise of the millennials and the implications it has for the workplace, let us take a quick look at the two immediately preceding generations: the baby boomers and the gen-Xers. We must, of course, be careful about stereotyping entire generations; however, with that caveat in mind, there is value in exploring broad generational traits so that we can better anticipate the kinds of intergenerational conflicts that may arise in legal departments and take action now to avoid having them derail efforts to build an outstanding team.

The baby boomers

The baby boomers are the large generation of people who grew up during the economic boom that took place in the period immediately after World War 2, which also corresponded to a period when there was a surge in births.[11]

Common characteristics that typify this generation of legal professionals include the following:

- *Courageous:* Baby boomers grew up during the counterculture years of the 1970s and are typically confident and unafraid to state their opinions; in the legal profession, they will not shirk from challenging established practices if they feel that it is justified.[12]
- *Hard working:* Baby boomers have a reputation for working very hard, keeping long hours at the office. They rose in the legal ranks at a time of abundance and expansion, when globalisation and rapid expansion characterised the profession, and career progression was perhaps somewhat easier than it has been for succeeding generations – provided you put in the hours. That has not been an issue for ambitious baby boomers, many of whom are deeply motivated by professional achievement and prepared to pay the price that comes with it.[13] Many of them were also raised learning to accept delayed gratification.

    Many baby boomers believe gen-Xers and millennials lack a proper work ethic and do not have a commitment to the workplace in the same way that they have had. Many of them believe in 'face time' at the office, and there is a sense among them that these other generations have failed to 'pay their dues'.[14]
- *Affluent and reformist:* As a consequence of the growth of the legal profession in the 1980s and 1990s and the prevalence of the low-cost public education that characterised their student years, most

baby boomers avoided the heavy burden of student debt that has saddled subsequent generations.[15] The baby boomer era also witnessed the expansion of female talent into the legal workplace, shifting norms that had prevailed among previous generations.[16]

- *Ambitious:* Baby boomers are better educated than previous generations and have leveraged that education to further their professional achievement; they are often quite competitive and driven to win.[17] As lawyers, they can be very task-oriented and will work relentlessly to achieve success in projects or challenges that they lead.[18] They have pushed for standard evaluation processes in the workplace in order to improve transparency and facilitate the weeding-out of the less successful from the successful.[19]

- *Self-actualising:* Less conformist and loyal than the generation that preceded them, baby boomers were raised at a time of middle-class affluence, when self-actualisation became fashionable and possible.[20] Consequently, many baby boomers find meaning in their work, seeing it as an important source of self-expression, although they have tended to soften the hierarchical and conformist management style that prevailed during the 'Mad Men' era of their parents.[21]

The gen-Xers

The generation-Xers are a smaller group than both the baby boomers and the millennials. Demographers consider gen-Xers to be a 'middle child', squeezed between two larger generations either side.[22]

They are even more educated than baby boomers: 29% of them have undergraduate or graduate degrees as opposed to 23% for the baby boomers.[23] They are also more socially, economically, racially and ethnically diverse.[24]

Gen-Xers grew up during the economic transition in developed nations from a manufacturing economy to a service economy.[25] Between 1978 and 1988, the number of female lawyers and doctors increased by 300%, and many gen-Xers grew up in dual-income households. Consequently, gen-Xers were sometimes referred to as 'latchkey kids', who learned to let themselves into their homes after school while their parents worked.[26]

They were the first generation to be bombarded with a steady diet of child-directed advertisements on TV. As *Specialty Retail Report* has observed in one of its analyses:[27]

> *Media's huge influence on this generation has been attributed to the rise of dual-career households when little Xers were growing up. Women continued to push their traditional boundaries, their path to the workplace and other venues paved in part by the feminist movement of the '70s.*

Later, as they entered universities, gen-Xers experienced the AIDS epidemic rather than the 'free love' that the baby boomers experienced. Many graduated from university in the wake of the Black Monday stock market crash, when few jobs were to be had. The music they grew up on reflected this collective angst and pent-up anger, with Punk Rock riding the early wave and Grunge riding a later wave.

Fortunately, many of the youngest members of this generation entered the workforce during the more prosperous 1990s, giving them an economic lift as they left school and entered the professions.

The group traits of generation-Xers include the following:

- *Independent-minded:* Having grown up in households where both parents worked, gen-Xers learned from an early age to be wary of authority and to be independent-minded.[28] In their professional lives, they have placed a more overt emphasis on freedom and a desire for increased responsibility at an early age. Many gen-Xers prefer to work independently and are sceptical of traditional work norms, such as face time in the office and regulated work hours.[29]
- *Work flexibility:* Generation X has been characterised by a marked rise in professional female talent, resulting in a push for reform and flexibility in workplace norms. Working from home and flexible arrangements to accommodate family schedules increased significantly during their rise. Gen-Xers coined the 'work hard, play hard' mentality.[30] They are willing to put in the hours but, unlike many baby boomers, they are less willing to seek professional success at the expense of their personal lives.[31] Having entered the

profession in the 1990s, during a time of rising affluence, many of them are relatively well off financially – affluent gen-Xers now outnumber affluent baby boomers[32] – and are therefore able to push for more balance.

- *Change agents:* Gen-Xers have grown up during a time of enormous social and economic change. They are more flexible and comfortable in a world that is constantly reinventing norms than previous generations have been. Many of them have been more open to having multiple employers during their lifetime – unlike the baby boomers, who have more often preferred to remain with the same employer for decades.[33]
- *Technologically adept:* Gen-Xers were the first generation to come of age as personal computers were introduced. While perhaps not as savvy on social media as millennials, gen-Xers are comfortable with technology in the workplace. They are more technologically fluent than baby boomers and are more able to adapt in that regard.

The millennials in more detail

Generational traits
The traits that are characteristic of the millennial generation have been shaped by a number of forces. In addition to the rise of the internet, the smartphone and social media, many millennials grew up in a home environment that felt relatively more sheltered than that of earlier generations, with parents who considered them to be special from birth onwards.[34]

This sense of specialness and security in the home contrasted with the uncertainties of the macro-environment, including the 'Twin Towers' trauma of September 11 2001, the subsequent 'War on Terror' and the worldwide economic crash of 2008.

The significant traits that apply to millennials are as follows:
- *Digital natives:* First and most obviously, millennials are the world's first true 'digital natives'. None of the millennials can remember a time before computers, which has shaped both how

they interact with technology and their approach to creativity and innovation.[35] They have grown up in the social media era and their outlook is heavily influenced by it. For instance, 88% of them get at least some of their news from Facebook, while 83% and 50% get it from YouTube and Instagram respectively.[36]

- *Diverse:* Millennials are also far more diverse in background than preceding generations. According to a 2014 study conducted by the US White House's Council of Economic Advisers, about 15% of the US population between the ages of 15 and 34 was born outside the United States, which is far higher than in 1950 and close to the 20% peak achieved in 1910.[37]

- *Well educated – yet in debt:* Millennials are exceedingly well educated, with 47% of them holding post-secondary degrees, more than any other generation in history.[38] In fact, millennials have higher college enrolment rates in all age groups than the rate for both gen-Xers and baby boomers, and completion rates are also increasing.[39] Yet even though many millennials attend college, an insufficient number of them are majoring in high-demand STEM (science, technology, engineering and mathematics) subjects.[40] Instead, many millennials are majoring in business, the social sciences and history, as well as the health professions and the visual and performing arts.[41]

  Unfortunately, all this education also means that millennials are carrying a fair amount of student debt. Roughly 50% of students took out student loans in 2013–14, as compared with only about 30% in the mid-1990s.[42]

- *Urban:* Millennials are more urban than any other generation.[43] Unlike earlier generations, millennials prefer city centres to suburbs. Consequently, and for the first time since the 1920s, city centres in the United States are growing faster than the suburban areas around them.[44] Also – and unlike baby boomers – millennials in the United States seem to prefer the West Coast to the East Coast, as well as emerging 'second cities' in other locations, with socially-conscious, creative places such as Austin, Texas, topping the list.[45]

Much of the available research on millennials comes from the United States, with comparable studies in Europe unfortunately being almost non-existent.[46] What does seem clear from the available research is that, while European millennials share many of the same traits as their American counterparts, there are differences. For instance, virtually all (99.7%) of the European millennials interviewed in one study spoke one or more foreign languages, with more than 80% speaking at least one additional European tongue and 22% speaking two or more.[47] In the United States, by contrast, only 21% of millennials speak a second language.[48]

By the time European youths graduate from university, they also seem quite open to moving and living – perhaps even permanently – outside their native country. In one survey, 65% of European millennials said they were ready to relocate with only minor reservations, with 18% indicating that they would welcome the opportunity entirely.[49]

Given their language traits and openness to moving across borders, European millennials may find it easier to adapt to cultural environments outside their home countries than US millennials.[50] The recent rise of Berlin as a hub for European millennials is certainly bearing this out.[51]

How these traits have shaped millennial lawyers

While researchers have found it more difficult to singularly characterise millennials' traits than they have for earlier generations, they have identified certain traits that are considered to be fairly characteristic of most millennials. Many are recognisable to anyone who deals regularly with millennials.

These all pose challenges to the conventional way of running a law firm or legal department. This is because they have implications for the way millennials in the legal profession approach their jobs, as described next.

Millennials are open to new ways of working

Millennials do not appear to accept the '9-to-5' lifestyle (or, in the case of most lawyers, the '9-to-9' lifestyle) – they seem far less willing to put up with it than baby boomers or gen-Xers. According to a study conducted by Bentley University, 77% of millennials feel that flexible working hours would make them more productive, while nearly 40% believe working remotely would do so.[52] One must be careful not to confuse that outlook with a less rigorous work ethic, because the Bentley study also found that 89% of millennials regularly check their emails after work hours. Perhaps as a result of their digital-native and social-media upbringing, they are 'always on' even if not always in.

Freelancing also seems to be attractive to this generation. Anyone who has recently used temporary attorneys and other staff from legal outsourcing firms will have noticed that the quality of the people who work for these outfits is overwhelmingly solid. Many of the attorneys who work there do so by choice because of the flexibility it affords them, not because they cannot get a traditional law firm job. In fact, many had traditional firm jobs but decided to leave those behind when they discovered they did not want the accompanying lifestyle.

Millennials are entrepreneurial

Millennials are unquestionably an entrepreneurial generation. In fact, more than two-thirds of them aspire to start their own business at some stage , while only 16% expect to remain in their current jobs for the rest of their careers.[53] Only 13% of them aspire to be CEOs or company presidents.[54] So you should consider polling your millennials to discover how many of them have the career goal of becoming a general counsel. You might be surprised.

Many ambitious millennials look to Facebook's Mark Zuckerberg and other technology founders, many of whom dropped out of college before graduating in order to focus on their fledgling businesses. To many US baby boomers and gen-Xers, who grew up dreaming of Wall Street and white-shoe firms, that seems a terrifying, if not suicidal, career strategy. Why drop out of Harvard or Stanford after so much effort? Baby boomers and gen-Xers generally find validation and security in a traditional organisational setting; millennials, less so.

Millennials are tech-savvy, open and innovative

As the first genuinely 'tech' generation, millennials are naturally tech-savvy. In a 2014 survey, 82% of hiring managers felt that "millennials are more technologically adept" and consider them, by a wide margin, to be more creative, adaptable and open to change in comparison with gen-Xers.[55]

Millennials are context- and relationship-driven

Millennials are, in some ways, more 'high maintenance' than other generations. They value connectivity and authenticity in respect of both their colleagues and their work. Eighty-four per cent of them agree with the statement "Knowing I am helping to make a positive difference in the world is more important to me than professional recognition" and 77% of them feel that their ability to excel in their job is contingent on deriving meaning from what they do.[56]

Anyone who has worked with millennials knows how important it is for them to have a meaningful relationship with their superiors, even though they tend to discount traditional hierarchies, demanding immediate, high-quality feedback. Yet many fail to get the feedback they crave, with only 19% reporting that they get routine feedback and only 17% reporting that the feedback they get is meaningful.[57]

What's the problem?

Despite these numerous positive traits, many millennials are failing to gain traction in the workplace. In fact, there seems to be a gap between supply and demand: many millennials are having trouble finding a traditional job even though hiring managers are having trouble hiring enough millennials.[58]

There are two causes for this employment gap. First, baby-boomer/gen-X managers often reject millennials based on an inappropriate way of evaluating candidates; and, secondly, many workplace cultures are outmoded, causing millennials to reject traditional careers.

As for the first cause, older generations often view millennials through the distorted lens of their own generation. For instance, hiring managers in one study perceived millennials to be four times more likely to be narcissistic than gen-Xers.[59] Could that be driven by the fact that millennials demand more mentorship from their bosses, are less respectful of hierarchy and more likely to value meaning and context than gen-Xers? How can we expect millennials, who grew up in an age of connectivity, context and information, to embrace the ethos forged in a time of less information and a more rigidly hierarchical society? More importantly, instead of viewing these qualities as narcissistic, we should welcome them.

The second cause for the employment gap is the nature of the traditional workplace itself, in which input is often valued as much as – or more than – the quality of the output; where people 'pay their dues' over many years, patiently climbing the promotional ladder by enduring years of routine work before being awarded a truly meaningful role.

This culture, where (to borrow Woody Allen's famous quote) "eighty per cent of success is showing up", is emblematic of the legal profession. Indeed, many who currently lead the profession began their careers in large law firms, where long hours were spent proofreading and doing due diligence or document review, often in windowless rooms. Their managers were distant, rarely giving much time to provide the context that millennials demand. As junior associates, today's leaders were expected to soak up knowledge through discipline and repetition, mostly by themselves. At the end of the rainbow, and many years later, lay the status and economic prize of a lifetime partnership.

Given their values, it may not be surprising that millennials are having difficulty finding this approach attractive. Even to many gen-Xers, working in a big firm with the prospect of partnership up ahead seems unattractive. Add to this the changing nature of the legal industry, with technology, offshoring and outsourcing eroding margins and security, and it is not too difficult to see that the profession may soon face a crisis where the best and brightest no longer seek a career in law.

Clearly, in a world where the majority of the talent pool comprises millennials, it is critical for general counsel to get this right.

How to attract millennials

To attract the best millennials, general counsel need to change both the way they hire and the way they work. Set out next are nine steps to getting there.

Remove the generational lenses

Approach Millennial candidates on their own terms and stop viewing them from the perspective of gen-Xers and baby boomers. Learn to get comfortable with the ways of working that characterise this generation.

If you aim to only hire those millennials who look and act like their predecessors, you will lose out on some of the best next-generation talent. This will require you to take some risks in terms of how incoming millennials will interface with the rest of your workforce, but the effort will be worth it in the long run. If you do well, some of your gen-Xers and baby boomers will themselves prefer the new millennial working norms.

Focus on output over input

Focus on rewarding your team for deliverables rather than for effort or for time in the office. To the extent that this conforms with your company policy, this may mean allowing more flexible working hours and permitting staff to work from home where that is possible without compromising quality. Incidentally, doing so will have the added benefit of attracting single parents to your department, thereby helping to boost your staff diversity.

Given modern communications and productivity technology, there is no need to be present at all times in an office location unless physical meetings have been scheduled, the job description calls for it (eg, assistants and receptionists) or there is team-based work to do. Consider allowing less formal attire (again, to the extent that is acceptable within the context of your broader company culture). Long commuting times, formal dress codes and time just spent in an office are repellent to the millennial mindset.

Provide context and meaning

Taking the time to provide millennials with the context for what they are doing is invaluable. Give them a sense of how their work fits in to the whole. Millennials will frequently be your most eager and hard-working employees, provided they understand why they are doing something and how that work is essential to the whole picture. They will be very discontented if they are locked in a room and asked to perform repetitive work without the benefit of any context.

Give a sense of ownership

Give your millennials – and, in fact, all of your employees – freedom within a safe framework to enable them to have a sense of ownership over what they are doing. The old notion of exclusively giving junior lawyers mundane and repetitive tasks, on the assumption that they are unable to do more sophisticated work, needs to change. It will fail to attract the talent you need, particularly in an age of profound technological disruption, where routine, repetitive work can increasingly be done by machines.

You need to emphasise the development of an emotional intelligence quotient (EQ), which is discussed further in the next chapter. You also need to develop skills in communication, analytics and other critical areas, rather than an ability to complete routine and repetitive tasks.

Provide variety

Millennials thrive on variety and new challenges. Be prepared to meet this demand by giving them a mix of work. Assign them to new areas of responsibility as frequently as you can reasonably do so. To do this means you will have to accept that they will make more mistakes up front, so be sure to provide new work assignments within a framework of supervision, so that the mistakes made will not be too destructive to the company. If you do this in the correct way, you will end up retaining millennial talent that is flexible, resilient and adaptive.

Upgrade your technology

Invest in intuitive technology that enables rather than hinders work. Millennials are less tolerant of outdated technology than gen-Xers or baby boomers are; and state-of-the-art technology is as attractive to them as outdated technology is repellent. To millennials, the level of technological sophistication in your team is critical to their willingness to stay.

One of the best ways to engage millennials is to ask them to be involved in decision-making on new technology and to serve as the mentors for the department in its use.

Ensure your legal leadership has the right skills

As discussed more fully in the next chapter, your leadership team needs to have both EQ and strong communication skills. Attracting and retaining millennials requires the ability and desire to both relate to them and communicate with them on terms they feel comfortable with. This is also essential in steering millennials to accept cultural norms that are essential for the rest of the office and for dealing with intergenerational conflicts.

Mentor and encourage

Encourage mentorship and promote managers who not only have the heart of teachers, but also the innate curiosity to learn from younger colleagues. Integrating millennials will also require developing the right skills in your gen-Xers and baby boomers, who need to provide feedback on a consistent basis, coach the millennials and be willing to learn themselves. These skills are anyway critical to remaining competitive as a firm.

Also consider abolishing 'one size fits all' feedback. Give feedback immediately, rather than wait until mid-year or year-end reviews – and take that approach not just for millennials but for everyone on your team.

Make the mentoring you establish go both ways. Have millennials mentor older colleagues and vice versa. Each generation has something to teach the other, and all might find the learning they get to be both useful and desirable. Multigenerational mentoring will also ensure that critical knowledge is captured as generations of workers transition in and out of the organisation.[60]

Embrace the gig economy

You need to embrace the fact that most of your talent will not be with you for life, and you should reorganise your workplace accordingly.

Co-founder and executive chairman of LinkedIn, Reid Hoffman, together with entrepreneurs Ben Casnocha and Chris Yeh, describe in their book *The Alliance* how you have an opportunity to build a lasting, innovative organisation if you treat your people less like permanent employees or family and more like free agents who join your department for single or successive assignments. They put it this way:[61]

[A] business is far more like a sports team than a family. Yet while a professional sports team doesn't assume lifetime employment, the principles of trust, mutual investment, and mutual benefit still apply. Teams win when their individual members trust each other enough to prioritise team success over individual glory; paradoxically, winning as a team is the best way for team members to achieve individual success.

You should also develop a departmental alumni network, so that when your talent ultimately leaves your department they remain part of your broader network. In the modern economy, employees may come back for further assignments in the future. Even if they do not, they may connect you with other talent you might wish to hire or to experts who can assist you in solving particular problems you might be facing. As such, ex-employees should become a part of your knowledge bank, which you can draw from as needed.

Balancing interests across the generational divide

Managing a multigenerational workplace can be difficult. Companies and, by extension, their legal departments have four generations working alongside each other, each with their own distinctive traits, values and attitudes about work.[62] While it is important to attract the right millennial talent by configuring your workplace to appeal to them, it is equally important not to alienate your existing team of gen-Xers and baby boomers.

It is incumbent upon you as general counsel to configure your workplace so that the diversity this generates can be harnessed in a productive way, while attracting more millennials, who will soon replace gen-Xers and baby boomers as the bulk of your talent pool. Baby boomers, for instance, might disagree with the notion that people should be able to work remotely or show up to work in less formal attire on days where there are no external meetings. You will need to balance these interests in the right way. Below are four approaches you might consider adopting.

Seek open-minded millennials

Seek millennial candidates who seem comfortable working alongside other generations and who display the same leadership qualities that you are seeking in your other team members, including curiosity and EQ, as noted in the next chapter. Avoid hiring even the most talented of millennials (or other generations) if they seem unwilling or unable to compromise in their approach to work.

Reconfigure your approach to compensation and benefits

Different generations on your team may value different things. As the American Management Association has observed:[63]

> [A]s more people retire later in life, many will want more time off as opposed to increased compensation. Younger people may value more flexibility in their careers, like assignments that foster new skill sets they can apply later in their careers. Older workers may want research assignments and paid sabbaticals during which they can engage in learning programs.

Given these differences, you might consider, within the confines of what your company policies permit, to reward people differently, depending on what they value most. If millennials value flexible working arrangements but baby boomers prefer research assignments, consider giving each of them what they want. This can be done by having regular conversations with your staff to learn what people find attractive. Of course, your ability to do this will depend on company policy and the size of your team. The larger and more dispersed your team is, the more difficult and bureaucratic such an approach may become.

Communicate in different ways

Consider adapting your communication channels to accommodate the different generational preferences that may exist. For instance, baby boomers tend to prefer face-to-face or verbal communication, while gen-Xers and millennials may be comfortable with email or social messaging.[64] By adopting both approaches into your communications plans, you will ensure that no one feels left out.

Hold regular awareness sessions

Assume there is a lack of awareness among your team about the differences between the generations, and organise regular awareness sessions accordingly. Let representatives from each generation conduct the sessions, which will provide each generation with "an opportunity to educate each other about each generation's own history, characteristics, milestone events, culture, language, and norms."[65]

How precisely you decide to approach this challenge will depend on your specific organisation and circumstances. But it is incumbent on you as the general counsel to ensure that you secure both an attractive work environment for millennials, who represent your organisation's future, and a harmonious intergenerational environment for all staff.

Leadership skills

The key to successful leadership today is influence, not authority.
(Kenneth Blanchard)[1]

Wﾍhat does it take to be a successful in-house lawyer today? Some skills never change and remain at the core of professional legal excellence. Foremost among these are superior judgement, legal acumen and experience. However, as the legal landscape shifts and becomes ever more complex, many non-legal skills are becoming equally important. While far from an exhaustive list, below are 10 skills that are essential for your people to possess.

It is important to appreciate that the successful in-house lawyer must both possess specific skills and be able to combine them in ways that allow her to be a businessperson as much as a lawyer. She needs to effectively become what Paul Hughes has called "a strategic partner with commercial insight, wrapped around a core of legal expertise".[2]

Professional excellence

You always need to hire people who are outstanding lawyers with superb technical and analytical skills.

For senior hires, you need highly experienced attorneys who are demonstrated leaders in the profession, whether from a law firm, a government setting or another in-house environment. They must possess gravitas and executive presence. They must have strong, logical minds that are able to apply abstract legal concepts to real-world situations. They must be able to deliver timely, well-reasoned and appropriate decisions.

For more junior positions, you need people who show the ability and promise of one day becoming such leaders, even if they may not yet be there.

The foregoing qualities are fairly obvious – and have always been important. But in today's environment the skills set out below are also required and are arguably just as important to professional success.

Other essential leadership skills

Innate curiosity

Good in-house lawyers need to be excellent learners who are innately curious, because both the legal profession and the businesses they serve are evolving at breakneck speed. Knowledge becomes stale very quickly, and information flows simultaneously along multiple trajectories. To stay at the forefront of these trends is critical and requires an enormous amount of commitment and dedication. That in turn can only be sustained if a lawyer is innately curious, possessing a strong desire to learn and evolve.

People like that usually possess the following three core traits (described further below) that you should look out for in candidates:
- they are constant learners;
- they are future literate; and
- they have a keen desire and ability to import and export good ideas.

Constant learners

The average lawyer will be content to restrict herself to the body of knowledge she acquired in the formal context of law school, perhaps a few subsequent formal courses and what she has learned in the day-to-day practice of her profession. She takes a narrow view of what learning means, how it has evolved, and the important role it plays in excellence. Her assessment is therefore way off mark.

In contrast, the best in-house lawyers are constantly learning new things in both formal and informal ways.

Formal v 'organic' learning Professional knowledge acquisition has evolved greatly over the past few years, from being largely based on formal learning (structured courses and textbooks) towards what can be termed 'organic' learning: the accumulation of knowledge through unstructured, informal means. The former takes place at a discrete period of time and then ends, and is focused on specific topics. The latter is ongoing, continual and peripatetic.

As lawyers, we often emphasise formal learning at the expense of the organic kind. More than almost any other profession, our educational affiliations stick with us; they continue to define who we are throughout our professional lives. Few of us exhibit the kind of avid curiosity and thirst for knowledge typically found among the organic learners of Silicon Valley, where what you know is more important than where you learned it. Moreover, our institutions reflect this bias: continuing legal education requirements, for instance, are mostly required to be taken in formal settings that focus on discrete, narrow legal topics.

There is, of course, nothing wrong with formal learning. Indeed, it is an essential component to any foundational understanding of the law. But our profession often fails to recognise the limitations of formal learning or seize upon the opportunities that organic learning present. Organic learning is better at equipping us to innovate or react quickly to changing circumstances – skills that are essential to thriving in today's environment.

Bill Gates, Steve Jobs and Mark Zuckerberg are classic examples of organic learners. All of them dropped out of school but not out of learning. Jobs said that dropping out of school allowed him to stop taking the required classes that did not interest him and begin attending the ones that looked interesting. Calligraphy, for instance, taught him:[3]

> *about serif and sans serif typefaces, about varying the amount of space between different letter combinations, about what makes great typography great. It was beautiful, historical, artistically subtle in a way that science can't capture, and I found it fascinating.*

A decade later, that knowledge became critical to his design of the first Macintosh computer, with its beautiful typography. To Jobs, technology alone was insufficient: "It's technology married with the liberal arts, married with the humanities, that yields us the results that make our hearts sing."[4]

That sort of approach to learning seems far from the kind of cloistered education we find in a traditional law school setting. We train our lawyers to worship formal learning at the expense of the organic kind. Consequently, many of us have an oddly old-fashioned and conservative view of education in which exclusivity rather than inclusiveness is the hallmark of erudition. The more exclusive the institution (and hence the fewer the number and variety of people you have interacted with during your time spent learning), the better your education presumably is. This ossified view of learning is reinforced in the selective hiring processes undertaken by many top law firms that view elite school affiliations as the ultimate measure of competence and skill.

These biases are oddly out of sync with the world around us. We no longer live in a place where formal learning is the sole – or even the primary – vessel for knowledge accumulation. The body of available knowledge needed to do our jobs well exceeds what can be learned in one class or course of study. Benjamin Franklin may have learned nearly all there was to know about 18th-century science and maths; but in the 21st century, even for the brightest intellectual, that would be impossible.

The internet v books The internet has become an optimal learning tool because it acts as a conduit for virtually every conceivable learning format, including books, podcasts and webcasts, magazines, talks, interviews, blogs and online courses.

The beauty of the internet lies in the fact that it combines both structured and organic learning. At the structured level, there are academic courses offered by leading institutions through vehicles such as EdX and Coursera. At the middle layer, there are podcasts and audible e-books from which we can learn new skills and ideas while doing the dishes or walking the dog. At the third level there is the outward aspect of social media that connects us to people, whether in our own fields or others.

As a society, we are becoming better at randomly interacting with people we do not know (eg, through Airbnb and Uber). That liberality of outlook is spilling over into sites such as LinkedIn, which allow for professionals in different fields to bump up against each other and generate new ideas and opportunities. It is incredibly important that we as lawyers recognise this power and seize it.

That said, books remain at the core of organic learning if you want to gain in-depth knowledge about a subject. There is something about the level of concentration that goes into reading a book that forces you to think about and process the information in a different way from other media.

One possible programme that you might consider for your team is the policy of HubSpot that reimburses people for any book they buy, provided they write a few paragraphs on what the book was about and what they learned.[5]

> *In my whole life, I have known no wise people (over a broad subject matter area) who didn't read all the time – none, zero.*
> (Charlie Munger)[6]

Success in the era we are in will belong to those lawyers who adopt constant learning as an inherent part of who they are. They will be 'information herbivores', constantly grazing on new knowledge that is available in virtually unlimited quantities, whenever desired.

Future literate

Good in-house lawyers must also be what Bryan Johnson, the founder of Braintree (now a subsidiary of PayPal), calls 'future literate'.[7] Those who will thrive in the 'new normal' do not just continually learn new things; they seek to apply that knowledge in order to try to anticipate rapidly shifting trends.

Being future literate is about staying 'ahead of the curve' so that you can try to advance the industry you work in, as well as the legal profession as a whole. Knowledge without application is useless; it will soon evaporate. But knowledge that is used to anticipate and shape the future is power.

Able to import and export good ideas

One of the most important ways to gather knowledge is to import and export good ideas (including best practice) through personal networks. Books and other materials provide food for thought, but people with experience are still the best teachers.

Importing ideas from outside the organisation 'Networking' has become a bit of a loaded term, particularly for a lot of lawyers. Often, people go about it the wrong way, assuming that networking is about getting something out of people, 'working a room' and 'schmoozing'. In fact, it's quite the opposite. It's about making friends, engaging in thoughtful dialogue and giving as much of your own time as you can comfortably allow to helping others.

By doing this, you inadvertently build a support system of experts who in turn may help you, even if you have no idea how or when or if they will when you first meet. Author of the critically acclaimed book entitled *A Lawyer's Guide to Networking*, legal management consultant and former general counsel Susan Sneider explains:[8]

> *Networking is building and sustaining relationships over time to provide value to others. For in-house counsel, internal corporate networking – both within and outside the legal department – is critical for job security, promotion, and status. Networking is about developing good personal relationships. The more in-house lawyers develop rapport with their business partners, the easier it is for them to fulfil the dual roles of advancing strategic business objectives and serving as the company's guardian. It is equally important to develop and sustain relationships with colleagues inside law firms and other corporations, and all manner of people outside your organisation including business executives, personal service providers, members of your athletic club and former college and law school classmates. Their connections and their different world orientation is critical for in-house counsel to learn about new ideas and new opportunities.*

In today's connected age, a candidate's personal network should be considered an asset that they bring to the role. You are, in a sense, not just hiring an individual; you are also hiring that individual's network and the strength of knowledge and experience it brings. As Reid Hoffman and colleagues observe in their book *The Alliance*, "network intelligence that leverages individual networks of your organisation's people is the most effective way for your organisation to engage with and learn from the outside world".[9]

You need to consider the strength of a candidate's network when interviewing them. Examine their profile on LinkedIn or Twitter. If they don't have one, be suspicious.

> *There are more smart people outside our company than inside it.*
> (Reid Hoffman, Ben Casnocha and Chris Yeh)[10]

Dispersing ideas within the organisation In-house lawyers must also be adept at importing and exporting good ideas within and across the organisation, not just from outside it. This applies at all levels, not just to the leadership. Indeed, where most legal departments fall short on the networking aspect is not among their senior leadership but among the rest of the staff.

Hoffman and colleagues like to think of each employee as a scout – able to receive, filter and decipher information from the outside world that can in turn help the organisation to adapt.[11] The legal department can be thought of as an ant colony: its strength lies in its interconnectedness, not in the power of any one individual however talented that person may be.

At the more junior levels of your organisation, it may be much harder for your team to network effectively outside the organisation. They may lack the budget to travel or the ability to be away much from their homes or offices. But that shouldn't stop them from importing and exporting ideas. They can, for instance, do an excellent job networking within the company by delivering training, inviting others from outside or inside the legal department to come and speak to them and colleagues at 'lunch and learn' sessions and the like. They can also form practice groups to learn from each other. One organisation, the General Counsel 50, which is designed to enable general counsel to confidentially share ideas and connect with each other, maintains a side network for the GCs' personal assistants. The assistants get together regularly by phone or in person to share ideas and best practice. Why not establish similar groups within your own company?

Given the natural reluctance and outright fear that some lawyers have when it comes to networking, you may need to nudge your people in the right direction. One practice you might consider is to pay for people to take anyone they like out to lunch once per month, provided they come back and tell you at least three things they learned.[12] Sometimes, the information picked up during such events may not seem that useful at first, but it's amazing what it can lead to in the long run.

Excellent communication

Your leaders must be outstanding communicators. In an era of constant change and mobile talent, it is critical that they be able to persuade and inspire the rest of your team. To succeed, they need to display three core communications skills:

- they must be excellent storytellers;
- they must be able to start with the why, leading from the heart and not just the head; and
- they must be clear, concise and business-focused writers.

Storytelling

Leaders need to be excellent storytellers. Unfortunately, despite the past glories of US TV lawyer Perry Mason, this is alien to the way many lawyers have been taught. As lawyers, we tend to emphasise technical jargon that leaves people cold.

What you say is ultimately less important than how you say it. To be effective, you need to learn to tell stories. The reason this is important is simple: our brains are wired to connect with stories. Good stories surprise us and stick with us. They connect us emotionally with the issue at hand in a way that mere facts alone can never do. In that sense, a powerful narrative can act as a peg and make the underlying ideas you are trying to convey more memorable and meaningful than they would otherwise be. Stories are persuasive where mere facts are not.

Good storytellers go beyond just giving an account. They know the difference between what happened and the story about what happened. They never recount events; they construct a story around the events. They are able to draw out a central, organising theme that makes the events meaningful. At its core – in its deepest sense – they are able to convey what the story is really about, and what the central problem or crisis is that needs to be addressed.[13]

Often, the best communicators will start with a question rather than a statement. Excellent communicators think carefully about the first and the last sentence. They provide examples rather than spell everything out. They focus their communication as much on what they want the audience to leave thinking and feeling, as they do on conveying information.

An example Imagine one of your leaders is giving a presentation on your company's Code of Conduct to an audience of bored executives, who are yawning while checking their emails. It is hot and late in the day, and they have been listening to people who have been killing them softly with PowerPoint presentations since eight o'clock that morning. She walks them through the Code of Conduct, with detailed slides on the nuances and finer points, with references to paragraphs and page numbers. Six months from then, no one will even remember that she gave the talk, let alone what was said.

Now imagine a different version of the story. Same room, same temperature, same time of day, except now she starts by firmly telling them that she is not going to walk them through the Code of Conduct, because they should already know it – and if they are still unfamiliar with it, then shame on them.

Instead, she stares at them for 20 seconds in silence. There is a tension in the room. People begin to look up from their iPhones. This is different! Then she shows a slide with just one picture on it; a picture of a man. There are no words, just the picture. She asks the audience to guess who the person is. Competitive instincts are now awake. Names get shouted out until the audience guesses correctly that the person is a former CEO of a highly regarded company who lost his job due to an ethics infraction. People are now engaged. Next, she shows another picture: a happy scene of a couple on their wedding day. She asks the audience to guess who this is. It is someone from the company who committed insider trading and is now facing prosecution. Someone in the audience shouts that they know him.

Next, she shows a slide with a picture of the front page of his SEC indictment. She quietly asks people how they think his wife is feeling now; what his kids must be going through. Then, she displays a slide with 100 anonymous faces. "Who are all these people?" she asks. "These are the 50 ethics cases she dealt with last year across the company. All of these people are now gone," she says quietly and firmly. "Some are facing legal action. Who do you think is responsible for this?" There is a long silence. She pulls out a mirror and walks down the aisle, showing everyone his or her own reflection. "We are responsible – as leaders we are responsible", she says. She leaves a long, pregnant pause as she lets that fact sink in. After the session, she distributes a hand-out with details on the Code of Conduct.

Which of these presentations will be most impactful? Which one will people remember the most when they face an ethical dilemma? American poet, memoirist and civil rights activist Maya Angelou, has said that "people will forget what you said, people will forget what you did, but people will never forget how you made them feel".[14]

The broad approach When you coach someone on communications, you should start by asking them to discard their carefully crafted slides and narrative; have them just tell their story. Ask them to do that a few times. Then ask them to tell you the 30-minute story in 60 seconds. This forces them, without thinking, to condense the story down to what is truly essential. Once you have distilled the essence, you can reconstruct the presentation – ideally with no words, just pictures.

Once that is done, the speaker will have a powerful story, backed by illustrative pictures that lend weight to her words. At that point – but only then – do you work back in the keywords that may be necessary to convey important details that must be included.

Focus on 'why'

In his famous TED talk entitled "Start with Why", Simon Sinek, an author, speaker and consultant who writes on leadership and management, explains why leading from the heart is so critical:[15] "People don't buy what you do; they buy why you do it." To take people with you, you must trigger those parts of the brain that drive behaviour. As Sinek notes, in the 1963 Civil Rights March on Washington, Dr Martin Luther King inspired millions by telling them why change was needed and he focused on the deeper truths that connected everyone; he didn't dwell on the 'how'.

Most in-house leaders will never rise to the level of storytelling excellence that Dr King displayed, but simply focusing on why something needs to happen can move mountains.

Demonstrate clear written communication

Your leaders must also be able to write in a clear and concise manner that is easily consumable by clients. Many lawyers struggle to determine what to leave out. They never take the time to boil their communications down to the essence, which is hard work. Mark Twain is once said to have remarked, "I didn't have time to write a short letter, so I wrote a long one instead."[16]

But writing the long letter can render your communication useless. Complex syntax and jargon-laden paragraphs usually conceal fuzzy thinking that has little practical application. Moreover, decision makers will simply discard a lengthy tome.

On average, 122 business emails are sent and received per user per day, and this average is growing at a 3% rate per year.[17] If you assume that people spend two minutes per message, an average business user is spending more than four hours per day just dealing with email. Be respectful of that time pressure. If you are unable to boil an email down to a few sentences or a paragraph, you should consider an alternative means of communication. Write a White Paper (a firm proposal on a topic) and attach it, summarising the main points in a sentence or two. Or pick up the phone and call the person.

Consider putting in place a policy that if someone sends you an email message that is unable to fit on your iPhone screen, you will delete it without reading it. They can set up a meeting instead if they want to discuss why they were sending you such a long message.

Tom Chi, founder of Google X and lead developer of Microsoft Outlook, has made a radical proposal that resonates with this author: what if you were to commit to only sending five emails a day?[18] How would that impact the nature and quality of your communications and your work?

You need communicators who can make an impact with their communications. Only those who can will be able to make a difference, regardless of how much they know.

Excellent business judgement

The best in-house lawyers are business oriented and not just technically proficient.

Understanding a client's needs and responding accordingly is essential in a world where substantive legal knowledge is rapidly becoming a commodity. Lawyers must join their clients on market visits, attend sales conferences and invite themselves to strategic business planning meetings. They need to be curious about, and have a passion for, the businesses they serve. They need to ask lots of questions. It is no longer enough to sit behind a desk in an ivory tower and dispense legal advice. Doing just that is a sure-fire way to become a corporate dinosaur.

Market visits

It can be enormously valuable to have your lawyers spend regular time in the market with your company's customers. This gives your lawyers a feeling for the market and also gives them the credibility they need in their work. If clients know they are dealing with someone who understands the business and has a passion for it, they will be more receptive.

The Coca-Cola Company's lawyers go out on regular market visits. Legal teams are divided into groups, and each group is given a designated area of a city to visit. They go out, with cameras and notepads at the ready, to visit supermarkets, restaurants, fitness centres and everything in between, to see which of the company's products are sold there, how they are presented, what the price communication is, what special offers (if any) are made, and how, if there are beverage coolers present, they are stocked. Then they reconvene and the lawyers must present what they have discovered, together with their recommendations for how to improve things, to the senior sales executives.

Some of those involved find this a bit unnerving at first, but once they have done it a few times, they feel they are part of the Coca-Cola sales team in addition to being lawyers. They understand the key sales drivers, and what the in-store challenges look like. They have met with and spoken to customers about their needs and frustrations, and they have considered the company's products from the perspective of consumers in the outlet.

Understanding how the business works gives your lawyers far better ability to tailor their advice and act in a pragmatic manner, as well as argue their case more forcefully from a position of knowledge rather than ignorance.

The business of the law

Outstanding in-house lawyers not only understand the business their company is in; they also understand the business of the law.

Of course, the core business they are in is to protect the company's assets and its reputation, while enabling it to conduct its business in the best manner possible. But they also need to understand how to run their own practice as a business. In-house lawyers must:

- be cost-creative, understanding how to leverage the principles of professional procurement to their team's own sourcing needs;
- own their numbers, knowing what their budget, headcount and external spend numbers look like;
- be familiar with the cost and efficiency opportunities that globalisation and technological disruption have brought to the profession, including through technology and process optimisation, and then seize the initiative and act on that knowledge;
- have a passion for the people they lead and be keen to learn more about how to motivate them, drive them forward and create the best possible work environment; and
- know how to write a business case so that, for example, they can collaborate with their business partners, secure needed resources, and effect changes in commercial behaviour. This is a skill that law schools and private practice should be teaching; it is critical in an

in-house legal leadership role. A proper business case will speak the language of the client, bringing persuasion by using the same terminology, fiscal discipline and structure that any other executive would use.

Being results-driven

Lawyers are typically intelligent, task-oriented and impatient high-achievers who are driven to win. They have largely succeeded in life by applying these traits to whatever gets thrown at them.[19] Given this environment, finding results-driven lawyers should be simple. Unfortunately, what constitutes an acceptable legal result can be way off what is actually needed in the real world.

For an in-house lawyer to deliver a sophisticated and highly regarded result, she needs to provide guidance that is both practical and actionable to her business partners, keeping in mind that they are trying to solve real-world problems while operating within real-world constraints. By contrast, most lawyers have been trained in law schools and firms to analyse every possible nuance, highlight ambiguities and point out all of the pitfalls. They are trained to be cautious and deliberative. While that may earn you an A grade in your law school exams, it may not be truly useful to a corporate client.

To be results-driven, an in-house lawyer must be demonstrably able to take her analysis and intelligence the extra mile and provide an actionable, commercially viable solution to the problem that is both legal and ethical. This requires her to unlearn certain ingrained habits from her legal training without losing them altogether. She must manage complex legal projects and adapt to changing environments, all the while keeping the end objective in mind and applying her legal skills in a carefully considered manner to achieve an optimal end result. This means that she needs to think like a businessperson who has legal expertise. If this is done correctly, it can be enormously powerful.

Lawyers can be fantastic business leaders. Jim Collins, the highly regarded business consultant and author of numerous best-sellers, including *Built to Last* and *Good to Great*, has highlighted exceptional CEOs in his various writings.[20] Of these, at least three were lawyers, two of whom are on Collins's list of the ten greatest CEOs of all time:

- Darwin E Smith of Kimberly-Clark, who led the company's transition from a paper company to a consumer products company, was corporate counsel at the company before becoming CEO;[21]
- William McPherson Allen, the legendary post-WW2 president of Boeing, who shored up the company's finances and moved it from being a propeller and bomber business to a jet engine and commercial aircraft behemoth, was a corporate counsel on the board of Boeing Airplane Company before he took over;[22] and
- Herb Kelleher, co-founder, chairman emeritus and former CEO Southwest Airlines, who built one of the most admired businesses in the United States, was a lawyer who created the concept together with a client and a banker.[23]

Although this might seem surprising at first glance, it is very reasonable because good lawyers:

- bring communication skills and an ability to analyse and synthesise a broad spectrum of information from across their company;
- combine left- and right-brain thinking by spotting issues and applying their imagination to the problems they face;
- ask the right questions (using what's known as the Socratic Method) and consider all sides of an issue before arriving at a solution; and
- focus, like good CEOs, more on protecting their flanks than on taking big risks – they take risks only once those risks have been empirically evaluated, and they are fact-driven.[24]

Table 4 gives a list of CEOs with a legal background.[25]

Table 4: CEOs with a legal background

CEO	Company	Prior GC	Legal background
Alexander, Anthony	FirstEnergy	✓	✓
Anderson, Richard	Delta Air Lines	✓	✓
Blake, Francis	Home Depot	✓	✓
Blankfein, Lloyd	Goldman Sachs Group		✓
Braly, Angela	WellPoint	✓	✓
Burke, Kevin	Consolidated Edison		✓
Chambers, John	Cisco Systems		✓
Chenault, Kenneth	American Express		✓
Conway, John	Crown Holdings		✓
Crane, David	NRG Energy		✓
Dauman, Philippe	Viacom	✓	✓
Diaz, Paul	Kindred Healthcare	✓	✓
Dillon, David	Kroger		✓
Earley, Anthony Jr	PG&E Corporation	✓	✓
Engles, Gregg	Dean Foods		✓
Ettinger, Jeffrey	Hormel Foods		✓
Farrell, Thomas II	Dominion Resources	✓	✓
Ferguson, Roger Jr	TIAA-CREF		✓
Finnegan, John	Chubb		✓
Frazier, Kenneth	Merck	✓	✓
Greenberg, Lon	UGI	✓	✓
Haldeman, Charles Jr	Freddie Mac		✓
Johnson, William	Progress Energy	✓	✓
Kandarian, Steven	MetLife		✓
Kearney, Christopher	SPX	✓	✓
Kinder, Richard	Kinder Morgan		✓
King, David	Laboratory Corp of America	✓	✓
Lipinski, John	CVR Energy		✓
Mathas, Theodore	New York Life Insurance		✓
McGee, Liam	Hartford Financial Services Group		✓
Moynihan, Brian	Bank of America	✓	✓
Ninivaggi, Daniel	Icahn Enterprises	✓	✓
O'Brien, Richard	Newmont Mining		✓
Otis, Clarence Jr	Darden Restaurants		✓
Rogers, James	Duke Energy	✓	✓
Roth, Michael	Interpublic Group		✓

continued on next page

CEO	Company	Prior GC	Legal background
Rubright, James	Rock-Tenn	✓	✓
Rust, Edward Jr	State Farm Insurance Company		✓
Skaggs, Robert Jr	NiSource		✓
Smisek, Jeffrey	United Continental Holdings	✓	✓
Sorenson, Arne	Marriott International	✓	✓
Starks, Daniel	St Jude Medical		✓
Steiner, David	Waste Management	✓	✓
Storch, Gerald	Toys R Us		✓
Temares, Steven	Bed Bath & Beyond	✓	✓

Past CEO	Company	Prior GC	Legal background
Jeffrey B Kindler	Pfizer	✓	
James L Gallogaly	Lyondell Basell	✓	
James L Gallogaly	Chevron Phillips Chemical Company	✓	

(Source: Morae Legal Corporation. Information compiled by Morae Legal Corporation using publicly available information)

On the flip side, legal training can also impede the ability to generate great results, because many lawyers:

- are too risk-averse;
- lack fluency in basic business concepts, including financial tools and calculations;
- possess a certain myopia that comes from their insularity and professional identity, and they can sometimes choose to be advisors rather than deciders; and
- are – sometimes unfairly – coloured by the stereotypical perceptions of non-lawyers, and need to have the skills to break through those assumptions and demonstrate that they can deliver.

In summary, outstanding in-house lawyers apply the strengths of their legal training to achieve actionable results for their clients and business partners. Mediocre lawyers end up hog-tied by the negative traits they possess.

In selecting your team, you need to pick those who possess the former qualities and avoid those with the latter.

Autonomy

Good in-house lawyers must be able to function autonomously yet understand when to advise management on how their work is progressing or on any unusual situations that require the input of either their legal department managers or their commercial clients.

The pros and cons of law firm training

Legal leaders differ on whether lawyers should only be hired for in-house roles once they have already achieved a certain amount of experience in a law firm or government setting.

Generally speaking, prior experience is key to in-house success. That is because successful in-house lawyers must be autonomous self-starters, yet most in-house environments lack the infrastructure that law firms possess to properly train new lawyers. Of course, there are always exceptions: occasionally, lawyers with little or no law firm experience will excel in-house because they are innate self-starters and quick learners.

But those exceptions aside, law firms are excellent places for junior lawyers to cut their teeth and gain the skills they need later in their in-house career. A good law-firm setting teaches young lawyers to apply professional rigour to their academic knowledge. It instils a sense of discipline and cements the work ethic that they honed in law school. They have the opportunity to seek mentorships, and a law firm training affords them a breadth of experience across a range of subjects that would be difficult to get anywhere else.

One problem, however, is that as outside counsel move in-house, they can come across as too technical, particularly if they are joining as generalists. Another challenge can be multitasking: law firm attorneys are incredibly busy people but it is often on a core group of matters that fill their day and prioritisation is fairly clear; by contrast, life in-house is one where the attorney is bombarded with hundreds of unrelated requests each day and needs to figure out how to allocate time between the various matters.

The pros and cons of government training

Government experience can also be enormously valuable. Former GE

General Counsel Ben W Heineman Jr has noted that US government experience was important to him because:[26]

> *working inside government gave people a 'finger-tips' understanding of broad issues with dimensions far beyond narrow legal questions and a feel for how public-sector institutions worked that they couldn't acquire as easily (although it was not impossible) from representing clients before government – in legislative, regulatory, or judicial venues.*

That said, government lawyers, like law firm attorneys, may possess traits that might at first cause friction in the corporate environment. For example, they may find it difficult to distance themselves from their former roles – eg, by being too quick to advocate self-reporting where that might be legally unnecessary or unwise under the circumstances.

In summary, the core competencies that in-house lawyers provide requires a level of autonomy that can only come with experience. Therefore, unless you have the infrastructure to train people in-house, you should generally recruit people who have at least three-to-five years of law firm, government or other relevant experience for junior roles and a minimum of 10–15 years of practice for more senior positions.

Courage

Legal leaders in a corporate setting must have the courage to speak up and prevent stupid or potentially illegal things from happening.

Not only do they need to know the difference between pragmatism and inappropriateness; they also need to have the guts to call out and stop decisions that are legally inappropriate, and to then stand their ground. Ultimately, every lawyer who serves in a leadership position in a company has to be willing to resign from their position at any time if they are thwarted in doing the right thing.

It is, of course, the ultimate responsibility of the general counsel to ensure there is an atmosphere of openness and transparency, where people feel comfortable bringing things forward where there is any doubt.

But that must not detract from the basic capability that all legal leaders must possess: the courage to resist and speak out against illegal, inappropriate or unethical behaviour, even where that will require them to go against their friends and colleagues.

Manipulative business partners

Resisting a senior business partner requires a depth and strength of character that not every lawyer possesses. Commercial leaders who themselves lack the right moral fibre can nevertheless be incredibly good at manipulating the weakest lawyers.

Such people often have a predatory instinct and can smell weakness in the air; they got to where they are by being excellent students of human character and effective persuaders. They will rarely openly fight a lawyer to prevent a legally necessary initiative. But some may use every trick in the book to manipulate them into a deep somnambulant state of non-action.

Here are some examples of the kinds of arguments to be aware of – ones that commercial leaders might successfully seek to employ to stall efforts:

- *The 'yes but later' argument:* "We should do what you say, of course ... but let's do it next quarter, not now, because there are core commercial priorities that would get disrupted if we change things mid-stream."
- *The 'yes but needs more clarity' argument:* "Yes, absolutely ... but first, we need to obtain more information because the proposal is half-baked. More specifically, we need answers to the following 100 questions that I've asked you (and when you're done answering those, we have another 100, and then another 100, etc)."
- *The 'you don't understand how the business works' argument:* "This is over-broad and doesn't reflect how we conduct business. It frankly displays some ignorance on your part. So before you roll this out, you need to go back to the drawing board and reconfigure it and propose it again." (Read: water it down to the point where it is rendered useless).
- *The 'passive-aggressive' approach:* "OK, I have my doubts and this

will be hard, but if we need to, let's do it" (said by the senior leader with body language that says this is not a priority and he remains deeply sceptical). Nothing actually happens. Some time later, another meeting is held, basically with the same result. Then nothing happens again. Repeat *ad infinitum.*

Lawyers in far-flung offices, who are thousands of miles from the general counsel, will be most vulnerable to these arguments. Their business partners are just down the hall and have an outsized influence on their behaviour.

We need to have a structure that ensures high standards at all times, because we are only as strong as our weakest link. This structure can be created, for instance, by ensuring that there is a direct reporting relationship up through the function for all lawyers, into the GC.

But that still leaves the need to ensure that we have selected only those lawyers who have the guts to stand up to the occasional bully, and the intelligence and flexibility to counteract any cunning, stealthy obfuscation and delaying tactics.

Flexible leadership style

Today's in-house counsel needs to maintain a flexible approach to leadership that leverages both different sources of power and different leadership styles. In turn, it requires Emotional Intelligence (EQ) to know when to leverage what source and style.

Erica Peitler, author of *Leadership Rigor,*[27] notes that there are three core sources of power that you can draw upon:

- *positional power,* which comes from the authority of your title and position within an organisation (which is clearly only useful for senior attorneys);
- *expert power,* which comes from your specialised skills (such as your legal expertise); and
- *personal power,* which comes from your ability to connect and inspire people, ask the right questions, listen, provide support and encouragement, and create a safe environment.

Your in-house leaders need to be aware of these different power sources and apply them appropriately to the context and audience. In addition, they need to understand and leverage a broad range of leadership styles.

Peitler further states that everyone has a particular style that they are most comfortable with. But to be successful, a leader must be able to match the best style to the right situation/person. For instance, some people may need 'big picture' directional leadership, whereas others may need more detailed hand-holding. The more senior a lawyer gets, the more he needs to get out of his comfort zone to develop his range of styles.

This skill is essential to success because it allows a lawyer to navigate virtually any situation with the right tone and approach.

Cultural intelligence

In a world that is increasingly global and interconnected, nothing is purely domestic. Everyone is connected and networked, and work is increasingly handled across physical and cultural borders. Lawyers who are unfamiliar with cultural differences or who have no tools to effectively navigate their way through the inevitable obstacles that arise as a consequence of such differences can derail delicate negotiations, repel promising talent and frustrate your ability to build a world-class department.

It is therefore critical that your lawyers possess cultural intelligence (CQ), so that they are able to understand the context, whether that involves gender expectations, communication styles or other aspects that may be unfamiliar to them.

> *If you go into every interaction assuming that culture doesn't matter, your default mechanism will be to view others through your own cultural lens and to judge or misjudge them accordingly.*
> (Erin Meyer)[28]

Set out next are some of the most important competencies that lawyers with good CQ will demonstrate.

Shrewdness over leadership styles

Good in-house lawyers will have an understanding of how different cultures approach leadership because that will deeply impact performance.

In some countries, such as France, many leaders employ an autocratic style in which the boss is generally expected to have the answers, while those who report up are expected to be compliant and not ask too many difficult questions.[29] Variations of the hierarchical approach exist in various parts of the world, including Latin America and the Middle East.[30] Team members in such cultures are unlikely to challenge the leader's decisions or engage in vigorous debate about the merits of a position put forward by the leader.

By contrast, consensus-driven leadership cultures such as are common in Norway and Sweden, typically have a flatter, more egalitarian approach, although with variations.[31] In such cultures, explicit displays of hierarchical order and power are frowned upon. Even though the boss ultimately casts the deciding vote, it is rarely openly acknowledged that this is the case. People at all levels are expected to weigh in; and when decisions are made they are often cast as having been arrived at by group discussion, even where the boss may ultimately cast the deciding vote.

Your legal leaders need to be familiar with the different approaches to leadership around the world, especially if they are going to be interacting with counterparties or business partners, or managing teams of people outside their own cultures. If they try to employ a consensus-driven and flat Scandinavian leadership style in a very hierarchical place such as France (or vice versa), they will be setting themselves up for failure.

Shrewdness over disagreement

Lawyers need to be aware of how people in a given culture view disapproval and open disagreement. Is open disapproval of an idea considered to be a rejection of the idea or of the person? Are open displays of disagreement viewed as a positive or a destructive force for the team? Your lawyers need to know the answers to these questions, and to saving or losing 'face', if they are going to act for you in a culturally sensitive manner.

Face The role of 'face' is critical in this context. In Confucian cultures such as China, Japan and South Korea, group harmony is considered to be critically important and it relies on everyone maintaining prescribed roles relative to each other (eg, father–son, husband–wife and ruler–subject).[32] When you openly disagree in that context, you risk upsetting social order, because your disagreement may be viewed as a suggestion that the person you disagree with has failed to live up to their prescribed role.[33] That may cause them to lose face, generating a sense of shame in the recipient and disunity in the group.

Consequently, disapproval or disagreement must be stated indirectly and very subtly. People from such cultures must therefore learn to understand the subtext by 'reading the air in the room', surveying the surroundings, paying attention to the little nuances and acting appropriately by picking up on very subtle or even indirect signals of disagreement.

By contrast, many Western cultures, such as the French, often view open and constructive disagreement as a positive thing. Rather than being viewed as an affront to the individual, it is typically seen as an honest effort to move the proposed idea forward, in order to harness the group's collective intelligence and experience.

As Meyer notes:[34]

> [S]tudents in the French school system are taught to reason via thesis, antithesis, and synthesis, first building up one side of the argument, then the opposite side of the argument, before coming to a conclusion. Consequently, French businesspeople intuitively conduct meetings in this fashion, viewing conflict and dissonance as bringing hidden contradictions to light and stimulating fresh thinking.

In such cultures, remaining passive or silent in the face of a proposal being brought forward that you disagree with might even be viewed as passive-aggressive, destructive or derelict.

Bridgewater Associates, a US hedge fund, typifies this view, having adopted a culture that attempts to forge "an idea meritocracy in which meaningful work and meaningful relationships are pursued through radical truth and radical transparency".[35] At Bridgewater, employees are encouraged to openly hash out tensions and speak their minds, requiring its people "to be extremely open, air disagreements, test each other's logic and view discovering mistakes and weaknesses as a good thing that leads to improvement and innovation".[36] As Bridgewater's founder, Ray Dalio, has said: "thoughtful disagreement radically improves understanding".[37]

High-context and low-context cultures Cultures that are sensitive to open disagreement, such as China and Japan, tend to be regarded as 'high-context' cultures, in which people have a high number of shared norms and context.[38] In such cultures, there is no need to spell out openly what is meant because everyone gets it. Homogenous cultures, such as Japan, typify this, with common norms and subliminal signalling ingrained from birth.

By contrast, cultures that are more likely to depersonalise open disagreement, such as Germany, the United States and the Scandinavian countries, tend to be recognised as 'low-context', where people are conditioned to convey information more explicitly, not assuming that others will implicitly understand the context.[39] As Erin Meyer notes, in these cultures, "effective communication must be simple, clear, and explicit in order to effectively pass the message".[40]

The United States has the lowest context culture in the world, made up as it is of immigrants who came to the country from a wide variety of backgrounds and cultures.[41] Action points and 'wrap-ups' are common at the end of meetings, to be clear on what has been agreed and who is responsible for what actions, and the deadlines that need to be met. Such summaries might be viewed as unnecessary or perhaps even patronising in high-context cultures.

Often, it can be very difficult for someone from a low-context culture to pick up on the subtle cues that are given at meetings in high-context cultures, which can create confusion. It can take many years to learn to listen properly, 'read the air' and figure out what is really being said and done in a cultural environment that is different from your own.

You want leaders who have that experience.

Trust

Another cultural difference that can be critical to understand is how trust gets built.

In task-based cultures, such as the United States, the United Kingdom, Germany, Denmark and Australia, trust in the commercial context is often built from the head – ie, through good work, excellent analysis and a track record of delivering on what has been promised.[42]

In relationship-based cultures, such as Nigeria, Brazil, Saudi Arabia and China, trust is built from the heart – ie, through personal bonds, friendship and affection.[43] In China, for instance, establishing personal relationships in this way in order to facilitate business trust is sometimes referred to as *guanxi*. As Kim Draemer has noted that "[m]any Chinese feel that *guanxi* can be a better indicator of character, ability and integrity than a diploma from an Ivy League school in America or a top university in China".[44]

This kind of trust can take much longer to build and develop. It takes more than one day to learn to trust someone at an emotional level; in cultures where emotional trust is critical you will need to invest in the relationship well in advance of any point at which you need to rely on the relationship. This requires the patience to go slow and nurture the relationship. You need to think long-term.

Many cultures fall somewhere in between these extremes, and complexity can be added in the form of familial, tribal or other cultural ties. It is critical for any global or international role that your lawyers understand and appreciate the differences between these approaches to trust building and that they take the time to develop the right strategies to build trust depending on the context.

Reasoning

Finally, your legal leaders should be familiar with the methods that people from different cultures typically employ to develop their arguments and persuade others that their ideas or proposals are well reasoned.

Deductive v inductive reasoning In many European countries, particularly Latin countries such as Italy and France, people will typically employ deductive reasoning to try to convince others of the soundness of their arguments. In these cultures, the focus is on clarifying principles first (ie, focusing in detail on the diagnosis of the problem) before turning to applications (ie, possible solutions).[45]

By contrast, other cultures, such as the United States and the United Kingdom, tend to employ what is known as inductive reasoning, in which general conclusions are drawn and the bulk of time is spent focusing on the solutions, and far less on the diagnosis.[46]

This may all seem theoretical, until the day comes when you, as a Frenchman, present what you think is a persuasive argument before a crowd of Americans, who lose interest halfway through your analysis of the antithesis; or the day when you, as an American, present to a room full of Frenchmen who clearly do not trust your recommendations because they view your rather cursory analysis of the problem as indicative of sloppy and superficial work.

Lawyers who have had significant foreign assignments usually display good CQ and will know how to modify their approach to fit the audience, so that they are more persuasive and effective as advocates.

Grit

Your legal leaders also need an innate sense of 'grit', which is defined as "passion and perseverance for long-term goals".[47] In essence, it is that certain quality that enables highly successful people to stay motivated and determined to succeed in respect of challenging goals, over long periods of time, despite setbacks and hardship. If you knock a gritty person down, they will just get right back up again, over and over again, until they succeed at what they set out to do.

As one study puts it:[48]

> *Grit entails working strenuously toward challenges, maintaining effort and interest over years despite failure, adversity and plateaus in*

progress. The gritty individual approaches achievement as a marathon; his or her advantage is stamina. Whereas boredom signals to others that it is time to change trajectory and cut losses, the gritty individual stays the course.

Grit is not the same thing as talent, which is how quickly you can improve a skill if you invest the time and effort to do so. Grit enables talent to blossom by driving the person to invest the time and effort needed to achieve success.

According to Angela Duckworth, a professor at the University of Pennsylvania and perhaps the leading authority on grit, getting from talent to achievement can be summarised in two simple formulae:[49]

talent × effort = skill

skill × effort = achievement

Notice how effort counts both in acquiring skill and in going on to achieve something with that skill. As Duckworth notes:[50]

What this theory says is that when you consider individuals in identical circumstances, what each achieves depends on just two things, talent and effort. Talent – how fast we improve in skill – absolutely matters. But effort factors into the calculations twice, not once. Effort builds skills. At the very same time, effort makes skill productive.

Our culture has a tendency to focus on talent and intelligence over grit. However, grit counts as much or even more. When the chips are down and you are in the middle of a crisis, you definitely want to be surrounded by gritty people.

While grit is related to self-control and conscientiousness, it is not the same thing. Gritty people tend to also score highly in relation to these other traits, but grit is a more reliable predictor of success with respect to challenging long-term goals than either self-control or conscientiousness. Thus, a conscientious and self-controlled person may perform a short-term objective (eg, a task at work) well, but may buckle in the face of a challenging obstacle that stands in the way of a long-term objective.

Grit can in fact be measured. Duckworth has developed a 'Grit Scale' that will determine the level of grittiness in a person, based on their agreement or disagreement (ranging from 'very much like me' to 'not like me at all') with the following 10 statements:

- "New ideas or projects sometimes distract me from previous ones."
- "Setbacks don't discourage me. I don't give up easily."
- "I often set a goal but later choose to pursue a different one."
- "I am a hard worker."
- "I have difficulty maintaining my focus on projects that take more than a few months to complete."
- "I finish whatever I begin."
- "My interests change from year to year."
- "I am diligent. I never give up."
- "I have been obsessed with a certain idea or project for a short time but later lost interest."
- "I have overcome setbacks to conquer an important challenge."

You can take the Grit Scale test yourself at http://angeladuckworth. com/grit-scale/.

While you may decide to spare those under consideration for your team from actually taking this test, there is value in keeping an eye out for grittiness levels in prospective candidates. Life is hard. The law is a tough field to be in, with many setbacks, frustrations and long nights. Grit counts toward success.

Final comment

Note that the nine traits described above (innate curiosity, excellent communications, excellent business judgement, results driven, autonomy, courage, flexible leadership, cultural intelligence and grit) are not specific to the legal profession. All senior executives, regardless of function, need to acquire them to some degree. Therein lies an important point: in a changing professional world, many of the core capabilities for success at the highest level are converging.

Part D: Critical threads

Change management

I have learned that if you must leave a place that you have lived in and loved and where all your yesteryears are buried deep, leave it any way except a slow way, leave it the fastest way you can. Never turn back and never believe that an hour you remember is a better hour because it is dead. Passed years seem safe ones, vanquished ones, while the future lives in a cloud, formidable from a distance.

(Beryl Markham)[1]

Change will run though and profoundly impact your ability to upgrade and transform your organisation. It is applicable across Parts B and C of this book.

As you embark on the efforts outlined in this book, your team is likely to experience the emotional and logistical hurdles of change. Change brings uncertainty; and that typically triggers a defensive reaction in most people, generating resistance. Providing people with as much detail as is available can be helpful, but resistance is still likely. Change management is one of the most challenging tasks in business, filled with complexity, including deep-seated emotional components.

Jeanie Daniel Duck refers to "all the human issues that swirl around change – both personally and professionally", as the 'change monster'.[2] If you don't deal with these issues effectively, you will end up fighting the monsters of change rather than achieving your objective.

The information in this book will only provide you with a start to understanding the complex topic of change management, so use this chapter as just a primer. Shelves of excellent books have been written on managing change, and it would be well worth your time to delve into some of them before embarking on your transformation. One book that you might find particularly helpful is Duck's *The Change Monster*.[3] You are also encouraged, if possible, to retain a change management expert to help you before you begin any transformation effort.

Never underestimate the impact change will have on you, your people and your organisation. Indeed, the biggest obstacle to change is probably going to be the very change you are trying to impact.

Lawyers are often the most change-resistant of professionals. By nature, lawyers are risk-averse, rule-driven creatures, raised on precedent and comfortable mainly within the status quo and where there is certainty of outcome.

Change, by contrast, is inherently messy, unpredictable and carries risk. In this sense, lawyers will provide more grief and demand more attention in a changing situation than the rest of the company. As the Legal Executive Institute has noted:[4]

> *Change is never easy, especially the type of systemic and dramatic change the legal industry is experiencing in the current market. And lawyers – not known for being open to change to begin with – are sometimes having a very difficult time with how their profession is evolving and how to envision what the lawyer and law firm of the future may look like.*

Expect major resistance, and budget into your time frame the need to manage that change in an effective way.

The objective of this chapter is to focus your attention on 10 key lessons about managing change. Consider these to be a brief introduction to a topic you will want to learn much more about before you embark on your own transformation.

Change is the natural state of being

> *There is nothing permanent except change.*
> (Heraclitus)[5]

It is easy to assume that change is an exceptional state. But in fact it is the only natural state. Nothing is ever truly static, whether you are looking at corporate life or life itself. Most of us intuitively appreciate that adaptation leads to success, while stasis leads to extinction. Yet, how quickly we discard this truth and how passionately we seek to preserve the status quo.

Consider the effort to preserve the beautiful flora and fauna of coastal California. This coastline is one of the most stunningly beautiful landscapes in the world, in addition to being among the most diverse of any grassland in North America.[6] But what we see as beautiful and untouched is in fact filled with alien species that have invaded the area over a long period of time.

The bottom line is that in practical terms we can no longer identify the original state. And to preserve something less than the original state requires a determination of which state should be preserved. The current state? The state from 100 years ago? The state that is objectively most worth preserving? And even if one could somehow actually decide which state to preserve, would it be certain that the chosen version is better than all future versions?

The same is true for organisations. How many of today's blue-chip companies are structured exactly as they were in 1950? The Dow Jones Industrial Average components have changed 51 times since its inception in 1896.[7] Pearson plc was once one of the world's largest building contractors. Over the years, it exited that industry and entered and exited numerous others, including at various times oil and electric power, financial services, manufacturing, investment trusts, media and publishing,[8] before becoming the world's leading education company that it is today, with operations in educational textbooks, digital learning technologies, assessments and English language learning.[9]

Would it have been better if Pearson, or any of the Dow Jones industrials, were preserved at a given point in time? And how would we know that any version preserved would be better than their future states?

Many of today's largest and most successful corporations were built on the backs of radical change. Ray Kroc bought McDonald's from the original McDonald brothers in 1961 after becoming frustrated with the brothers' desire to limit the number of restaurants.[10] By the time Kroc passed away 23 years later, McDonald's had 7,500 outlets and annual sales of more than $8 billion.[11]

When an organisation is undergoing change, it can be easy to think that anything other than the current state is undesirable. To succeed in life and business, you must embrace change by fostering the resilience and adaptation necessary to evolve. Nature and business are unkind to those who resist.

Start with why change is necessary

Before you begin any transformation, you need to make sure your people are not just on board with what is happening, but also with why it must happen. Change is not about blueprints; it is about winning hearts, which leads to winning minds. You have to get people to trust you and buy in to the change. It is not uncommon in change management that the team will follow the leader's plans less because they agree, and more because they trust the leader.

Great consumer goods companies do the same thing. They appeal to your emotions rather than your logic. They focus on why you really want to buy their product. That is far more powerful than appealing to the rational part of your brain by pointing out functional features.

Take expensive Swiss watches. A Patek Philippe Nautilus Collection Stainless Steel wristwatch retails for about US$50,000. For that, you get a watch that will tell you the hours, minutes, sub-seconds, date and phase of the moon.[12] By contrast, a Timex Men's Classic Digital Dress Silver Tone wristwatch retails for just under US$25 and features a 100-hour chronograph, 100-hour countdown timer, alarm, month/day/date display and a nightlight.[13] So why pay $49,975 more for the Patek Philippe? Because the Patek Philippe is far more effective in signalling wealth and taste, which is the real reason why you want to buy it. It satisfies a deep emotional need, which has nothing to do with your head and everything to do with your heart.

To win the hearts and minds of your people as you embark on your change journey, you too must avoid merely explaining in rational terms what the change will be and how it will happen. Of course, you have to do that too; but you need to start with the 'why'. People need to understand why they should believe you; why they should follow your call for change; why they should uproot themselves and resist the natural urge to maintain the status quo.

So where to begin? Start by discussing why the proposed change is necessary to the firm. Make it dramatic and urgent. Use imagery. Paint a picture that fits your situation. Is it a burning platform? Or a lazy river with rapids ahead? Start with a story because stories appeal to the heart, not just the head (see the chapter entitled "Leadership skills"). Whatever your story is, illustrate the consequences of not changing. There are many examples of firms or entire industries that did not adapt to change well: Wang word processing, Kodak film, Blockbuster Video, as well as manufacturers of typewriters and carbon paper. Unlike those firms, Western Union morphed from sending telegrams to wiring money with outlets in grocery stores and it is more profitable than ever.

Once you have achieved an understanding among your audience of the need for the change, the 'why' can help you focus on the 'how'. Only at that point can you begin openly discussing thought processes, trade-offs and alternatives considered. Always come back to the 'why' until you are certain people have begun to accept it. Test the audience's understanding of it so you know everyone has grasped the need for the change. They don't have to like it or even agree with it, but they must acknowledge understanding.

People adopt change at different speeds and for a variety of reasons. Do not expect 100% agreement at once simply because the logic is obvious to the supporters. Give people time to adjust and continue to reinforce the 'why' regularly. Adjustment to the new normal will eventually happen for almost everyone – but there may come a point where some people get left behind. While not a desirable goal, it is not unexpected. To gain success with the majority of your people, be patient, allow for slower movement than you might like and make sure you let the dissenters feel that their voices have been heard and understood. That may require you to build a spirit of agreement around them. As Larry Marks, a senior strategic consultant and expert on change management, notes:[14]

> You will likely have naysayers and you must be gentle in how you bring them along. Engage the influencers (bosses, co-workers, social leaders) and cultural leaders in the organisation to lead the slow adopters to acceptance. Once the influencers are on board, the naysayers will begin to fall in line.

You may never get total buy-in, but if the majority of the social leaders are for it, the rest will usually follow in fairly short order. Leaders lead, but as Larry Marks further observes:[15]

> *More than strong management and leadership are required for a successful initiative. Change management is a process with a rigour that requires precision. It involves quantifications; goal analysis and agreement; managerial style development; open, productive communication; and the flexibility to change what is not working as the process moves forward.*

Make sure you take note of this as you move into your transformation effort.

Change is an inherently emotional process

Change invariably comes packed with a lot of big emotions, including fear, elation, depression and exhaustion. It is important to recognise this as a natural part of the process; so you should know that the emotional roller coaster your team is about to get on has its own cycle of stages. Recognising those stages makes them easier to manage.

Anyone who has moved from one country to another can attest to the effect of 'culture shock', which is the emotional reaction you experience upon relocating. There is a cycle to culture shock, including an early 'honeymoon' phase, when you arrive in the new country, to a low period in the middle and an adjustment at the back end, when you settle in and feel at home.[16] Culture shock is far more manageable if you can recognise the emotional cycle and learn to adapt to its phases.

Organisational change also has its emotional cycles and the more you acquaint yourself with them, the better you will be at coping with the process. Jeanie Daniel Duck describes five basic phases of the change process: stagnation, preparation, implementation, determination and fruition:[17]

- *Stagnation* happens when organisations no longer innovate or provide the right products or technologies. There can be denial, and people may prefer to continue working as before; but eventually it becomes clear that change is needed to survive.
- That ushers in *preparation*, in which the decision is made to

change. This is an in-between phase, which brings with it uncertainty and insecurity. People realise that change is coming but they are still trying to determine what the change means for them or the organisation as a whole. This is a phase that is filled with difficult work and trade-offs, particularly if there is a lack of alignment or the phase goes on for too long.

- When the organisation is clear about where they need to head, *implementation* begins. The company announces its transformation plan and execution commences. At this stage, people experience the same fear, uncertainty and exhaustion that they felt during preparation, except that now they also feel confused, apathetic, resentful, inadequate and volatile. There may also be positive emotions such as relief, exhilaration, excitement and recognition.
- At this point, *determination* kicks in. This is a critical juncture because the change has been formally implemented but has not yet really taken root. People begin to experience change fatigue, exhaustion and disillusionment. In addition, some may begin to put up real resistance as they realise that the change will actually require them to work differently. An enormous amount of courage and commitment is needed to push through and secure the new ways of working. Many organisations will, at this stage, retreat.
- Finally, if the organisation has been able to successfully slog through the determination phase, it will experience *fruition*, when the organisation is transformed. This is a happy period, where the new normal sets in.

Complacency, however, lurks just around the corner. Unless people recognise that change is a constant process, stagnation will inevitably rear its ugly head again. Forward movement stops – and once stopped, it is difficult to resume. Momentum is your friend. A commonly heard phrase from many organisations is: "We have a commitment." Always ask yourself what happed to the previous commitment and try to discover why it is no longer in force.

Convey Duck's above cycle of five phases to your people. Introduce them, before you begin, to the phases that they could well go through. If you do, you may help them recognise that what they are about to experience is part of a normal emotional cycle. That in turn will help them to navigate the emotional depths that the proposed change will trawl them through.

Regularly track your team's emotional state

Because change is so emotional, it is critical that you regularly track and discuss how people are feeling about the change that is under way. Your team will need to exchange and receive information in order to process what is happening, and agree on the direction. If you fail to do this, people will travel at different speeds through the various stages of the change curve. The majority of people may still be in the determination phase, while senior management has moved on to fruition.

Leaders often overlook this aspect because they forget how much more information they possess relative to the rest of the organisation. It can be easy to get disconnected from the emotions that people are experiencing elsewhere in the organisation. Talking about headcount reductions in a strategy meeting at the executive level is a very different experience emotionally from attending your tenth farewell party for an old friend and colleague who is being let go during a restructuring. Change should not be something that people feel is happening to them; it should be a process that they participate in.

To get to that place, you need to create a safe space in which your people can air how they are feeling. If you transparently share how the team is feeling, you will also create trust, which breeds engagement. Better to get the negativity out in the open in a safe environment than to let it fester under the surface. Sunlight is the best disinfectant.

This is a delicate process and it is easy to cross the line from getting the problems out in the open to open revolt as all the complaints are voiced in one room. It is for this reason that it is often best to engage a professional change management expert to help you navigate the process.

The best place to start is by means of two-way communication. Fundamentally, communication equals trust. People need to recognise that they are not alone, that their voices are heard and that they have a stake in what is happening. You need to really listen to what is being said and then respond to it. This will require you, as a leader, to make yourself vulnerable. You need to be willing to be open and honest about the strengths and potential weaknesses of the change. In every case where a weakness is discussed, the leader must be ready to present a logical approach to how that will be handled.

Open conversation and visibility are good, but be very careful about anonymous surveys. If you are not going to share the results with the group, that can be workable but argues against transparency. If you share the results and they are heavily negative, you a creating a new unifying wave of resentment.

The next step is to create small discussion groups, ideally led by people from outside the team or even outside the organisation. The groups can be asked to share in a guided and reasonably confidential manner their thoughts and concerns about the change that is happening, using the feedback from the survey as a guide. The discussions need to strike the right balance between being structured and unstructured. On the one hand, they should focus on the topics of interest from the survey, as well as some free-form discussions around what is working well and what is not, how to fix problems, etc. On the other hand, the sessions should not be scripted so tightly that people feel unable to speak their minds freely.

The focus groups should be supplemented by regular 'unplugged' sessions, in which senior leaders from your team travel around your organisation and conduct small off-the-record meetings over coffee, with no more than four or five people at a time – preferably away from the work premises, in a café or other comfortable surroundings.

These smaller sessions can be unscripted opportunities for people to share their thoughts and ask questions. It allows people who may not otherwise have access to you to feel connected. Unlike the focus groups, these sessions can and should be completely unstructured and held on a regular and ongoing basis, even after the transformation is complete. It is important, though, that the leaders who will be conducting these sessions are trained on how to get the desired results and how to handle conflicts in the discussions. Difficult, awkward and potentially inflammatory issues may arise and leaders need to have some acquaintance with how best to respond in such situations. The best instructors to give this kind of training are experts – usually change management professionals from within or outside your organisation.

After running the survey, the discussion groups and the unplugged sessions, you should analyse the feedback to identify broad trends or key recurring themes, such as concern, excitement and personal anxiety over what the change "means to me". Once you have these, you should relay them back to the whole team and openly track how everyone is doing. These feedback themes invite discussion, and the regular unplugged sessions will be a useful tool for monitoring things on an ongoing basis. The goal is to get people to feel that they are a part of the change, rather than a victim.

Conduct the transformation-specific surveys and discussion groups on a regular basis during the transformation, so that everyone knows how everyone is feeling and what the issues are. In that way, everyone owns the solutions and you build a sense of trust and transparency, which is essential for the right outcome. Just as importantly, make sure the team members receive updates on any progress with the change and on anticipated results.

Do not let your team freeze up

Have you ever had that nightmare in which you dream that you are being pursued by something dangerous and, just as the dangerous thing (person, tiger, monster) is about to pounce on you, you find yourself unable to move? That can be an actual living nightmare if it happens during your transformation. The fear of change can freeze you or your team.

There will be times in your journey when it becomes incredibly difficult to move forward. The level of complexity, the energy required and the emotional toll can cause your team to flounder. You may be tempted to declare a pause or declare victory without actually embedding the change. If the change is perceived as dangerous, people may actually freeze up by disengaging – carrying on as before and nodding in agreement at meetings, but not doing much to actually effect the change in their daily work.

Freezing up is a natural response to danger. In nature, animals typically respond to danger in one of three ways: fight, flee or freeze. The kakapo, a large, nocturnal parrot in New Zealand, defends itself by freezing up and standing very still until the danger has moved on. That worked fine while the parrot's only natural predator was a (now extinct) giant eagle. But when European settlers – and their cats, rats and stoats – arrived, it led to the kakapo's near extinction.[18]

Similarly, freezing up can be disastrous in a transformation. In a changing environment, you need to constantly adapt to the problems you experience. Freezing up minimises your ability to do so.

If you stand still too long in a fight, you will get hit, so you need to move your feet and not make yourself a target. Similarly, during a transformation, you must also keep moving. If you stand still too long, you will lose momentum and things will start to unravel. It is important that you recognise the signs of fatigue and resist the siren calls to "let it go – you've changed enough". Push on through with what you set out to do, no matter how exhausting or painful it feels. It will be a lot worse in the long term if you give in at this point.

Never look back

Looking back is an exercise in bitterness compounded by myopia. Everything seems so much better in the past when you are facing a present – and an uncertain period of time into the future – that is full of disruption and uncertainty. But you cannot drive forward when you are looking in your rear view mirror. The rear view mirror is only 20 centimetres across while the windscreen is nearly two metres wide. Your vision must be focused to succeed.

Sir Winston Churchill is said to have remarked: "If you're going through hell, keep going."[19] How right he was.

Change can give you the best work of your career

Change can be a negative experience, but it can also be tremendously exhilarating and provide you with some of the most rewarding work of your career.[20] You may discover new truths about yourself and what you are capable of. You may find sources of courage and creativity you never knew you possessed.

Change can also present you with incredible career opportunities that may never otherwise have happened. To spot these, however, you have to suspend your disbelief, step forward and embrace the change – sometimes, success lies in recognising the inevitability of the change and working with it rather than against it.

In Norway, people traditionally spend their summers at cabins that dot the beautiful coastline. In the mornings, right after waking up, people will run out to the rocks and dive into the cold, clear water. Rain or shine. Those moments of suspension in the air before your body hits the bracing water can be difficult. But once you have quite literally taken the plunge, you emerge deeply refreshed and energised.

Encourage your team to dive in. The longer you wait, the harder it gets.

Focus on what you can control; don't worry about the rest

We can watch our diet and exercise regularly but we are unable to ensure that our health will last. We can take steps to save for our retirement – but will that prevent the next financial meltdown? Life is inherently full of uncontrollable variables.

Transformation and change are equally fraught with uncertainty and the potential for major meltdowns beyond your control. But in both life and transformation, you need to focus on the elements that you can influence and avoid worrying about the ones that you can't. This can be a hard lesson for lawyers, who are trained to think and worry about risk. They see a stove and immediately think of third-degree burns instead of a delicious bowl of soup.

Try to sort out the controllable risks you face as you navigate your transformation from the ones you have little or no ability to influence. Then focus your efforts on the former and try to stop worrying about the latter. Letting go of what you know is outside of your control allows you to unleash your energy on the problems over which you have influence. If the entire company is undergoing a transformation, emphasise to your team that even though they are unable to control how the whole thing is going, they can control how well their team navigates their own process.

There is a morale aspect to this as well. If you spend time worrying about the uncontrollable, you begin to feel powerless and demotivated. Focusing on what is within your control will empower you and give you a sense of pleasure in your work.

Every culture has its admirable traits. I used to live in Japan, and one of the traits that I have admired the most about the Japanese is their incredible devotion to ensuring perfection in their work. I recall seeing a cleaner who scrubbed the stairs with an incredible focus and vigour for a long, long time, concentrating on one spot with a toothbrush-sized utensil. Nothing seemed to distract him from his task; he was completely at ease and yet fully devoted to doing his job. This trait is also very common at many levels within corporate organisations in Japan; people are fully dedicated to completing their work as well as they possibly can. When they undertake a task, whatever that task may be, they do it deliberately and completely. If you find yourself washing dishes, for example, focus on being the best possible dishwasher you can be; strive for perfection in that task. While you will never attain perfection in dishwashing (or anything else), something truly valuable comes from striving for it with both deliberateness and focus.

While we cannot all find emotional and psychological peace in everything we do, there is a lesson here for teams in a time of change. Encourage people to focus on and find meaning in their daily work, regardless of the change going on around them. If they apply their efforts to the things that are within their control, they will find the quiet, inner satisfaction that comes with making the world a better place, one bit at a time. That in turn infects your whole culture with something positive and valuable.

You are in charge of you

During a time of transformation, remind yourself and the people you lead that you are more than just your job; you are the sum of many parts, including family, hobbies, friends and interests, as well as work. When so much of what is happening around you at work is outside your control and could impact your job, it can be hard to put things in perspective. But if you reflect deeply on it, a material change in your role or your work need not change who you are – unless you let it.

Remind people that *they* are in charge of themselves. Not their managers. Not their company. Not the team. Regardless of what happens to them, they have choices as to how they react and what steps they take.

The anchorwoman of a local TV news station and her colleagues all had their jobs terminated when the station was sold to a new owner, who decided to change the format and cancel the news show. Once she had overcome the initial shock of being out of work, the anchorwoman realised that she was not synonymous with her former job. She had many other skills and interests that she could cultivate. The more she thought it through, the more she realised that this was an opportunity to move in a new direction. She set to work using her investigative skills to explore what options were available to her. Ultimately, she settled on public and media relations and went on to become the owner of a successful public relations consultancy.

By contrast, one of her colleagues, a former star reporter, gradually slid into depression. He was never fully able to dissociate himself from his old job. As a result, he could never move on from viewing his own value as having been inextricably connected to his former job, even though he had similar media and investigative skills that he could have transformed into something new.

In a transformation situation, it is important that you focus on doing what you can to effect the change, without letting the fear control you of what the change might mean for your current role. You are ultimately responsible for your own engagement, and you answer to yourself and no one else in how you respond.

Of course, it is easier said than done. But you will have a better chance of surviving in your job and in life if you can relax and add value than if you cower under your desk. You might be unable to compartmentalise job stress, but you can learn to keep things in perspective and react in the way that is best for you.

This is the 'new normal'

The greatest legacy of a successful transformation lies in learning to embrace change and adapt to a world that is constantly changing, rather than in effecting just the change of the moment.

If you focus only on the change in front of you, you will fool yourself into believing that the uncertainty you are facing is transitory and that, once the change has been implemented, you can go back to stasis. But nothing could be further from the truth. Successful transformation is only attained when understanding the change process becomes embedded as a perpetual way of life within your organisational culture. Change is the constant!

The trick is finding a way to ensure that you have a built-in process that allows you to innovate, process and effect change. Expatriates who successfully move every few years from one country to the next have learned to work the uncertainty of where they will be in a few years' time into their family culture. They know they will eventually move again and so they put in place a process to facilitate the next move: they maintain an up-to-date list of valuables for the insurance valuation that the movers require; they preserve only what they actually cherish, keeping their household possessions to a relatively constant size; and once they know the location of the next move, they have a smooth process to investigate schools or other key installations before searching for housing. They know exactly what is needed and desired.

Similarly, in your team you should create a cultural expectation that nothing stays static. Instil a process to identify, adopt and implement new ideas. That will go some way towards preparing everybody for change and ensuring that when it happens it does so more on your own terms. In cases where change happens unexpectedly, at least you will have in place a process for implementing it.

Summary

The above principles may be a helpful start in getting yourself and your team over the finish line and readjusting how you deal with change going forward. But, as noted earlier, consider further reading on the subject before you embark on your journey. Never underestimate the power and impact that change will have on your team.

Strategic direction

If you don't know where you're going, you'll end up someplace else.

(Yogi Berra)[1]

Maintaining a sense of strategic direction is critical to your effort. If you embark on a journey without a map, you are likely to reach your destination with substantial delays and you will only have yourself to blame if you end up somewhere else. In terms of your strategic direction, you will need a roadmap that is tailored to your own team, its culture and its circumstances.

One place you can start on that effort is to consider a few principles, look at the efforts of others, and combine these principles and experiences with your own thoughts about your particular journey. This chapter will provide you with a basic overview of some of the principles that need to be included in your strategic planning, as well as some specific elements that may be useful for you to consider including in your plan.

'Strategy' is a massive topic and a comprehensive examination of it is beyond the scope of this book. But since it greatly informs how you roll out a transformation, you need to at least be introduced to it here. Engaging a consultant to help you map out your strategic roadmap may be helpful if you are starting from scratch.

Roadmap principles

Let us consider a few basic principles so that we are clear on what we mean by a 'roadmap' to help you execute your strategy. In essence, it means having a clearly articulated and carefully thought-out plan that encompasses a vision, a mission and strategic priorities for your team and that allows you to determine where you are heading and how you will get there.

To help you think about these various components of the roadmap, consider an analogy related to the armed forces of a country. The general orders the army to win the war; the colonel orders the troops to win the battle; the captain orders the platoon to take the hill; and the sergeant orders the charge. The general is talking about the vision; the colonel about the mission; the captain about the strategic priority; and the sergeant about the tactical steps.

Let us consider each of these in turn.

Vision

An organisation's 'vision' spells out what it wants to be or do in the future. It goes to the heart of where the organisation is heading, defining its ultimate destination. It should be short, simple, memorable and motivational, and convey in a clear and inspiring way the company's direction – what the organisation ultimately aspires to be. It is a kind of 'North Star' that guides everyone; it gives people a sense of clarity of purpose.

Having a true vision is absolutely essential because it tells you where you want to go. To serve its purpose, the vision needs to be a true one. It must be thoughtfully considered and accurately reflect the organisation's ambition. Too many companies either have fluffy, meaningless visions that are unconnected to their true purpose, or overly complex visions that no one in the company understands or remembers.

Visions need to be short, sharp and to the point. Everybody should be able to get the idea immediately, whether they are employees, customers or unfamiliar with the business altogether. The vision for Pearson, for example, is "to help people make more of their lives through learning".[2] For Amazon, it is "to be Earth's most customer centric company; to build a place where people can come to find and discover anything they might want to buy online".[3] As you can see, a vision is at its core an aspirational statement, but it is clear and memorable.

Should you have a legal department vision? The answer is 'yes' but it is a qualified yes. As a support function, the legal team's vision must remain completely aligned with the company's vision lest you end up on a journey towards a different destination from the company you serve. The legal department should therefore have the same vision that the company has.

The one caveat might be where your company lacks a vision or has one that you find incomprehensible or misaligned with the company's true destination. In that case, your best bet might be to raise that with your CEO in order to get clarity and perhaps start a conversation within your broader organisation about where you are heading. If there is a strong need for you to consider crafting your own vision statement, that is a sign that you might want to consider changing jobs, because your company is clearly adrift, lacking direction or purpose.

Mission

A 'mission' is based more in the present and spells out what we, as lawyers, will do to help achieve the company's vision. To be useful, it needs to be specific to your team. The company will probably also have a mission, but here you can deviate from the broader organisation-wide mission and have in place one for the legal department. That is because it will allow you to better align your skills with the organisation's direction and destination.

In considering the best mission for your legal team, conduct the following analysis:

- *Unique capabilities:* Ask yourself what unique capabilities your team possesses that give you competitive advantages. In other words, what functional skills does your team possess that no one else (inside or outside the company) has?
- *Core role:* Ask yourself what the core role you, as in-house counsel, must play in order to help your company achieve its vision. What do you do that no one else (inside or outside the company) can do in order to support the company's vision?
- *Combining the two:* Combine your unique capabilities with your core role to form your mission.

Unique capabilities

As you take time to think through what your unique capabilities are, it will become apparent fairly quickly that you are the only legal experts inside the company. But go deeper and ask yourself what capabilities you possess that differentiate you from outside counsel. What makes you uniquely capable to supply the company with legal services? In other words, why should the company have an in-house legal team? Why not just go directly to outside law firms for all the company's legal needs? How are you adding unique value?

You might decide that there are two special capabilities that only you can provide. These are pragmatism and proactivity. These capabilities could be considered your unique selling points – the skills, talent and experience that really separate you from outside providers of all types.

Proactivity Only you as insiders are present when your business partners are making formative decisions. Thus, only you can proactively identify issues before they become problems and be part of that decision-making process.

If, for example, you are sitting in a strategic or tactical planning meeting with your internal business partners and someone were to propose something that would be legally inadvisable, only you would be able to raise that observation there and then and thus enable the company to recalibrate its actions so as to remain legally compliant and minimise risk.

Contrast this with the reactive approach of law firms or other providers, which are unable to be present as insiders when decisions are made. Without counsel present, your business partners might proceed with possibly illegal or inappropriate actions and be forced to deal with the consequences, including reputational harm. Moreover, they would have to retain expensive outside legal counsel after the fact, to clean things up as best they could once things had blown up.

Pragmatism Your insider status also means you have a unique opportunity to infuse your advice with pragmatism. Your intimate knowledge of the business by virtue of your insider status allows the development of practical solutions that combine both the legal and business needs of the company.

If you do your job well, you will be solving problems in addition to providing legal advice. By contrast, outside counsel must serve many clients and be less familiar with your company, its culture and its circumstances – making it harder to judge legal risk with the same keen understanding of the business exigencies as inside lawyers can.

You may decide there are additional unique capabilities that the internal legal department brings to your company. The point is to think carefully about the question and articulate a compelling answer to it that your business partners understand and accept. The day a consultant approaches your CEO and suggests outsourcing the legal department in order to save money, you want to be sure that he decides to stick with you because he understands the unique capabilities you provide to the company, including leadership, vision, perspective, intimate knowledge of how your business operates, market conditions and the culture of your company.

Core role

Once you have identified your unique capabilities, focus on the second step. Ask yourself what your unique role is in helping your company to achieve its vision.

You might, for instance, conclude that, as in-house counsel, you play two roles exceptionally well: you enable the company to conduct its business; and you protect the company's assets and reputation in the best way possible. It is in navigating the tension between these sometimes contradictory roles – what Ben W Heineman Jr refers to as the 'partner –guardian tension'[4] – that the in-house lawyer adds the most value for the company's clients.

> *The greatest challenge for General Counsel and other inside lawyers is to reconcile the dual – and at times contradictory – roles of being both a partner to the business leaders and a guardian of the corporation's integrity and reputation.*
> (Ben W Heineman Jr)[5]

You might decide that your core role is entirely different from the above, which is illustrative and intended to get the conversation started in your organisation. The point is to engage in the conversation.

Combine the two

Put your unique capabilities and your core role together to arrive at your mission. Using the above examples, for instance, you might decide that your legal department mission is "to provide proactive and pragmatic legal advice that enables our business and protects our assets and reputation".

Strategies and tactics

Once you have identified your mission, you will need to underpin it with strategies and tactics in order to drive it forward.

If the company's vision is your destination and your mission is what you will do to help achieve that vision, then your strategies are the outline plans to help achieve your mission, and tactical steps are the specific actions that you will take. You are likely to need to engender more than one strategy and set of tactics to help you. Your strategies and tactics, therefore, need to be unique to your team.

To determine what your strategies should be, you want to think carefully about the following questions:

- What are you doing today that will help you to achieve your mission?
- What is holding you back from achieving your mission and what steps can you take to help move things forward?

You need to effectively take an inventory of what is working and what is holding you back. The inventory should be laser-focused on getting the legal department to a place where it can achieve its mission.

This effort should, to the extent possible, be data-driven and not just anecdotal. You can generate this data through internal research, such as questionnaires or interviews of your business partners, to determine where there are gaps. This process will be greatly facilitated by your ability to track and manage your own key metrics, such as budget and expenditure ratios (eg, spend by matter, type, internal to external), training, contract management (volume, hours spent, type), customer satisfaction, engagement and the like.

Once you have developed your strategies, you will be in a position to outline what your tactical business plan priorities should be. You should pick priorities that are aligned with your strategies, which in turn are aligned with and support your mission, which in turn is how you as a team will help your organisation achieve its vision.

For example, let us say your mission is "to provide proactive and pragmatic legal advice that will enable and protect the business". After taking your inventory, you might conclude that one thing you are doing today that helps you to do that is that your department is good at informing itself and the company about upcoming regulations, because that enables you to react with enough speed to be proactive. 'Anticipate changes in the regulatory landscape' might therefore be one of your strategies.

If, by contrast, you were to decide that you are not doing enough business partner training in areas such as brand protection or diversity, and that this was preventing you from achieving your mission because it was hindering its proactive element, then you might adopt a strategy around improving the quality and frequency of your business partner training.

Regardless of what you select, you will want to measure and track how you are progressing. It is much simpler to be data-driven if you are actively collecting and tracking your key metrics. Indeed, there is a symbiosis between the two efforts, since the metrics you decide to track will, in part, be driven by your strategic priorities, and vice versa.

Examples of strategic priorities

The strategies you adopt each need to be unpacked further than just the top-line statement, so that you really understand what is needed to make them meaningful and leverage them for business planning and other purposes.

Let us suppose that your legal department has developed three core strategies to assist you in achieving your mission "to provide proactive and pragmatic legal advice that will enable and protect the business":

- to develop your people;
- to provide the right advice at the right time; and
- to leverage global strength.

Let us unpack each to see how they might play out as tactical steps.

Example strategy 1: Develop your people

Without well-trained, capable people we are unable to provide proactive and pragmatic legal advice that enables and protects the business, so we need to ensure that our people are able to fully develop their potential.

We have embraced five ways to ensure this happens (as described further below):

- providing leadership;
- building frameworks;
- nurturing diversity;
- creating a safe haven; and
- importing/exporting excellence.

Providing leadership

To empower our people, we will develop and promote leadership across our team at two levels: servant leaders and leaders of self.

Servant leaders Those who lead other people must do so as servant leaders. They lead solely to serve their teams, and 'service' in this context is used in the same way that parents serve their children – not by giving them everything they want, but by developing them, encouraging them to reach their full potential, nudging them and ultimately helping them to soar. Servant leaders therefore:

- eliminate administrative obstacles that hold their people back;
- build the means for their people to achieve career success; and
- provide cover when their people legitimately need it.

Leaders of self Sole contributors – ie, those who are not leaders of other people – must be 'leaders of self'. This requires them to:

- develop themselves by actively learning and identifying, creating and seeking out career opportunities;
- take the initiative, whether in developing client relationships, resolving matters within their control or displaying a desire to excel; and
- become active co-creators of the surrounding culture, helping to build and reinforce it.

It should go without saying that servant leaders must also be strong leaders of self.

Building frameworks

We should maintain performance routines (such as the setting of objectives, the conducting of reviews and the coaching of staff or partners) to ensure people have clearly defined, attainable and measurable goals that are both meaningful and connected to our vision and mission. Only then will everyone be investing in the vision.

Building the right frameworks also means recognising those who live out the values of the firm. This is not just about increasing monetary reward; sometimes the most powerful recognition is praise given for a job well done.

Nurturing diversity

We need an open, diverse culture, where no one is afraid to challenge orthodoxy. This gives our team better decision-making. But we must also reinforce unity of purpose once we have decided where we are going.

Creating a safe haven

Our people need to feel safe. Everyone on the team needs to feel they are covering each other's backs. The best way to encourage people to do amazing things for others is to foster an environment where others would do the same for them. This starts with our leadership.

Importing/exporting excellence

We must nurture curiosity about our profession, our company and the world beyond by developing:

- *Avid learners:* We need those who continually find ways to learn new things and borrow better ways of working. The more we know, the more we can contribute.
- *Networking:* We need networkers who seek out new thinking and bring that back into our team. To do this, we need to give people time to develop their personal networks, both internally and externally.

We should actively put in place various measures to encourage these imperatives. For instance, we will allow each person on the team to take anyone to lunch or dinner once per month, provided they come back and share with us at least three things they have learned.

Example strategy 2: Provide the right advice at the right time

In order to provide the right advice, we need to develop legal and business expertise. But that is insufficient: we need also to be prepared to continually grow that expertise as our business evolves. If we fail to do this, we will become stale – and no one needs solutions to yesterday's problems.

Our expertise must also be paired with pragmatism. We are here to help our business achieve its goals. While guard rails are important – we mustn't allow the company to do anything illegal or unethical – being overly conservative can also be very damaging. This balance can be difficult for lawyers to achieve. Constant reinforcement from our legal leadership is needed.

Providing our advice at the right time is all about ensuring that we strive to be proactive as discussed earlier. This requires us to be embedded in all areas of the business, with seats at the decision-making table.

Example strategy 3: Leverage your global strength

The goal is not necessarily to be a global powerhouse but to act as if we were one by drawing on the wealth of knowledge that exists across the team, regardless of size.

If we learn to communicate openly within the team, we often find there is someone with a deeper knowledge or understanding of an issue than we have. If, however, we keep quiet, people will lose that strength and be left trying to solve problems alone.

To do this correctly, we need better communications, work exchanges, rotational assignments and cross-team projects. Initiatives like these will broaden the knowledge base, connect people and leverage diversity. They can also make our team a more fun place within which to work.

When and how to execute your strategic direction

Your vision, mission, strategies and tactical steps are, at some level, aspirational. But as Laozi said, "The journey of a thousand miles begins with a single step."[6] If the first step is to know where you want to go, the second step is executing your plan. But when and how do you do that?

When?

You should start to formulate and execute your strategic direction only after you have completed your evaluation of your first 100 days and your risk analysis, and you have appointed your leadership team. If you try to create a strategic direction any earlier, you will have difficulty knowing where you need to head. And if you try to do it much later, you will flounder until it is done.

The word 'start' in the preceding paragraph is significant. The roadmap process is not one that starts and stops after the first phase of your journey has begun. Rather, it is an ongoing process that needs to be continually recalibrated as you develop your culture and as your business evolves.

In order to ensure that your roadmap is a living document, you will also need to embed a commitment of continual improvement in your strategic planning process. Consider applying 'lean inspired' principles to your business planning process by focusing all departmental efforts on identifying and promoting department activities that will help fulfil your strategic priorities, and on identifying and reducing/eliminating other activities.

In other words, use your roadmap to frame where your department and your people need to devote more time and effort and what they should stop or spend less time executing. This can be as simple as making sure that your people are constantly prioritising their time and resources based on the roadmap. If this is embedded, it can go a long way in helping people navigate their huge workload by giving them a framework and licence to decide how to prioritise in the daily deluge they face, secure in the knowledge that you and the leadership will back them up.

How?

With respect to the 'how', you might want to start with your leaders in an offsite session and then take the outcome to the broader legal function for a full review and vetting. The process needs to be inclusive if there is to be legitimacy and enthusiasm behind it. You need collective input and involvement if you want real alignment behind the end result.

Another important issue to consider as you are formulating your roadmap is how it fits with your formulation of your culture and values, as outlined in Part C.

At one level, your roadmap has to be a reflection of your culture, in that it needs to take its starting point in your current reality and build upon it. At another level, however, your strategy needs to be an aspirational map that will direct your efforts to move your culture towards a sophisticated level at which you are comfortable, identifying the things you need to focus on and build as you move forward. In this sense, if your roadmap is to be a living document and not just something you complete to check a box before putting it away in a drawer, it needs to be crafted through collective input and with your values and culture in mind.

Today's workplace requires flexible, empowered, intellectually curious and high-performing teams of professionals who lead themselves and their colleagues forward with creativity, pragmatism and effectiveness. This primer on the principles that should underlie a roadmap, together with the concrete example of how that might play out, will hopefully provide you with ideas on which to build your own roadmap – one designed for your own specific circumstances.

Part E: Conclusion

Concluding remarks

They always say time changes things,
but you actually have to change
them yourself.
(Andy Warhol)[1]

The basic model being proposed

The volatile and complex environment that companies and their legal advisers find themselves in has raised the stakes for today's general counsel. Pressures are growing, threats are more diffuse and the costs of getting it wrong are rising. Internal demand for legal support is increasing, but legal department resources are shrinking.

To succeed as general counsel, you must, in addition to being a strategic partner–guardian, be able to build, lead and inspire an outstanding legal team. It is only by doing this that you can manage the professional convergence and role overload that comes with the job.

There are, however, plenty of opportunities amidst the threats that can help you build an excellent organisation. The innovation revolution is unbundling the traditional law firm model and disaggregating the one-stop-shop approach to handling legal matters. Today, you can efficiently allocate your work to the best-suited provider, ranging from your own in-house team to law firms and alternative legal services partners. New technologies allow you to better communicate and be productive, provide self-service options and improve the overall efficiency and transparency of your operations.

It can be difficult to identify these opportunities and build an outstanding team while at the same time navigating the intense challenges of a day-to-day substantive practice. Where and how to begin? This book has answered that question by providing you with a model for building a high-performing legal team.

There is a method and sequencing to the approach we have considered. You should start with the hardware. Assess your core risks and talent, and design an integrated team structure around that; unify your budget and optimise your spend; rationalise your service delivery model; select the right outside partners; and identify the technologies that will support your efforts. By tackling these things first, you will gain the credibility you need to focus on the software, the less tangible but critical components of culture and talent. You will need to develop and reinforce your subculture; identify and tweak your unwritten cultural assumptions; manage the generational context; and recruit legal leaders who have the skills and qualities needed to run a high-performance 21st-century legal team.

In the real world, there will of course be interplay between the hardware and the software; steps will get mingled. But if you are in doubt, you should return to the basic sequencing.

Throughout your effort, you must also pay attention to change management and strategic direction. Failing to address these will scuttle your endeavours.

Looking forward

As has been evident throughout this book, the pace of change – particularly in the past decade – has been relentless. We live in exponential times. More change happens in a year or two today than historically happened in a lifetime. In 2006–07 alone, for instance, Apple's iPhone, the Kindle, Airbnb and Android were introduced; Facebook began to scale; computing storage capacity accelerated greatly, making big data possible; the internet reached one billion users; IBM started building its artificial-intelligence and machine-learning computer, named Watson; and Intel introduced non-silicon materials into microchips, enabling Moore's Law to continue.[2]

The legal world has also been impacted by these events, and the future of the profession will no doubt see a lot more change. Indeed, as Professor Susskind has noted, "by 2035 ... it is neither hyperbolic nor fanciful to expect that the legal profession will have changed beyond recognition".[3] One thing, however, seems fairly certain: whatever issues tomorrow's general counsel must wrestle with, they will still need an outstanding team of individuals to back them up.

Accelerating your legal team's performance is therefore the best way to both address today's challenges and prepare for those of tomorrow. The tasks may change, but general counsel will always need to stay on top of hardware and software, while managing change and ensuring strategic direction.

The road is hard and intense. The results will be worth it.

Chapter notes

Introduction

1 *"Sea Change: How Corporate Governance Demands are Elevating the General Counsel's Job"*, General Counsel Leaders Circle, Target Topic, July 2014 (available at www.gcleaderscircle.org/wp-content/uploads/2014/07/GCLC-Target-Topic-GC-Corp-Governance-final-July-2014.pdf; accessed 31 October 2016).

2 Ben W Heineman Jr, *The Inside Counsel Revolution: Resolving the Partner–Guardian Tension*, Ankerwycke, 2016.

3 Steven Johnson, *Where Good Ideas Come From: The Natural History of Innovation*, Penguin Group USA, 2010, location 127 in the e-book edition.

4 Irving Wladawsky-Berger, "The Rise of the T-Shaped Organization", *The Wall Street Journal CIO Journal*, 18 December 2015 (available at: http://blogs.wsj.com/cio/2015/12/18/the-rise-of-the-t-shaped-organisation/; accessed 23 October 2016).

5 See http://psychology.iresearchnet.com/industrial-organisational-psychology/job-satisfaction/role-overload-and-underload/ for a discussion of role overload and underload.

6 Ben W Heineman Jr, note 2 above, p361.

7 From Merriam-Webster Dictionary (see www.merriam-webster.com/dictionary/model; accessed 28 October 2016).

The changing context

1 Quotation from www.brainyquote.com/quotes/keywords/disruption.html; accessed 21 November 2016.

2 Valentina Pasquali, "Compliance Goes Global: The Unavoidable Costs of Increasing Regulation", *Global Finance Magazine*, May 2015 (article available at: www.gfmag.com/magazine/may-2015/unavoidable-costs-increasing-regulation-compliance-goes-global; accessed 20 November 2016).

3 *Ibid*.

4 See: www.uschamber.com/above-the-fold/the-growing-burden-federal-regulations/ for the 1950 statistic and https://regulatorystudies.columbian.gwu.edu/reg-stats for the 2015 statistic (both sites accessed 1 October 2016).

5 See http://financialservices.house.gov/dodd-frank (accessed 1 October 2016).

6 See https://thinkprogress.org/5-numbers-to-know-as-dodd-frank-wall-street-reform-celebrates-its-5th-birthday-e145f4360b7c#.x2ws4y5vd (accessed 1 October 2016).

7 Pasquali, note 2 above.

8 *Id*.

9 Pasquali, note 2 above, p1.

10 See: https://en.wikipedia.org/wiki/Facilitating_payment (accessed 3 November 2016).

11 Leuan Jolly, *"Data protection in the United States: overview"*; available through Practical Law.com, Thompson Reuters, at http://us.practicallaw.com/6-502-0467 (accessed 3 November 2016).

12 *Ibid*.

13 Lindsay Fortado, "Cartel Fines in US and China Rise to Record Levels", *Financial Times*, 13 January 2016 (available at www.ft.com/content/1c56c27c-b9f3-11e5-b151-8e15c9a029fb; accessed 1 October 2016).

14 See, for example, "Corporate bribery – The anti-bribery business", *The Economist*, 9 May 2015 (available at: www.economist.com/news/business/21650557-enforcement-laws-against-corporate-bribery-increases-there-are-risks-it-may-go; accessed 2 December 2016); and Alexander Sword, "8 of the biggest European antitrust fines imposed on tech firms for business practices", *Computer Business Review*, 21 April 2016 (available at www.cbronline. com/news/mobility/8-of-the-biggest-european-antitrust-fines-imposed-on-tech-firms-for-business-practices-4870212/; accessed 2 December 2016).

15 Pasquali, note 2 above.

16 Susan Lund, James Manyika and Jacques Bughin, "Globalization is Becoming More about Data and Less about Stuff", *Harvard Business Review*, 14 March 2016 (available at: https://hbr.org/2016/03/globalisation-is-becoming-more-about-data-and-less-about-stuff/; accessed 27 October 2016).

17 *Ibid*.

18 "Air Cargo", *Cartel Digest*, Shearman and Sterling LLP (available at www.carteldigest.com/cartel-detail-page.cfm?itemID=19/; accessed 1 November 2016).

19 *Ibid*.

20 *Ibid*; and Kathrina Szymborski, "Four Takeaways from the Ongoing Air Cargo Price Fixing Litigation", *Antitrust Update*, Patterson Belknap, 23 December 2014 (available at: www.antitrustupdateblog.com/ four-takeaways-from-ongoing-air-cargo-price-fixing-litigation/; accessed 2 December 2016). The European Commission's fines were subsequently overturned on appeal – see Christian Oliver, "EU court overturns €790m air cargo cartel fines", *Financial Times*, 16 December 2015 (available at www.ft.com/content/ 81f27278-a410-11e5-873f-68411a84f346/; accessed 2 December 2016). However, it was reported in *Politico* in October 2016 that the European Commission appeared poised to issue new sanctions in relation to the matter – see Nicholas Hirst, "Commission closes in on air cargo cartel fines: Decision will galvanise damages claims of as much as €7 billion filed across Europe", *Politico*, 10 October 2016 (available at www.politico.eu/article/commission-closes-in-on-new-air-cargo-cartel-fines-air-canada-british-airways-cathay-pacific-cargolux-japan-airlines-lan-chile-martinair-sas-singapore-airlines-qantas/; accessed 1 November 2016).

21 Samuel R Miller, Kristina Nordlander and James C Owen, "U.S. Discovery of European Union and U.S. Leniency Applications and Other Confidential Investigatory Matters", *The CPI Antitrust Journal*, March 2010 (available at www.sidley.com/~/media/Files/Publications/2010/03/US%20Discovery%20of%20European%20Union%20and%20US%20Lenien cy%20A__/Files/View%20Article/FileAttachment/2010%2003%2014%20%20Competition%20Policy%20International%20%20No__/; accessed 5 November 2016).

22 John C Dickey, "Top 10 Issues for Cross-Border M&A and Strategic Investments in 2013", *Dykema*, 5 April 2013 (available at

www.dykema.com/resources-alerts-Top-10-Issues-for-Cross-Border-M-and-A-and-Strategic-Investments-in-2013_4-2013.html; accessed 1 November 2016).

23 *Ibid*.

24 *Ibid*.

25 *Ibid*.

26 Lund, Manyika and Bughin, note 16 above.

27 Martin Reeves, Simon Levin and Daichi Ueda, "The Biology of Corporate Survival", *Harvard Business Review*, Jan–Feb 2016 (available at: https://hbr.org/2016/01/the-biology-of-corporate-survival/; accessed 5 November 2016).

28 "Business Transformation and the Corporate Agenda", KPMG, 2014 (available at www.kpmg.com/US/en/IssuesAndInsights/Articles Publications/Documents/business-transformation-corporate-agenda.pdf; accessed 5 November 2016).

29 CEB, *The New Legal Operating Model* (2016), pp11, 12 and 56. Reproduced with permission. The assumptions applying to the analysis are as follows:
· Internal process productivity growth:
  · 6% annual median growth in in-house legal department budgets (2010–2014)
  · 2% median increase in in-legal department
  · Estimated annual growth rate: 5%–10%
· Law firm productivity growth:
  · 2%–3% annual growth in profit/lawyer (2011–2015)
  · Most law firms spend 2%–4% of firm revenue on technology
  · Estimated annual growth rate: 5%–10%
Sources: CEB Legal Budget Diagnostic (2010–2014); CEB and Wolters Kluwer ELM Solutions 2014 and 2015 Real Rate Report; ILTA/Inside 2014 Legal Technology Purchasing Survey; Norton Rose Fulbright Litigation Trends Annual Survey (2013, 2014, 2015); and a CEB analysis.

30 Richard Susskind, *Tomorrow's Lawyers: An Introduction to Your Future*, Oxford University Press (2013), p90 in the e-book edition.

31 Richard Susskind and David Susskind, *The Future of the Professions: How Technology Will Transform the Work of Human Experts*, Oxford University Press, 2015, p71 (citing Richard Susskind, *The End of Lawyers*, 2008).

32 Basha Rubin, "Legal Tech Startups Have a Short History and a Bright Future", *Tech Crunch*, 6 December 2014 (available at https://techcrunch.com/2014/12/06/legal-tech-startups-have-a-short-history-and-a-bright-future/; accessed 3 November 2016).

33 *Ibid*.

34 For an overview, see Richard Susskind, note 30 above, p528 in e-book edition.

35 Gavriel Hollander, "A Shore Thing?", *Legal Week*, 3 October 2014 (available at www.axiomlaw.com/Docs/2014.10.03_-_Legal_Week_Article_on_Near-shoring.pdf; accessed 5 November 2016).

36 See www.dorsey.com/services/legal_mine.

37 Richard Susskind, note 30 above, p557 in e-book edition. Susskind refers to this as 'leasing'.

38 Jody Greenstone Miller and Matt Miller, "The Rise of the Supertemp", *Harvard Business Review*, May 2012 (available at https://hbr.org/2012/05/the-rise-of-the-supertemp/; accessed 5 November 2016).

39 Richard Susskind, note 30 above, p547 in e-book edition.

40 See Cathy Reisenwitz, "What is Lean Law? A Conversation with Expert Kenneth A. Grady", Capterra Legal Software Blog, 9 June 2015 (available at http://blog.capterra.com/what-is-lean-law-a-conversation-with-expert-kenneth-a-grady/; accessed 5 November 2016).

41 See Steven Johnson, *Where Good Ideas Come From: The Natural History of Innovation*, Riverside Books (a Division of Penguin Group (USA) Inc), 2010.

42 Matthew Ridley, *The Rational Optimist: How Prosperity Evolves*, Harper Collins, 2010, p6.

43 As Steven Johnson has noted: "It's not that the network itself is smart; it's that the individuals get smarter because they're connected to the network." Johnson, note 41 above, location 674 in e-book edition.

44 Irving Wladawsky-Berger, "The Rise of the T-Shaped Organization", *The Wall Street Journal CIO Journal*, 18 December 2015 (available at http://blogs.wsj.com/cio/2015/12/18/the-rise-of-the-t-shaped-organisation/; accessed 21 October 2016).

45 Andy Boynton, "Are You an 'I' or a 'T'?", *Forbes Magazine*, 18 October 2011.

46 Tim Brown, as quoted in Wladawsky-Berger, note 44 above.

47 Wladawsky-Berger, note 44 above.

48 Gillian Tett, *The Silo Effect: The Peril of Expertise and the Promise of Breaking Down Barriers*, Simon and Schuster, 2015.

49 See http://psychology.iresearchnet.com/industrial-organisational-psychology/job-satisfaction/role-overload-and-underload/ for a discussion of role overload and underload.

Talent and risk assessments

1 Quotation from www.movemequotes.com/tag/first-things-first/.

2 Aristotle, as quoted at: http://lightarrow.com/five-motivational-quotes-to-inspire-you-to-build-good-habits/; accessed 16 August 2016.

3 Lee Cockerell, *Time Management Magic: How to Get More Done Every Day – Move From Surviving to Thriving*, Emerge Publishing, 2014.

4 Mark Roellig, "OMG! Was That Just a Dream? I Just Became a General Counsel. What Do I Do Next?", Massachusetts Mutual Life Insurance Company, p1. ©2010 Mark Roellig (www.gcr.executiveboard.com). Roellig's article is an excellent primer on your first 100 days in the general counsel role and what to do during that time.

5 Some of the thoughts outlined here are taken from Roellig's article, note 4 above.

6 Tool questions are provided and reproduced courtesy of Bobby Katz.

7 See www.transparency.org/research/cpi/overview/.

8 The concept of scaling risk as described here has been used with the permission of Pearson plc.

9 Based on a conversation with Matt Kettel, VP Compliance and Risk Assurance, Pearson plc, on 6 October 2016.

10 Cass Sunstein and Reid Hastie, "Happy Talk and the Dangers of Groupthink", *Time Magazine*, 14 January 2015

11 *The UK Corporate Governance Code*, April 2016, ©

The Financial Reporting Council Ltd 2016 (available at www.frc.org.uk/Our-Work/Publications/Corporate-Governance/UK-Corporate-Governance-Code-April-2016.pdf; accessed 3 August 2016).

12 Gillian Tett, *The Silo Effect: The Peril of Expertise and the Promise of Breaking Down Barriers*, Simon and Schuster, 2015.

Designing an integrated team structure

1 Quotation from www.brainyquote.com/quotes/keywords/ team.html; accessed 21 November 2016.

2 Ben W Heineman Jr, *The Inside Counsel Revolution: Resolving the Partner-Guardian Tension*, Ankerwycke, 2016, p365.

3 CLOC (Corporate Legal Operations Consortium), Corporate Legal Operations Officers Summary version 1.0, updated 10 July 2015 (available at www.iltanet.org/HigherLogic/System/DownloadDocumentFile.ashx?…07f1…1/; accessed 8 October 2016).

4 Statistics and chart in Table 3 from Melissa Maleske, "GCs' Embrace of Legal Ops Refocuses In-House Departments", *Law360*, 27 January 2016 (available at www.law360.com/articles/751500/gcs-embrace-of-legal-ops-refocuses-in-house-departments/; accessed 1 October 2016), citing the ACC Chief Legal Officers 2016 Survey. Used with permission.

5 Mark Roellig, "OMG! Was That Just a Dream? I Just Became a General Counsel. What Do I Do Next?", Massachusetts Mutual Life Insurance Company. ©2010 Mark Roellig (www.gcr.executiveboard.com).

6 Stanley M Davis and Paul R Lawrence, "Problems of Matrix Organizations", *Harvard Business Review*, May 1978 (available at https://hbr.org/1978/05/problems-of-matrix-organisations/; accessed 28 August 2016).

7 Global Integration, "Solid line and dotted line reporting: What are solid line and dotted line reporting in a matrix organization structure?" (available at: www.global-integration.com/matrix-management/matrix-structure/solid-line-reporting-dotted-line-reporting-matrix-organisation-structure/; accessed 28 August 2016).

8 Reference.com, "What is a dotted line reporting relationship?" (available at www.reference.com/business-finance/dotted-line-reporting-relationship-5155ce2a5850b1e0/; accessed 28 August 2016).

9 Global Integration, note 7 above.

10 Robert Cusumano, "Solid, Dotted and Matrixed: Reporting Lines for Legal", *Inside Counsel*, 25 February 2016 (available at www.insidecounsel.com/2016/02/25/solid-dotted-and-matrixed-reporting-lines-for-lega/; accessed 28 August 2016).

11 For a helpful discussion, see Evans Incorporated, "To Centralise or Decentralise? Key Considerations", Evans Incorporated Blog (available at www.evansincorporated.com/centralising-and-decentralising/; accessed 12 September 2016). This website contains a helpful table that lists the pros and cons of a centralised versus a decentralised approach, including the ones listed.

12 *Id.*

13 For a good, concise discussion of the right metrics to consider, see Patrick Johnson, "Top Ten Metrics That Your Legal Department Should Be Tracking", ACC.com, 4 March 2013 (available at www.acc.com/legalresources/publications/topten /ttmtyldsbt.cfm; accessed 12 September 2016).

14 See Evans Incorporated, "To Centralise or Decentralise? Key Considerations", Evans Incorporated Blog (available at www.evansincorporated.com/centralising-and-decentralising/; accessed 12 September 2016).

Law firms

1 Richard Susskind, *Tomorrow's Lawyers: An Introduction to Your Future*, Oxford University Press, 2013, location 90 in e-book.

2 A CEB analysis provided to the author by CEB indicates that the demand for legal services from corporate legal departments will rise by 30% between 2016 and 2020 – see the chapter entitled "The changing context" in Part A of the current publication. See that chapter also for a discussion of the increasing costs of getting it wrong.

3 Ross Dawson, "Future Timeline: The Restructuring of the Global Legal Services Industry", Future Exploration Network, 2 May 2016 (available at http://futureexploration.net/blog/2016/05/future-timeline-the-restructuring-of-the-global-legal-services-industry.html; accessed 1 October 2016).

4 Kyle McEntee, "Law Grads Still Face a Tough Job Market", *Bloomberg Law*, 4 May 2016 (available at https://bol.bna.com/law-grads-still-face-a-tough-job-market/; accessed 1 October 2016).

5 Amy Rebecca, "Law School Graduates Find it Tough to Cash in on New Degrees", GoodCall, 12 July 2016 (available at www.goodcall.com/news/law-school-graduates-find-tough-cash-new-degrees-07901/; accessed 1 October 2016).

6 See *Chambers Student* (UK edn), "Trends affecting the legal profession" (available at www.chambersstudent.com/where-to-start/trends-affecting-the-legal-profession; accessed 14 January 2017). The 'silver circle' is generally seen to consist of the following law firms: Ashurst; Berwin Leighton Paisner; Herbert Smith Freehills; SJ Berwin (now part of King & Wood Malleson); Macfarlanes; and Travers Smith. See *Chambers Student* (UK edn), "The Silver Circle" (available at www.chambersstudent.com/law-firms/types-of-law-firm/the-silver-circle; accessed 14 January 2017).

7 *Id.*

8 See the discussion in the chapter entitled "The changing context" in Part A of this publication.

9 Clayton M Christensen, Dina Wang and Derek van Bever, "Consulting on the Cusp of Disruption", *Harvard Business Review*, October 2013 (available at https://hbr.org/2013/10/consulting-on-the-cusp-of-disruption/; accessed 20 November 2016).

10 Altman Weil, "2015 Law Firms in Transition: an Altman Weil Flash Survey", pii (available at www.altmanweil.com/dir_docs/resource/1c789ef2-5cff-463a-863a-2248d23882a7_document.pdf; accessed 2 October 2016).

11 Susskind, note 1 above, location 163 in the e-book version. This fits well with my own experience: in the three years since I arrived as general counsel at Pearson, we have reduced our overall legal spend by 40%.

12 Stephen Rauf, "Legal Market Faces Major Transition – Top Trends Review", Accenture Spend Trends, November 2016 (available at https://spendtrends. accenture.com/legal-market-faces-major-transition-top-trends-review/; accessed 30 November 2016).

13 *Id.*

14 Thomson Reuters, "A Revolution in Legal Services", Thompson Reuters, 7 July 2015 (available at https://blogs.thomsonreuters.com/answerson/revolution-legal-services/; accessed 2 October 2016).

15 Information provided to author by Silvia Hodges Silverstein of Buying Legal, 12 November 2016.

16 Susskind, note 1 above, location 202 in e-book.

17 American Bar Association Commission on the Future of Legal Services, Issues Paper Regarding Alternative Legal Structures, 8 April 2016 (available at www.americanbar.org/content/dam/aba/images/office_president/alternative_business_issues_paper.pdf; accessed on 9 October 2016).

18 Victoria Prussen Spears, "Globalization's Impact on Legal Services: The American Bar Association Weighs In", *Intellectual Property and Technology Law Journal*, August 2012 (available at www.meyerowitz communications.com/writings-victoria-spears_2_2612848882.pdf; accessed 14 January 2017), citing ABA Committee on Ethics & Professional Responsibility, Formal Opus 08-451 (2008). See also Paul Burquest, Marie De Malzac and Mark Hillman, "Legal Services Outsourcing Matures, Offering Cost and Quality Benefits", Accenture Spend Trends, May 2016 (available at https://spendtrends. accenture.com/legal-services-outsourcing-matures-offering-cost-and-quality-benefits/; accessed 11 November 2016).

19 American Bar Association Commission, note 17 above.

20 Rauf, note 12 above.

21 Maria Jose Esteban and Professor David B Wilkins, "The re-emergence of the Big 4 in law", Thompson Reuters Industry Trends, 27 April 2016, (available at https://blogs.thomsonreuters.com/answerson/big-4-accounting-firms-legal-services/; accessed on November 15, 2016).

22 *Id.*

23 *Id.*

24 Thomas Connelly, "Big Four accounting giants are expanding their legal services arms globally – and solicitors are getting worried", *Legal Cheek*, 28 January 2016 (available at www.legalcheek.com/2016/01/big-four-accountancy-giants-are-expanding-their-legal-services-arms-globally-and-the-law-society-is-getting-worried/; accessed 15 November 2016).

25 The Law Society of England and Wales, "The Future of Legal Services", *Legal Cheek*, January 2016 (available at www.lawsociety.org.uk/news/stories/future-of-legal-services/; accessed 15 November 2016).

26 Susskind, note 1 above, location 316 in e-book.

27 Mary Crane, "How to Set Your Consulting Fees", *Forbes Magazine*, 11 June 2006 (available at www.forbes.com/2006/11/06/bostonconsulting-marsh-mckinsey-ent-fin-cx_mc_1106pricing.html; accessed 15 November 2016).

28 Information provided to the author by Kyle McNeil, Head of Business Development and US Sales at Axiom, 17 November 2016.

29 Information provided to the author by Silvia Hodges Silverstein, Executive Director at the Buying Legal Council, 12 November 2016.

30 Susskind, note 1 above, location 768 in e-book.

31 Comments made to the author by James Neath, Associate General Counsel, Global Litigation and Environmental at BP on 9 November 2016.

32 Esteban and Wilkins, note 21 above.

33 *Id.*

34 *Id.*

35 The author is grateful for the input of James Neath for these examples, provided to him by Neath on 9 November 2016.

36 Comments made to the author by James Neath on 9 November 2016.

37 Information provided to the author by Kyle McNeil, Head of Business Development and US Sales at Axiom, on 17 November 2016.

38 Comments made to the author by James Neath on 9 November 2016.

39 Susskind, note 1 above, location 547 in e-book.

40 See https://en.wikipedia.org/wiki/Hawthorne_effect/; accessed 17 November 2016.

41 Comments made to the author by James Neath on 9 November 2016.

42 Insights given to the author by James Neath on 9 November 2016.

43 The table shown in Figure 7 is based on one presented in "A Higher Bar", by Jason Heinrich, Michael Heric, Neal Goldman and Paul Chichocki, *Bain and Company Insights*, 8 October 2014 (available at www.bain.com/publications/articles/a-higher-bar.aspx; accessed 8 October 2016). The article accompanying the table is an excellent read, providing good insights into how to transform a legal department.

44 Information provided to the author by Kyle McNeil, Head of Business Development and US Sales at Axiom, on 17 November 2016.

45 *Id.*

46 Josh Stark, "Making Sense of Blockchain Smart Contracts", *CoinDesk*, 4 June 2016 (available at www.coindesk.com/making-sense-smart-contracts/; accessed 15 November 2016). A definition of 'blockchain' has been taken from "CIO Explainer: What is Blockchain?" by Steven Norton, *The Wall Street Journal*, 2 February 2016 (available at http://blogs.wsj.com/cio/2016/02/02/cio-explainer-what-is-blockchain/; accessed 15 November 2016).

47 *Id.*

48 *Id.*

49 *Id.*

50 JB Wogan, "Who's an Employee? The Uber-Important Question of Today's Economy", Governing the States and Localities, June 2016 (available at www.governing.com/topics/mgmt/gov-uber-employee-lawsuits-sharing-economy.html; accessed 15 November 2016).

51 *Id.*

52 The figures in the two charts were provided to the author by Morae Legal Corporation on 16 October 2016, citing the Ninth Annual Blickstein Group Law Department Operations Survey (2016) (available at http://blicksteingroup.com/ldo-

survey/). Reproduction with the kind permission of Morae Legal Corporation.

53 Information provided to the author by Joy Saphla of Morae Legal Corporation on 9 October 2016.

54 "Billing Rates Across the Country", *The National Law Journal*, 13 January 2014 (available at www.nationallawjournal.com/id=1202636785489/ Billing-Rates-Across-the-Country?slreturn= 20161030222330/; accessed 30 November 2016).

55 Sara Randazzo, "Law Firm Cravath Raising Starting Salaries to $180,000 – Change is Likely to Spawn a Wave of Copycat Moves from the New York Firm's Competitors", *The Wall Street Journal*, 6 June 2016 (available at www.wsj.com/articles/law-firm-cravath-raising-starting-salaries-to-180-000-1465241318/; accessed 30 November 2016).

56 Martha Neil, "First Year Associate Pay Will be $180K at Multiple BigLaw Firms Following Cravath's Lead", *ABA Journal*, 8 June 2016 (available at www.abajournal.com/news/article/cravath_raises_first_year_associate_pay_to_180k_effective_july_1/; accessed on November 30, 2016).

57 Altman Weil, note 10 above.

58 Information provided to the author by Joy Saphla of Morae Legal Corporation on 9 October 2016. Reproduced with the kind permission of Morae Legal Corporation.

59 Altman Weil, note 10 above, piii.

60 *Ibid.*

61 Comments obtained by the author during an interview with Joy Saphla on 1 October 2016.

62 *Id.*

63 Available at www.acc.com/_cs_upload/vl/membersonly/SampleFormPolicy/1362010_1.pdf/.

64 Rauf, note 12 above.

65 The author wishes to acknowledge the helpful input and advice received for this list of additional policies from James Neath, Associate General Counsel, Global Litigation and Environmental at BP.

Alternative legal services providers

1 Conversation between the author and Julia Shapiro, CEO of Hire an Esquire, on 15 October 2016.

2 "2015 Law Firms in Transition Survey", © 2015 Altman Weil Inc (available at www.altmanweil.com/dir_docs/resource/30fbe3fb-3300-4bef-86e7-1b2d72b3bbeb_document.pdf; accessed 9 October 2016).

3 Jordan Furlong, as quoted in "What is NewLaw and How it is Changing the Legal Industry Forever!" by Ilina Rejeva, *LegalTrek*, 26 April 2016 (available at https://legaltrek.com/blog/2016/04/what-is-newlaw-and-how-it-is-changing-the-legal-industry-forever/; accessed 9 October 2016).

4 The background for this section was taken from conversations that the author had on 21 October 2016 with Julia Shapiro, CEO of Hire an Esquire, and Bill Stone, Managing Member of Outside GC.

5 Albert Yoon, "Competition and the Evolution of Large Law Firms", 63 *DePaul L Rev* 697 (2014), p701 (available at http://via.library.depaul.edu/law-review/vol63/iss2/17).

6 *Id.*

7 Conversation between the author and Julia Shapiro, CEO of Hire an Esquire, on 15 October 2016.

8 Information contained in this section was provided by Denise Nurse of Haleburys during an interview with the author on 11 November 2016.

9 See www.mlaglobal.com/legal-recruiting-services/legal-solutions/secondment; accessed 9 November 2016.

10 Drew Combs, "Disruptive Innovation: Look out Firms, Axiom is trying to beat you at your own game", *The American Lawyer*, July/August 2012 (available at: www.axiomlaw.com/Images/Attorneys/001081201 Axiom.pdf; accessed 16 October 2016).

11 See www.axiomlaw.com/what-we-do/solution/corporate-transactions; accessed 16 October 2016.

12 Drew Combs, note 10 above.

13 See www.beatoncapital.com/2013/09/2018-year-axiom-becomes-worlds-largest-legal-services-firm/; accessed 16 October 2016; and Casey Sullivan, "The World's Largest Law Firm Will Have 7,300+ Lawyers", *Bloomberg Law: Big Law Business*, 17 November 2015 (available at https://bol.bna.com/the-worlds-largest-law-firm-will-have-7300-lawyers/; accessed 15 November 2016).

14 *Id.*

15 Based on an interview by the author with Hire an Esquire CEO Julia Shapiro on 21 October 2016.

16 Information provided by Denise Nurse of Haleburys during an interview with the author on 11 November 2016.

17 *Id.*

18 Information provided to the author by Kyle McNeil, Head of Business Development and US Sales, Axiom, on 29 November 2016.

19 Source: UnitedLex , "Cost Predictability in e-Discovery: The New Normal", (provided to the author by UnitedLex on 21 April 2016).

20 *Id.*

21 Information provided to the author by Kyle McNeil, Head of Business Development and US Sales, Axiom, on 29 November 2016.

22 *Id.*

23 Source data provided to the author by Joy Saphla of Morae Legal Corporation on 7 November 2016.

Selecting the right partners

1 Sun Tzu, *The Art of War.* Quotation from http://corporatepartnering.com/4-wisdom.htm; accessed 20 November 2016.

2 Silvia Hodges Silverstein, "What We Know and Need to Know About Legal Procurement", *South Carolina Law Review*, Vol 67, p485.

3 *Ibid*, p492.

4 *Id.*

5 Stephen Rauf, "Industry-Leading Commercial Practices in Selecting Outside Legal Counsel", Accenture SpendTrends, December 2016 (available at https://spendtrends.accenture.com/industry-leading-commercial-practices-in-selecting-outside-legal-counsel/; accessed 30 December 2016).

6 Information provided to the author by James Neath, Associate General Counsel, Global Litigation and Environmental at BP on 9 November 2016.

7 *Id.*

8 *Id.*

9 Frank Strong, "Trends in Legal Spend from a Law Department Survey", LexisNexis Business of Law

Blog, 19 November 2015 (available at http://businessoflawblog.com/2015/11/law-department-survey/; accessed 8 October 2016).
10 Information provided to the author by Silvia Hodges Silverstein, Executive Director of the Buying Legal Council, 12 November 2016.
11 Silvia Hodges Silverstein, note 2 above, p485.
12 *Id.*
13 Information provided to the author by Silvia Hodges Silverstein, Executive Director of the Buying Legal Council, 12 November 2016.
14 Lawcadia, "Guide to Legal Procurement Asia-Pacific – Part 1: an Introduction to Legal Procurement", citing Silvia Hodges Silverstein, "Research Report: The State of Legal Procurement" in SH Silverstein (ed), *Legal Procurement Handbook* (pp126–132), USA: Buying Legal Council (available at http://lawcadia.com/wp-content/uploads/2016/07/Guide-to-Legal-Procurement-Part-1.pdf?utm_medium=email&utm_campaign=Guide%20to%20Legal%20Procurement&utm_content=Guide%20to%20Legal%20Procurement+CID_208b7b5087e7e60c0190d74157dba8d5&utm_source=Lawcadia%20enews&utm_term=Download%20the%20Guide%20now/; accessed 8 October 2016).
15 BP is one example. Information provided to the author by James Neath, Associate General Counsel, Global Litigation and Environmental at BP on 9 November 2016. Pearson plc also uses KPIs as part of its law firm selection process.
16 Information provided to the author by James Neath, Associate General Counsel, Global Litigation and Environmental at BP on 9 November 2016.
17 *Id.*
18 Information provided to the author by James Neath, Associate General Counsel, Global Litigation and Environmental at BP on 9 November 2016.
19 Firm size is usually one of the most important price drivers, with location coming second. Information provided to the author by Silvia Hodges Silverstein, Executive Director of the Buying Legal Council, on 12 November 2016.
20 Information provided to the author by James Neath, Associate General Counsel, Global Litigation and Environmental at BP on 9 November 2016.
21 Vivian Hunt, Dennis Layton and Sarah Prince, "Why Diversity Matters", McKinsey & Company, January 2015 (available at www.mckinsey.com/Insights/Organisation/Why_diversity_matters?cid=other-eml-alt-mip-mck-oth-1501/; accessed 19 August 2016).
22 The legal procurement organisation named Buying Legal Council has developed a best-practices RFP format with recommended questions. Go to www.buyinglegal.com for more information.
23 Rauf, note 5 above.
24 *Id.*

Technology
1 Erik Brynjolfsson and Andrew McAfee, *The Second Machine Age: Work, Progress, and Prosperity in a Time of Brilliant Technologies*, WW Norton & Company, 2014, p102 of the e-book edition.
2 Interview of Victoria Lockie by the author on 21 November 2016.
3 Appian, "What is Process Improvement in

Organizational Development?", Appian, 2016 (available at www.appian.com/about-bpm/process-improvement-organisational-development/; accessed 21 November 2016).
4 *Id.*
5 Dorothy Leonard-Barton and William A Kraus, "Implementing New Technology", *Harvard Business Review*, November 1985 (available at https://hbr.org/1985/11/implementing-new-technology/; accessed 21 November 2016).
6 *Id.*
7 Dale Carnegie Training, training course entitled "Change Management & the Strategic Planning Process Improvement" (outline available at www.dalecarnegie.com/strategic-planning-process/; accessed 21 November 2016).
8 Brynjolfsson and McAfee, note 1 above, p120 of the e-book edition.
9 Bill Teuber, "The Coming of the Second Machine Age", *The Huffington Post*, 22 January 2014 (available at www.huffingtonpost.com/bill-teuber/the-coming-of-the-second-machine-age_b_4648207.html; accessed on 21 November 2016).
10 Brynjolfsson and McAfee, note 1 above, pp583–596 of the e-book edition.
11 Quoted in Brynjolfsson and McAfee, note 1 above, p580 of the e-book edition.
12 See Brynjolfsson and McAfee, note 1 above, p669 of the e-book edition, quoting Ray Kurzweil, *The Age of Spiritual Machines: When Computers Exceed Human Intelligence*, London: Penguin, 2000, p36.
13 See Brynjolfsson and McAfee, note 1 above, p657 of the e-book edition. Those authors cite the story as retold by inventor and futurist Ray Kurzweil in his book *The Age of Spiritual Machines: When Computers Exceed Human Intelligence*, London: Penguin, 2000, p36.
14 "Your smartphone is millions of times more powerful than all of NASA's combined computing in 1969", ZME Science, 13 October 2015 (available at www.zmescience.com/research/technology/smartphone-power-compared-to-apollo-432/; accessed 21 November 2016).
15 *Id.*
16 Tom Simonite, "Moore's Law is Dead. Now What?", *MIT Technology Review*, 13 May 2016 (available at www.technologyreview.com/s/601441/moores-law-is-dead-now-what/; accessed 21 November 2016).
17 Madhumita Murgia, "End of Moore's Law? What's Next Could be More Exciting", *The Telegraph*, 25 February 2016 (available at www.telegraph.co.uk/technology/2016/02/25/end-of-moores-law-whats-next-could-be-more-exciting/; accessed November 21, 2016).
18 "Internet of Things (IoT)", TechTarget IoT Agenda (available at http://internetofthingsagenda.techtarget.com/definition/Internet-of-Things-IoT/; accessed 21 November 21, 2016).
19 Antonio Regalado, "The Economics of the Internet of Things", *MIT Technology Review*, 20 May 2014 (available at www.technologyreview.com/s/527361/the-economics-of-the-internet-of-things/; accessed 21 November 2016).
20 *Id.*
21 Susan Gunelius, "The Data Explosion Minute by Minute", ACI, 12 July 2014 (available at

https://aci.info/2014/07/12/the-data-explosion-in-2014-minute-by-minute-infographic/; accessed 30 December 2016). Gunelius's blog also contains an interesting infographic that can be accessed via the same link.

22 See https://en.wikipedia.org/wiki/Cloud_computing/ (accessed 21 November 2016).

23 Id.

24 Eric Griffith, "What is Cloud Computing?", PC Magazine, 3 May 2016 (available at www.pcmag.com/article2/0,2817,2372163,00.asp; accessed 21 November 2016). The definition of 'backbone' is taken from http://searchtelecom.techtarget.com/definition/backbone/, accessed on the same date.

25 See www.salesforce.com/uk/blog/2015/11/why-move-to-the-cloud-10-benefits-of-cloud-computing.html (accessed 21 November 2016).

26 Michael Copeland, "What's the Difference between Artificial Intelligence, Machine Learning and Deep Learning?", nvidia, July 2016 (available at https://blogs.nvidia.com/blog/2016/07/29/whats-difference-artificial-intelligence-machine-learning-deep-learning-ai/, accessed 21 November 2016).

27 Id.

28 Id.

29 See www.techopedia.com/definition/190/artificial-intelligence-ai/ (accessed 21 November 2016).

30 Robert D Hof, "Deep Learning – With massive amounts of computational power, machines can now recognize objects and translate speech in real time. Artificial intelligence is finally getting smart", MIT Technology Review (available at www.technologyreview.com/s/513696/deep-learning/; accessed 21 November 2016).

31 See http://whatis.techtarget.com/ definition/machine-learning; see also https://hackernoon.com/ the-self-learning-quant-d3329fcc9915#.x31cxnoan; both accessed 22 November 2016.

32 Copeland, note 27 above.

33 Christof Koch, "How the Computer Beat the Go Master", Scientific American, 19 March 2016 (available at www.scientificamerican.com/article/how-the-computer-beat-the-go-master/; accessed 22 November 2016).

34 Id.

35 Id.

36 Julie Sobowale, "How Artificial Intelligence is Transforming the Legal Profession", ABA Journal, 1 April 2016 (available at www.abajournal.com/magazine/article/how_artificial_intelligence_is_transforming_the_legal_profession/; accessed 22 November 2016).

37 Id.

38 Richard Susskind, Tomorrow's Lawyers: An Introduction to Your Future, Oxford University Press, 2013, location 263 in the e-book version (citing Ray Kurzweil, The Singularity is Near: When Humans Transcend Biology, New York: Viking Books, 2005).

39 David A Mindell, Our Robots Ourselves: Robotics and the Myths of Autonomy, Viking Books, 2015, p8 in the e-book edition.

40 Id.

41 See Mindell, note 40 above, p9.

42 Richard Susskind, Tomorrow's Lawyers: An Introduction to Your Future, Oxford University Press, 2013.

43 Part 3 of Richard Susskind's book, Tomorrow's Lawyers: An Introduction to Your Future, Oxford University Press, 2013, contains a fascinating discussion of this point, including consideration of some of the new jobs for lawyers that he sees coming as a result of the changes underway within the profession.

44 Id.

45 Cited in "How and Why Millennials are Shaping the Future of Remote Working" by Sarah Sutton Fell, insight, 21 April 2016 (available at: http://workplaceinsight.net/millennials-shaping-future-remote-working/; accessed 22 November 2016).

46 See http://us.practicallaw.com/.

47 See, eg, www.cebglobal.com/compliance-legal.html.

48 See, eg, www.novatuscontracts.com/novatus-contract-management-software/.

49 See www.americanbar.org/groups/departments_offices/legal_technology_resources/resources/charts_fyis/casemanagementcomparison.html.

50 See, eg, www.legaltracker.com/effortless-e-billing/.

51 Stephen Rauf, "Legal Market Faces Major Transition – Top Trends Review", SpendTrends, November 2016 (available at: https://spendtrends.accenture.com/legal-market-faces-major-transition-top-trends-review/; accessed 30 November 2016).

52 Sobowale, note 37 above.

53 Id.

54 See www.nexlp.com/ediscovery/ (accessed 22 November 2016).

55 Sobowale, note 37 above.

56 Id.

57 Id.

58 Debra Cassens Weiss, "In a first, a BigLaw firm announces it will use artificial intelligence in one of its practice areas", ABA Journal, 9 May 2016 (available at www.abajournal.com/news/article/in_a_first_a_biglaw_firm_announces_it_will_use_artificial_intelligence_in_0/; accessed 22 November 2016).

59 Baker & Hostetler seems to be the first law firm to use Ross. See Cassens Weiss, note 58 above.

60 Interview of Victoria Lockie by the author on 21 November 2016.

Culture

1 Dharmesh Shah, "Why Company Culture is Crucial" HubSpot (Stanford University e-Corner podcast series, season 11 episode 14), 10 February 2016 (available at http://ecorner.stanford.edu/podcasts/3615/Why-Company-Culture-is-Crucial; accessed 30 October 2016).

2 See John P Kotter and James L Heskett, Corporate Culture and Performance, The Free Press (a division of Simon & Schuster Inc), 1992, location 69 in e-book version.

3 Live on-stage interview of Robert Richman, heard by the author at a Pearson event in Miami, Florida, on 5 February 2015.

4 Angela Duckworth, Grit: The Power of Passion and

Perseverance, Scribner (an imprint of Simon & Schuster Inc), 2016, p262 in e-book.

5 *Ibid*, pp242–243 in the e-book.

6 See Kotter and Heskett, note 2 above, location 86 in e-book.

7 Paper by Alicia Boisnier and Jennifer A Chatman, "The Role of Subcultures in Agile Organizations", Haas School of Business, University of California, Berkeley, 24 May 2002 (available at http://citeseerx.ist.psu.edu/viewdoc/download?doi=10.1.1.196.9740&rep=rep1&type=pdf; accessed 6 November 2016).

8 *Id*.

9 *Id*.

10 *Id*.

11 Rajesh Anandan, "3 Reasons Why Culture is Your Most Important Asset", Unreasonable (available at https://unreasonable.is/3-reasons-why-culture-is-your-most-important-asset/; accessed 18 September 2016).

12 Patrick M Lencioni, "Make Your Values Mean Something", *Harvard Business Review*, July 2002 (available at https://hbr.org/2002/07/make-your-values-mean-something/; accessed 18 September 2016).

13 See https://en.wikipedia.org/wiki/Enron (accessed 18 September 2016).

14 David Burkus, "A Tale of Two Cultures: Why Culture Trumps Core Values in Building Ethical Organizations", *The Journal of Values Based Leadership*, Vol 4, Issue 1, Winter/Spring 2011 (available at www.valuesbasedleadershipjournal.com/issues/vol4issue1/tale_2culture.php; accessed 9 November 2016).

15 See https://en.wikipedia.org/wiki/Jeffrey_Skilling#cite_note-18/ and https://en.wikipedia.org/wiki/Kenneth_Lay/, both accessed 9 November 2016.

16 Clayton M Christensen, James Allworth and Karen Dillon, *How Will You Measure Your Life?*, Harper Business, 2012, p3.

17 PBS Frontline, transcript of *Blackout* programme 1916, original airdate 5 June 2001 (available at www.pbs.org/wgbh/pages/frontline/shows/blackout/etc/script.html; accessed 9 November 2016).

18 Robert A Prentice, "Ethical Decision Making: More Needed Than Good Intentions", *Financial Analysts Journal*, Vol 63, No 6, 2007.

19 Martha Lagace, "Enron's Lessons for Managers", *Working Knowledge*, Harvard Business School, 12 July 2004 (available at http://hbswk.hbs.edu/item/enrons-lessons-for-managers/; accessed 9 November 2016).

20 *Id*.

21 Burkus, note 14 above.

22 See www.thesmokinggun.com/file/enrons-code-ethics (accessed 18 September 2016) in relation to Enron's corporate code of ethics.

23 Levi Nieminen, "Values with Teeth: Create More Meaningful Values Statements", Gotham Culture, 16 July 2015 (available at http://gothamculture.com/2015/07/16/values-with-teeth-create-more-meaningful-values-statements/; accessed 18 September 2016).

24 Richard Pearson, "Why Company Culture Matters More to Employees than Pay", Business.com, 15 January 2015 (available at www.business.com/company-culture/why-company-culture-matters-more-to-employee-than-pay/; accessed 18 September 2016).

25 Kotter and Heskett, note 2 above, location 126 in e-book.

26 Pearson, note 24 above.

27 Ginger Christ, "Millennials Value Quality of Work Life Over Money", *EHS Today*, 12 April 2016 (available at http://ehstoday.com/safety-leadership/millennials-value-quality-work-life-over-money; accessed 18 September 2016).

28 Anandan, note 11 above, citing Kotter and Heskett, note 2 above, at location 174 in e-book (which contains other statistics relevant here).

29 *Id*.

30 Richman interview, note 3 above.

31 *Id*.

32 Kotter and Heskett, note 2 above, location 114 in the e-book version.

33 For a good discussion of some of these ideas and how start-ups should shape culture, listen to Dharmesh Shah, note 1 above.

34 Richman interview, note 3 above.

35 *Id*.

36 Shah, note 1 above. Shah has done a brilliant job of writing down the company's culture in a deck he calls the HubSpot Culture Code.

37 *Id*.

38 See http://blog.cultureamp.com/blog/what-is-culture-hacking/.

39 Robert Richman, "The Culture Blueprint: A Guide to Building the High-Performance Workplace" (Creative Commons Attribution – ShareAlike 4.0 International Licence), locations 404-405 and 1665 in the e-book version.

40 Alan Iny, "A New Paradigm for Creativity", Smart People podcast, episode 252, ART19 (available at https://art19.com/shows/smart-people/episodes/a3d90a30-eeae-4fb6-82ac-fb4b5889493a/; accessed 3 December 2016).

41 Luc de Brabandere and Alan Iny, *Thinking in New Boxes: A New Paradigm for Business Creativity*, ©The Boston Consulting Group, Random House, 2013, location 1151 of the e-book edition.

42 The ideas presented are taken from or inspired by de Brabandere and Iny, note 41 above. See in particular location 1107 of the e-book edition.

43 Brabandere and Iny, note 41 above, location 1107 of the e-book edition.

44 Barbara Gago, "What is Culture Hacking?", CultureAmp (available at http://blog.cultureamp.com/blog/what-is-culture-hacking/; accessed 6 November 2016).

45 Richman, note 39 above, location 418 in the e-book version.

46 *Id*.

47 Gago, note 44 above.

48 David A Kaplan, "Mars Incorporated: A Pretty Sweet Place to Work", *Fortune*, 17 January 2013 (available at http://fortune.com/2013/01/17/mars-incorporated-a-pretty-sweet-place-to-work/; accessed 9 November 2016).

49 See www.mars.com/global/about-us/five-principles/responsibility/; accessed 9 November 2016.

50 Observed by the author during visits to Mars's corporate headquarters in 2013.

51 See Kotter and Heskett, note 2 above, location 69 in the e-book version.

52 *Id*.

53 Dianna Hartley, "Check Out Amazon's Process of

Screening New Hires", The Hiring Site Blog, 24 January 2014 (available at http://thehiringsite. careerbuilder. com/2014/01/21/check-amazons-process-screening-new-hires/; accessed 18 September 2016).

54 Greg Benzinger, "Amazon's Current Employees Raise the Bar for New Hires", The Wall Street Journal, 7 January 2014 (available at www.wsj.com/articles/ SB10001424052702304753504579285133045398 34/; accessed 18 September 2016).

55 Shah, note 1 above.

56 Id.

57 Mike Swift, "A Look Inside Facebook's 'Bootcamp' for New Employees", The Star.com/San Jose Mercury News, 18 April 2012 (available at www.thestar.com/business/2012/04/18/a_look_insi de_facebooks_bootcamp_for_new_employees.html ; accessed 18 September 2016).

58 Id.

59 David Novak, Taking People with You: The Only Way to Make Big Things Happen, Penguin Group (USA) Inc, 2012, p190

60 Ibid, p2.

61 Richman, note 39 above, location 267 in the e-book version.

62 Kotter and Heskett, note 2 above, location 105 in the e-book version.

63 Richman, note 39 above, location 456 in the e-book version.

64 For a discussion of the sources of power, including personal power, listen to Erica Peitler in her discussion entitled "How to Lead", in the Smart People podcast, episode 175, of 26 January 2015 (available at www.smartpeoplepodcast.com/ 2015/01/26/episode-175-erica-peitler/).

65 Malcolm Gladwell, The Tipping Point: How Little Things Can Make a Big Difference, Little Brown Book Group. 2000.

66 Ibid, pp19 and 259.

67 Novak, note 59 above, p190.

The generational context and the rise of the millennials

1 Parts of this chapter are adapted with permission from an article published by the author in ACC Docket entitled "The Care and Feeding of Millennials", 22 March 2016 (available at www.accdocket.com/ articles/the-care-and-feeding-of-millenials.cfm; accessed 30 December 2016).

2 Cover liner to the music album The Scarecrow by John Mellencamp.

3 Different studies provide different date ranges for these groups, but for our purposes we will use the dates given. See https://en.wikipedia.org/wiki/ Millennials for data on millennials; https://en.wikipedia.org/wiki/Generation_X for gen-Xers, and https://en.wikipedia.org/wiki/ Baby_boomers for baby boomers (all accessed 20 November 2016).

4 As with other generational groups, there is a broad range of definitions as to when this group began, ranging from the mid-1990s to the early 2000s. For our purposes, we will consider their starting date to be the early 2000s – see https://en.wikipedia.org/ wiki/Generation_Z; accessed 20 November 2016.

5 See Alex Williams, "Move over Millennials, Here

Comes Generation Z", The New York Times, 18 September 2015 (available at www.nytimes.com/2015/ 09/20/fashion/move-over-millennials-here-comes-generation-z.html?_r=0/; accessed 16 September 2016).

6 Sally Kane, "Baby Boomers in the Workplace", The Balance, 11 August 2016 (available at www.thebalance.com/baby-boomers-2164681/; accessed 20 November 2016).

7 Richard Fry, "Millennials Overtake Baby Boomers as America's Largest Generation", Pew Research Center Fact Tank, 25 April 2016 (available at www.pewresearch.org/fact-tank/2016/ 04/25/millennials-overtake-baby-boomers/; accessed 17 September 2016).

8 Lauren Stiller Rickleen, "How the Millennial Generation Works", American Bar Association, 2016 (available at www.americanbar.org/ publications/young_lawyer_home/young_lawyer_ archive/yld_tyl_may08_rikleen.html; accessed 20 November 2016).

9 PwC report entitled Millennials at Work: Reshaping the Workforce (available at www.pwc.com/m1/en/services/consulting/docume nts/millennials-at-work.pdf; accessed 17 September 2016).

10 See www.bentley.edu/newsroom/latest-headlines/mind-of-millennial/; accessed 17 September 2016.

11 Kane, note 6 above.

12 Id.

13 Id.

14 Id.

15 Id.

16 Id.

17 Id.

18 Id.

19 Id.

20 Id.

21 Id.

22 Robert Klara, "Five Reasons Marketers Have Largely Overlooked Generation X: They're at the Peak of Their Careers but Many Brands Have Forgotten Them", AdWeek, 4 April 2016 (available at www.adweek.com/news/advertising-branding/5-reasons-marketers-have-largely-overlooked-generation-x-170539/; accessed 20 November 2016).

23 "Generation X", Specialty Retail Report, Summer 2003 (available at http://specialtyretail.com/issue/2003/07/running-a-cart-or-kiosk/generation-x/; accessed 20 November 2016).

24 Id.

25 Sally Kane, "Common Characteristics of Generation X Professionals", The Balance, 11 May 2016 (available at www.thebalance.com/common-characteristics-of-generation-x-professionals-2164682; accessed 19 September 2016).

26 Kane, note 25 above.

27 Specialty Retail Report, note 23 above.

28 Kane, note 25 above.

29 Id.

30 Id.

31 West Midland Family Center, Generational Differences Chart (available at www.wmfc.org/ uploads/GenerationalDifferencesChart.pdf; accessed 20 November 2016).

32 "Gen X Now Reportedly the Largest Generation

of Affluents", MarketingCharts, 22 September 2015 (available at www.marketingcharts.com/ traditional/gen-x-now-reportedly-the-largest-generation-of-affluents-59501/, accessed 20 November 2016).

33 Doug White and Polly White, "What to Expect from Gen-X and Millennial Employees", *Entrepreneur*, 23 December 2014 (available at www.entrepreneur.com/ article/240556/; accessed 20 November 2016).

34 Darrin J DeChane, "How to Explain the Millennial Generation? Understand the Context", *Inquiries*, 2014, Vol 6 No 3, pp2–3 (available at www.inquiriesjournal.com/articles/878/2/how-to-explain-the-millennial-generation-understand-the-context/; accessed 17 September 2016).

35 See www.whitehouse.gov/sites/default/ files/docs/millennials_report.pdf.

36 See www.americanpressinstitute.org/ publications/reports/survey-research/millennials-social-media/.

37 See www.whitehouse.gov/sites/default/ files/docs/millennials_report.pdf.

38 See www.americanpressinstitute.org/ publications/reports/survey-research/millennials-social-media/.

39 Dr Patricia Buckley, Dr Peter Viechnicki and Akrur Barua, "A new understanding of Millennials: Generational differences reexamined", Deloitte University Press, October 2015 (available at https://dupress.deloitte.com/dup-us-en/economy/issues-by-the-numbers/ understanding-millennials-generational-differences.html; accessed 17 September 2016).

40 *Id.* This study shows that only a slightly higher proportion of millennials is studying biological and biomedical sciences and computer and information sciences than gen-Xers, despite years of rhetoric aimed at increasing these rates. When they are compared with baby boomers, millennials trail in all STEM (science, technology, engineering and mathematics) majors except computer and information sciences.

41 Buckley *et al*, note 39 above.

42 See www.whitehouse.gov/sites/default/ files/docs/millennials_report.pdf.

43 See www.nielsen.com/us/en/insights/ news/2014/millennials-prefer-cities-to-suburbs-subways-to-driveways.html.

44 *Id.*

45 *Id.*

46 Elisabetta Corvi, Alessandro Bigi and Gabrielle Ng, *The European Millennials versus the US Millennials: Similarities and Differences*, ResearchGate, January 2007 (available at www.researchgate.net/publication/273630817_The_ European_Millennials_Versus_the_US_Millennials _Similarities_and_Differences; accessed 15 January 2017).

47 *Id.*

48 *Id.*

49 *Id.*

50 *Id.*

51 See "Why are Millennials Flocking to Live in Berlin?", *The Guardian*, 4 August 2015 (available at www.psfk.com/2015/08/cities-millennials-live-in-berlin.html; accessed 15 January 2017).

52 See www.bentley.edu/newsroom/latest-headlines/mind-of-millennial/ (accessed 17 September 2016).

53 *Id.*

54 *Id.*

55 See www.slideshare.net/oDesk/2015-millennial-majority-workforce/.

56 See www.mindtickle.com/blog/10-millennial-personality-traits-hr-managers-cant-ignore/.

57 Amy Adkins and J Brandon Rigoni, "Managers: Millennials Want Feedback but Won't Ask for It", *Business Journal*, 2 June 2016 (available at www.gallup.com/businessjournal/192038/manager s-millennials-feedback-won-ask.aspx; accessed 17 September 2016).

58 See http://millennialbranding.com/2014/2015-millennial-majority-workforce-study/.

59 A Millennial Majority Workforce study (available at www.slideshare.net/oDesk/2015-millennial-majority-workforce/; accessed 17 September 2016).

60 American Management Association, "Leading the Four Generations at Work" (available at www.amanet.org/training/articles/Leading-the-Four-Generations-at-Work.aspx; accessed 20 November 2016).

61 Reid Hoffman, Ben Casnocha and Chris Yeh, The Alliance: *Managing Talent in the Networked Age*, Harvard Business Review Press, 2014, p145 in the e-book edition.

62 American Management Association, note 60 above.

63 *Id.*

64 *Id.*

65 *Id.*

Leadership skills

1 Kevin Kruse, "100 Best Quotes on Leadership", *Forbes Magazine*, 16 October 2012 (available at www.forbes.com/sites/kevinkruse/2012/10/16/quot es-on-leadership/#50bf58697106/ (entry 33 in list); accessed 20 November 2016).

2 Paul Hughes, "A Dangerous Game of Bluff", *GC Magazine*, Winter 2014 (available at www.legal500.de/assets/pages/gc/winter-2014/a-dangerous-game-of-bluff.html; accessed 18 August 2016).

3 Commencement Address delivered by the late Steve Jobs at Stanford University, 12 June 2005 (text taken from http://news.stanford.edu/2005/ 06/14/jobs-061505/; accessed 18 August 2016).

4 Quote by the late Steve Jobs on 2 March 2011, recited on Dartblog (Dartmouth's Daily Blog) and available at www.dartblog.com/data/ 2011/03/009449.php; accessed 18 August 2016.

5 HubSpot actually doesn't require people to report back on the book at all, but I believe it makes sense to ask people to formulate some thoughts around what they have read and share that back with the team. For HubSpot's policy, see http://blog.hubspot.com/blog/ tabid/6307/bid/34234/The-HubSpot-Culture-Code-Creating-a-Company-We-Love.aspx#sm.0001hmacy28qzf17x002ir3l9nh2p.

6 Charlie Munger, billionaire investor, businessman, philanthropist, Vice Chairman of Berkshire Hathaway, as quoted on 25iq.com at: https://25iq.com/2015/07/26/a-dozen-things-charlie-munger-has-said-about-reading/; accessed 19 August 2016.

7 Quoted in the podcast "Fireside Chat with Braintree Founder, Bryan Johnson", University of Chicago Booth School of Business podcast series, 28 May 2015.

8 Quote provided to the author by Susan Sneider on 20 November 2016.

9 Reid Hoffman, Ben Casnocha and Chris Yeh, *The Alliance: Managing Talent in the Networked Age*, *Harvard Business Review* Press, 2014, p870 in the e-book edition.

10 *Id.*

11 *Ibid*, p882 in the e-book edition.

12 LinkedIn runs such a program. See *Ibid*, p1030 in the e-book edition.

13 Based on notes taken from a conversation attended by the author at a General Counsel 50 event on 19 March 2015 with Lea Thau, creator and host of *Strangers*.

14 See www.goodreads.com/quotes/5934-i-ve-learned-that-people-will-forget-what-you-said-people/.

15 See: https://www.youtube.com/watch?v=sioZd3AxmnE/.

16 See: www.goodreads.com/quotes/21422-i-didn-t-have-time-to-write-a-short-letter-so/; accessed 24 September 2016.

17 *Email Statistics Report, 2015-2019 – Executive Summary*, The Radicati Group Inc, March 2015 (available at www.radicati.com/wp/wp-content/uploads/2015/02/Email-Statistics-Report-2015-2019-Executive-Summary.pdf; accessed 24 September 2016).

18 Podcast by World 50 with Tom Chi on "Innovation and Leadership" (available at https://soundcloud.com/world50/world-50-podcast-tom-chi/s-67Own/; accessed 24 September 2016).

19 Based on notes taken by the author from a lecture given by Professor Scott Westfall at Harvard Law School on 6 May 2016.

20 See Jim Collins, "The 10 Greatest CEOs of all Time", Fortune, 21 July 2003 (available at www.jimcollins.com/article_topics/articles/10-greatest.html; accessed 20 November 2016); and Jim Collins, "Foreword to the 25th Anniversary Edition of Stephen Covey's *The 7 Habits of Highly Effective People* (available at www.jimcollins.com/article_topics/articles/The-7-Habits-of-Highly-Effective-People.html; accessed 20 November 2016).

21 See www.nytimes.com/1995/12/28/us/darwin-e-smith-69-executive-who-remade-a-paper-company.html; accessed 19 August 2016.

22 See https://en.wikipedia.org/wiki/William_McPherson_Allen/; accessed 19 August 2016.

23 See https://en.wikipedia.org/wiki/Herb_Kelleher/; accessed 19 August 2016.

24 Based on notes taken from a conversation attended by the author at a General Counsel 50 event on 3 March 2016 with Jim Collins.

25 Data in Table 4 provided by Joy Saphla, Morae Legal Corporation, to the author on 16 October 2016. Used with permission.

26 Ben W Heineman Jr, *The Inside Counsel Revolution: Resolving the Partner-Guardian Tension*, Ankerwycke, 2016, p364.

27 Erica Peitler, *Leadership Rigor: Breakthrough Performance and Productivity—Leading Yourself,*

Teams and Organizations, Circle Takes the Square Publishing, 2014.

28 Erin Meyer, *The Culture Map: Breaking Through the Invisible Boundaries of Global Business*, PublicAffairs™ (a member of the Perseus Books Group), 2014.

29 Gus Lubin, "24 Charts of Leadership Styles Around the World", *Business Insider*, 6 January 2014 (available at www.businessinsider.com/ leadership-styles-around-the-world-2013-12/; accessed 24 August 2016).

30 *Id.*

31 *Id.*

32 Meyer, note 28 above, p198.

33 Meyer, note 28 above, p199.

34 *Id.*

35 Bridgewater, "Principles & Culture" (available at www.bridgewater.com/; accessed 24 August 2016).

36 *Id.*

37 Dalio quotation given in John Gapper, "Bridgewater is troubled over 'radical transparency'", *Financial Times*, 10 February 2016 (available at www.ft.com/cms/s/0/789399f0-cf62-11e5-831d-09f7778e7377.html#axzz4HxmWCvTW/; accessed 19 August 2016).

38 Brian Neese, "Intercultural Communication: High and Low Context Cultures", Southeastern University Online Learning, 17 August 2016 (available at http://online.seu.edu/high-and-low-context-cultures/; accessed 24 August 2016).

39 *Id.*

40 Meyer, note 28 above, p34.

41 *Id.*

42 Erin Meyer, "Building Trust Across Cultures", INSEAD Knowledge, 13 February 2015 (available at http://knowledge.insead.edu/blog/insead-blog/building-trust-across-cultures-3844/; accessed 24 August 2016).

43 *Id.*

44 Kim Draemer, "Guanxi: Your Super Business Card in China", *The Huffington Post*, 5 May 2015 (available at www.huffingtonpost.com/kim-dramer-/guanxi-your-super-business-card-in-china_b_7126460.html; accessed 19 August 2016).

45 Meyer, note 28 above, p96.

46 *Id.*

47 See https://en.wikipedia.org/wiki/Grit_(personality_trait)/; accessed 24 August 2016.

48 Angela L Duckworth, Christopher Peterson, Michael D Matthews and Dennis R Kelly, *Grit: Perseverance and Passion for Long-Term Goals*, 10 January 2007, p1087 (available at www.dropbox.com/s/0y545gn2withb5e/Duckworth PetersonMatthewsKelly_2007_PerseveranceandPassion.pdf?dl=0/; accessed 24 August 2016).

49 Angela Duckworth, Grit: The Power of Passion and Perseverance, Scribner (an imprint of Simon & Schuster Inc), 2016, p41.

50 *Ibid*, p42.

Change management

1 Quotation from www.goodreads.com/quotes/tag/uncertainty/, citing her autobiography *West with the Night*.

2 Jeanie Daniel Duck, *The Change Monster: The Human Forces That Fuel or Foil Corporate Transformation and Change*, Random House, 2001, p5.

3 Jeanie Daniel Duck, *The Change Monster: The Human Forces That Fuel or Foil Corporate Transformation and Change*, Random House, 2001.

4 "Podcast: Dr. Larry Richard on the Legal Industry's 'Stress of Change', Part 1", Thompson Reuters Legal Executive Institute, 18 July 2016 (available at http://legalexecutiveinstitute.com/podcast-dr-larry-richard/; accessed 1 October 2016).

5 A quotation from Heraclitus found at BrainyQuote.com (available at www.brainyquote.com/quotes/authors/h/heraclitus.html; accessed 18 June 2016).

6 See www.sonoma.edu/cei/prairie/prairie_desc/species.shtml (accessed 25 June 2016).

7 See https://en.wikipedia.org/wiki/Historical_components_of_the_Dow_Jones_Industrial_Average/ (accessed 25 June 2016).

8 See www.fundinguniverse.com/company-histories/pearson-plc-history/ (accessed 25 June 2016).

9 See https://en.wikipedia.org/wiki/Pearson_PLC and www.pearson.com (both accessed 16 June 2016).

10 See https://en.wikipedia.org/wiki/Ray_Kroc (accessed 4 July 2016).

11 *Id.*

12 See www.finestwatches.com/patek-philippe-nautilus-collection-11407.html (accessed 4 July 2016).

13 See https://jet.com/product/detail/a4e436a1fa314e5f86c46643ac8d3b19?jcmp=pla:ggl:cwin_apparel_accessories_a3:apparel_accessories_jewelry_watches_a3_top:na:PLA_346046820_23693759100_pla-176135711100:na:na:na:2&code=PLA15&ds_c=cwin_apparel_accessories_a3&ds_cid&ds_ag=apparel_accessories_jewelry_watches_a3_top&product_id=a4e436a1fa314e5f86c46643ac8d3b19&product_partition_id=176135711100&gclid=CLOVtqCb2sOCFRRZhgodZcMF2A&gclsrc=aw.ds (accessed 4 July 2016).

14 Interview by the author with Larry Marks on 25 November 2016.

15 *Id.*

16 See https://en.wikipedia.org/wiki/Culture_shock/ (accessed 4 July 2016).

17 Daniel Duck, note 3 above.

18 See www.doc.govt.nz/kakapo/ (accessed 10 July 2016).

19 See www.brainyquote.com/quotes/quotes/w/winstonchu103788.html (accessed 10 July 2016). Some have questioned whether the quote should actually be attributed to someone other than Churchill – see, eg, http://quoteinvestigator.com/2014/09/14/keep-going/ (accessed 10 July 2016).

20 Daniel Duck, note 3 above, p108 of the e-book edition.

Strategic direction

1 Taken from www.goodreads.com/quotes/tag/destination/ (accessed 1 October 2016).

2 See www.pearson.com/about-us.html (accessed 10 July 2016).

3 See www.facebook.com/Amazon/info?tab=page_info/ (accessed 10 July 2016).

4 *Id.*

5 Ben W Heineman Jr, *The Inside Counsel Revolution: Resolving the Partner-Guardian Tension*, Ankerwycke, 2016.

6 Quotation by the Chinese philosopher Laozi (circa 604BC –531BC) in the Tao Te Ching, chapter 64. See https://en.wiktionary.org/wiki/a_journey_of_a_thousand_miles_begins_with_a_single_step (accessed 10 July 2016).

Concluding remarks

1 Quotation from www.brainyquote.com/quotes/topics/topic_change4.html/.

2 Thomas L Friedman, *Thank You for Being Late: an Optimist's Guide to Thriving in the Age of Accelerations*, New York: Farrar, Strauss and Giroux, 2016, p324 in the e-book edition.

3 Richard Susskind, *Tomorrow's Lawyers: An Introduction to Your Future*, Oxford University Press, 2013, location 1898 in the e-book edition.

Further reference material

There follows a list of suggested books, articles and podcasts that provide additional helpful material. Some are referenced in the chapter notes while others are additional recommendations. They are listed in the order of the first author's surname.

Books

Dianna Booher, *Creating Personal Presence: Look, Talk, Think, and Act Like a Leader*, (Berrett-Koehler Publishers Inc, San Francisco, 2011).

Erik Brynjolfsson and Andrew McAfee, *The Second Machine Age: Work, Progress, and Prosperity in a Time of Brilliant Technologies* (WW Norton & Co, New York and London, 2014).

Dale Carnegie, *How to Win Friends and Influence People* (Simon & Schuster, New York, 1936, 1964 and 1981).

Clayton M Christensen, James Allworth and Karen Dillon, *How Will You Measure Your Life?* (Harper Business, New York, 2012).

Lee Cockerell, *Time Management Magic: How to Get More Done Every Day – Move From Surviving to Thriving* (Emerge Publishing, Tulsa, 2014).

Jim Collins, *Good to Great: Why Some Companies Make the Leap and Others Don't* (Harper Business, New York, 2001).

Jim Collins, *Great by Choice: Uncertainty, Chaos, and Luck – Why Some Thrive Despite Them All* (Harper Business, New York, 2011).

Jeanie Daniel Duck, *The Change Monster: The Human Forces That Fuel or Foil Corporate Transformation and Change* (Random House, New York, 2001).

Luc de Brabandere and Alan Iny, *Thinking in New Boxes: A New Paradigm for Business Creativity* (© The Boston Consulting Group, Random House, New York, 2013).

Avinash K Dixit and Barry J Nalebuf, *Thinking Strategically: The Competitive Edge in Business, Politics and Everyday Life* (WW Norton & Co, New York and London, 1991).

Angela Duckworth, *Grit: The Power of Passion and Perseverance* (Scribner, New York, 2016).

Thomas L Friedman, *Thank You for Being Late: An Optimist's Guide to Thriving in the Age of Accelerations* (Farr, Strauss and Giroux, New York, 2016).

Malcolm Gladwell, *The Tipping Point: How Little Things Can Make a Big Difference* (Little Brown Book Group, Boston, 2000).

Joseph Grenny, Kerry Patterson, David Maxfield, Ron McMillan and Al Switzler, *Influencer: The New Science of Leading Change* (2nd edn) (McGraw-Hill, United States, 2013).

Simon Hazeldine, *Neuro-sell: How Neuroscience Can Power Your Sales Success* (Kogan Page, Great Britain and United States, 2014).

Chip Heath and Dan Heath, *Switch: How to Change Things When Change is Hard* (Broadway Books, New York, 2010).

Kristi Hedges, *The Power of Presence: Unlock Your Potential to Influence and Engage Others* (American Management Association, New York, 2012).

Ben W Heineman Jr, *The Inside Counsel Revolution: Resolving the Partner–Guardian Tension* (Ankerwycke – an imprint of the American Bar Association, 2016).

Reid Hoffman, Ben Casnocha and Chris Yeh, *The Alliance: Managing Talent in the Networked Age* (Harvard Business Review Press, Boston, 2014).

Steven Johnson, *Where Good Ideas Come From: The Natural History of Innovation* (Penguin Group, New York, 2010).

Steven Johnson, *How We Got to Now: Six Innovations That Made the Modern World* (Penguin Group, New York, 2014).

Parag Khanna, *Connectography: Mapping the Future of Global Civilization* (Random House, New York, 2016).

John P Kotter and James L Heskett, *Corporate Culture and Performance* (Free Press, New York, 1992).

Adele B Lynn, *The EQ Difference: A Powerful Plan for Putting Emotional Intelligence to Work* (American Management Association, New York, 2010).

Erin Meyer, *The Culture Map: Breaking Through the Invisible Boundaries of Global Business* (PublicAffairs™, a member of the Perseus Books Group, Philadelphia, 2014).

David A Mindell, *Our Robots Ourselves: Robotics and the Myths of Autonomy* (Viking, New York, 2015).

David Novak, *Taking People with You: The Only Way to Make Big Things Happen* (Penguin Group Inc, New York, 2012).

Daniel H Pink, *Free Agent Nation: The Future of Working for Yourself* (Warner Books, New York, 2001).

Daniel H Pink, *A Whole New Mind: Moving from the Information Age to the Conceptual Age* (Riverhead Books, New York, 2005).

Robert Richman, *The Culture Blueprint: A Guide to Building the High-Performance Workplace* (Creative Commons Attribution – ShareAlike 4.0 International Licence).

Matt Ridley, *The Rational Optimist: How Prosperity Evolves* (Harper Collins, New York, 2010).

Peter M Senge, *The Fifth Discipline: The Art and Practice of the Learning Organization* (Doubleday/Currency, New York, 1990).

Susan R Sneider, *A Lawyer's Guide to Networking* (2nd edn) (American Bar Association, Chicago, 2016).

Richard Susskind, *Tomorrow's Lawyers: An Introduction to Your Future* (Oxford University Press, Oxford, 2013).

Richard Susskind and Daniel Susskind, *The Future of the Professions: How Technology Will Transform the Work of Human Experts* (Oxford University Press, Oxford, 2015).

Gillian Tett, *The Silo Effect: The Peril of Expertise and the Promise of Breaking Down Barriers* (Simon and Schuster, New York, 2015).

Michael D Watkins, *The First 90 Days: Proven Strategies for Getting Up to Speed Faster and Smarter* (Harvard Business Review Press, Boston, 2013).

Jim Whitehurst, *The Open Organization: Igniting Passion and Performance* (Harvard Business Review Press, Boston, 2015).

Articles

American Bar Association Commission on the Future of Legal Services, "Issues Paper Regarding Alternative Legal Structures", 8 April 2016 (available at www.americanbar.org/content/dam/aba/images/office_president/alternative_business_issues_paper.pdf).

David Burkus, "A Tale of Two Cultures: Why Culture Trumps Core Values in Building Ethical Organizations", *The Journal of Values-Based Leadership,* Vol 4 Issue 1, Winter/Spring 2011 (available at www.valuesbasedleadershipjournal.com/issues/vol4issue1/tale_2culture.php).

Clayton M Christensen, Dina Wang and Derek van Bever, "Consulting on the Cusp of Disruption", *Harvard Business Review*, October 2013 (available at https://hbr.org/2013/10/consulting-on-the-cusp-of-disruption/).

Council of Economic Advisers, "15 Economic Facts About Millennials", October 2014 (available at www.whitehouse.gov/sites/default/files/docs/millennials_report.pdf).

Stanley M Davis and Paul R Lawrence, "Problems of Matrix Organizations", *Harvard Business Review*, May 1978 (available at https://hbr.org/1978/05/problems-of-matrix-organizations/).

Angela L Duckworth, Christopher Peterson, Michael D Matthews and Dennis R Kelly, "Grit: Perseverance and Passion for Long Term Goals", 10 January 2007 (available at www.dropbox.com/s/0y545gn2withb5e/DuckworthPetersonMatthewsKelly_2007_PerseveranceandPassion.pdf?dl=0/).

General Counsel Leaders Circle, "Sea Change: How Corporate Governance Demands are Elevating the General Counsel's Job", *Target Topic*, July 2014 (available at www.gcleaderscircle.org/wp-content/uploads/2014/07/GCLC-Target-Topic-GC-Corp-Governance-final-July-2014.pdf).

Harvard Business School, "Enron's Lessons for Managers", *Working Knowledge,* 12 July 2004 (available at http://hbswk.hbs.edu/item/enrons-lessons-for-managers/).

Silvia Hodges Silverstein, "What We Know and Need to Know About Legal Procurement", *South Carolina Law Review*, Vol 67, p485.

Robert D Hof, "Deep Learning – With massive amounts of computational power, machines can now recognize objects and translate speech in real time. Artificial intelligence is finally getting smart", *MIT Technology Review* (available at www.technologyreview.com/s/513696/deep-learning/).

Gavriel Hollander, "A Shore Thing?", *Legal Week*, 3 October 2014 (available at www.axiomlaw.com/Docs/2014.10.03_-_Legal_Week_Article_on_Near-shoring.pdf).

Vivian Hunt, Dennis Layton and Sarah Prince, "Why Diversity Matters", McKinsey & Co, January 2015 (available at www.mckinsey.com/Insights/ Organization/Why_diversity_matters?cid=other-eml-alt-mip-mck-oth-1501).

Patrick Johnson, "Top Ten Metrics That Your Legal Department Should Be Tracking", ACC.com, 4 March 2013 (available at www.acc.com/ legalresources/publications/topten/ttmtyldsbt.cfm).

Christof Koch, "How the Computer Beat the Go Master", *Scientific American*, 19 March 2016 (available at www.scientificamerican.com/ article/how-the-computer-beat-the-go-master/).

KPMG, "Business Transformation and the Corporate Agenda", 2014 (available at https://assets.kpmg.com/content/dam/kpmg/pdf/ 2013/11/business-transformation-corporate-agenda.pdf).

The Law Society of England and Wales, "The Future of Legal Services", January 2016 (available at www.lawsociety.org.uk/news/stories/future-of-legal-services/).

Patrick M Lencioni, "Make Your Values Mean Something", *Harvard Business Review*, July 2002 (available at https://hbr.org/2002/07/make-your-values-mean-something/).

Dorothy Leonard-Barton and William A Kraus, "Implementing New Technology", *Harvard Business Review*, November 1985 (available at https://hbr.org/1985/11/implementing-new-technology/).

Susan Lund, James Manyika and Jacques Bughin, "Globalization is Becoming More about Data and Less about Stuff", *Harvard Business Review*, 14 March 2016 (available at https://hbr.org/2016/03/ globalization-is-becoming-more-about-data-and-less-about-stuff/).

Steven Norton, "CIO Explainer: What is Blockchain?", *The Wall Street Journal*, 2 February 2016 (available at http://blogs.wsj.com/cio/2016/02/02/cio-explainer-what-is-blockchain/).

Valentina Pasquali, "Compliance Goes Global: The Unavoidable Costs of Increasing Regulation", *Global Finance Magazine*, May 2015 (available at www.gfmag.com/magazine/may-2015/unavoidable-costs-increasing-regulation-compliance-goes-global/).

Martin Reeves, Simon Levin and Daichi Ueda, "The Biology of Corporate Survival", *Harvard Business Review*, Jan–Feb 2016 (available at https://hbr.org/2016/01/the-biology-of-corporate-survival/).

Antonio Regalado, "The Economics of the Internet of Things", *MIT Technology Review*, 20 May 2014 (available at www.technologyreview.com/s/527361/the-economics-of-the-internet-of-things/).

Cathy Reisenwitz, "What is Lean Law? A Conversation with Expert Kenneth A, Grady", *Law Practice Management*, 9 June 2015 (available at http://blog.capterra.com/what-is-lean-law-a-conversation-with-expert-kenneth-a-grady/).

Mark Roellig, "OMG! Was That Just a Dream? I Just Became a General Counsel. What Do I Do Next?" (©2010 Mark Roellig) (available at www.gcr.executiveboard.com).

Tom Simonite, "Moore's Law is Dead. Now What?", *MIT Technology Review*, 13 May 2016 (available at www.technologyreview.com/s/601441/moores-law-is-dead-now-what/).

Julie Sobowale, "How Artificial Intelligence is Transforming the Legal Profession", *ABA Journal*, 1 April 2016 (available at www.abajournal.com/magazine/article/how_artificial_intelligence_is_transforming_the_legal_profession/).

Josh Stark, "Making Sense of Blockchain Smart Contracts", CoinDesk, 4 June 2016 (available at www.coindesk.com/making-sense-smart-contracts/).

Cass Sunstein and Reid Hastie, "Happy Talk and the Dangers of Groupthink", *Time Magazine*, 14 January 2015 (available at http://time.com/3668083/happy-talk-groupthink-leadership/).

Bjarne Tellmann, "The Care and Feeding of Millennials", *ACC Docket*, 22 March 2016 (available at www.accdocket.com/articles/the-care-and-feeding-of-millenials.cfm).

Irving Wladawsky-Berger, "The Rise of the T-Shaped Organization", *The Wall Street Journal CIO Journal*, 18 December 2015 (available at http://blogs.wsj.com/cio/2015/12/18/the-rise-of-the-t-shaped-organization/).

Albert Yoon, "Competition and the Evolution of Large Law Firms", 63 *DePaul L Rev* 697 (2014), p701 (available at http://via.library.depaul.edu/law-review/vol63/iss2/17).

Podcasts

Tom Chi on "Innovation and Leadership", a World 50 podcast (available at https://soundcloud.com/world50/world-50-podcast-tom-chi/s-67Own/).

Alan Iny on "A New Paradigm for Creativity", a Smart People podcast, episode 252 (available at https://art19.com/shows/smart-people/episodes/a3d90a30-eeae-4fb6-82ac-fb4b5889493a).

David Mindell on "Our Robots, Ourselves", an Econtalk podcast, 30 November 2015 (available at www.econtalk.org/archives/2015/11/david_mindell_o.html).

Erica Peitler on "How to Lead", a Smart People podcast, episode 175, 26 January 2015 (available at www.smartpeoplepodcast.com/2015/01/26/episode-175-erica-peitler/).

Larry Richard on "The Legal Industry's 'Stress of Change', Part 1", Thompson Reuters, Legal Executive Institute, 18 July 2016 (available at http://legalexecutiveinstitute.com/podcast-dr-larry-richard/).

Matt Ridley on "Trade, Growth and the Rational Optimist", an Econtalk podcast, 18 October 2010 (available at www.econtalk.org/archives/2010/10/ridley_on_trade.html).

Dharmesh Shah of HubSpot on "Why Company Culture is Crucial", Stanford e-Corner podcast series, season 11 episode 14, 10 February 2016 (available at http://ecorner.stanford.edu/podcasts/3615/Why-Company-Culture-is-Crucial).

Simon Sinek on "Start with Why", a TED Talk (available at www.youtube.com/watch?v=sioZd3AxmnE).

Daniel Susskind and Richard Susskind on: "The Future of the Professions: How Technology Will Transform the Work of Human Experts", public lecture at the Department of Management of the London School of Economics, 30 November 2015 (available at www.lse.ac.uk/website-archive/publicEvents/events/2015/11/20151130t1830vOT.aspx).

Gillian Tett on "The Silo Effect: Why Putting Everything in its Place Isn't Such a Bright Idea", public lecture at the Department of Management of the London School of Economics, 14 October 2014 (available at www.lse.ac.uk/website-archive/publicEvents/events/2015/10/20151014t1830vSZT.aspx).

Index

GC stands for 'general counsel'. Page references to Figures or Tables are in italics. References to Notes will be followed by the letter 'n' and Note number.